Just The facts101

Textbook Key Facts

Egypt Justice System and
National Police Handbook

Table of Contents

Just The Facts101

Exam Prep for

Egypt Justice System and National Police Handbook

Just The Facts101 Exam Prep is your link from
the textbook and lecture to your exams.

**Just The Facts101 Exam Preps are unauthorized and comprehensive reviews
of your textbooks.**

Just The Facts101 Exam Prep

eAIN 444686

Foundations of Business

A business, also known as an enterprise, agency or a firm, is an entity
involved in the provision of goods and/or services to consumers. Businesses are
prevalent in capitalist economies, where most of them are privately owned and
provide goods and services to customers in exchange for other goods, services,
or money.

:: Loans ::

In finance, a _____ is the lending of money by one or more individuals,
organizations, or other entities to other individuals, organizations etc. The
recipient incurs a debt, and is usually liable to pay interest on that debt
until it is repaid, and also to repay the principal amount borrowed.

Exam Probability: **Low**

1. *Answer choices:*
(see index for correct answer)

- a. Loan servicing
- b. Loan
- c. Federal Perkins Loan
- d. Revolving Loan Fund

Guidance: level 1

:: Goods ::

In most contexts, the concept of _____ denotes the conduct that should be preferred when posed with a choice between possible actions. _____ is generally considered to be the opposite of evil, and is of interest in the study of morality, ethics, religion and philosophy. The specific meaning and etymology of the term and its associated translations among ancient and contemporary languages show substantial variation in its inflection and meaning depending on circumstances of place, history, religious, or philosophical context.

Exam Probability: **High**

2. *Answer choices:*
(see index for correct answer)

- a. Durable good
- b. Experience good
- c. Good
- d. Anti-rival good

Guidance: level 1

:: Monopoly (economics) ::

A _____ is a form of intellectual property that gives its owner the legal right to exclude others from making, using, selling, and importing an invention for a limited period of years, in exchange for publishing an enabling public disclosure of the invention. In most countries _____ rights fall under civil law and the _____ holder needs to sue someone infringing the _____ in order to enforce his or her rights. In some industries _____ s are an essential form of competitive advantage; in others they are irrelevant.

Exam Probability: **High**

3. *Answer choices:*
(see index for correct answer)

- a. Demonopolization
- b. Rate-of-return regulation
- c. Tesco Town
- d. Statute of Monopolies

Guidance: level 1

:: Supply chain management ::

_____ is the process of finding and agreeing to terms, and acquiring goods, services, or works from an external source, often via a tendering or competitive bidding process. _____ is used to ensure the buyer receives goods, services, or works at the best possible price when aspects such as quality, quantity, time, and location are compared. Corporations and public bodies often define processes intended to promote fair and open competition for their business while minimizing risks such as exposure to fraud and collusion.

Exam Probability: **High**

4. *Answer choices:*

(see index for correct answer)

- a. Procurement
- b. Service parts pricing
- c. Pharmacode
- d. Institute for Supply Management

Guidance: level 1

:: Analysis ::

_____ is the process of breaking a complex topic or substance into smaller parts in order to gain a better understanding of it. The technique has been applied in the study of mathematics and logic since before Aristotle , though _____ as a formal concept is a relatively recent development.

Exam Probability: **Low**

5. *Answer choices:*

(see index for correct answer)

- a. Situational analysis
- b. Analysis
- c. Psychopolitical validity
- d. Configurational analysis

Guidance: level 1

:: Logistics ::

_____ is generally the detailed organization and implementation of a complex operation. In a general business sense, _____ is the management of the flow of things between the point of origin and the point of consumption in order to meet requirements of customers or corporations. The resources managed in _____ may include tangible goods such as materials, equipment, and supplies, as well as food and other consumable items. The _____ of physical items usually involves the integration of information flow, materials handling, production, packaging, inventory, transportation, warehousing, and often security.

Exam Probability: **Medium**

6. *Answer choices:*
(see index for correct answer)

- a. Logistics
- b. Savi Technology
- c. Terminal Operating System
- d. Logistics in World War I

Guidance: level 1

:: Mathematical finance ::

In economics and finance, _____ , also known as present discounted value, is the value of an expected income stream determined as of the date of valuation. The _____ is always less than or equal to the future value because money has interest-earning potential, a characteristic referred to as the time value of money, except during times of negative interest rates, when the _____ will be more than the future value. Time value can be described with the simplified phrase, "A dollar today is worth more than a dollar tomorrow". Here, `worth more` means that its value is greater. A dollar today is worth more than a dollar tomorrow because the dollar can be invested and earn a day's worth of interest, making the total accumulate to a value more than a dollar by tomorrow. Interest can be compared to rent. Just as rent is paid to a landlord by a tenant without the ownership of the asset being transferred, interest is paid to a lender by a borrower who gains access to the money for a time before paying it back. By letting the borrower have access to the money, the lender has sacrificed the exchange value of this money, and is compensated for it in the form of interest. The initial amount of the borrowed funds is less than the total amount of money paid to the lender.

Exam Probability: **Low**

7. *Answer choices:*
(see index for correct answer)

- a. Stochastic discount factor
- b. Incomplete markets
- c. Index arbitrage
- d. Earnings response coefficient

Guidance: level 1

:: Payments ::

A _____ is the trade of value from one party to another for goods, or services, or to fulfill a legal obligation.

Exam Probability: **Low**

8. *Answer choices:*
(see index for correct answer)

- a. Deficiency payments
- b. Tuition payments
- c. Payment

- d. Market transition payments

Guidance: level 1

:: Financial risk ::

_____ is a type of risk faced by investors, corporations, and governments that political decisions, events, or conditions will significantly affect the profitability of a business actor or the expected value of a given economic action. _____ can be understood and managed with reasoned foresight and investment.

Exam Probability: **Medium**

9. *Answer choices:*
(see index for correct answer)

- a. Political risk
- b. Risk metric
- c. Diversification
- d. Financial risk

Guidance: level 1

:: Competition regulators ::

The _____ is an independent agency of the United States government, established in 1914 by the _____ Act. Its principal mission is the promotion of consumer protection and the elimination and prevention of anticompetitive business practices, such as coercive monopoly. It is headquartered in the _____ Building in Washington, D.C.

Exam Probability: **High**

10. *Answer choices:*
(see index for correct answer)

- a. Queensland Competition Authority
- b. Competition Bureau
- c. Superintendency of Industry and Commerce
- d. Australian Competition and Consumer Commission

Guidance: level 1

_____ is a relationship between two parties, usually based on a contract where work is paid for, where one party, which may be a corporation, for profit, not-for-profit organization, co-operative or other entity is the employer and the other is the employee. Employees work in return for payment, which may be in the form of an hourly wage, by piecework or an annual salary, depending on the type of work an employee does or which sector she or he is working in. Employees in some fields or sectors may receive gratuities, bonus payment or stock options. In some types of _____ , employees may receive benefits in addition to payment. Benefits can include health insurance, housing, disability insurance or use of a gym. _____ is typically governed by _____ laws, regulations or legal contracts.

Exam Probability: **Medium**

11. *Answer choices:*
(see index for correct answer)

- a. Employment
- b. delayering
- c. Shift work sleep disorder
- d. Psychological contract

Guidance: level 1

The _____ of a corporation is all of the shares into which ownership of the corporation is divided. In American English, the shares are commonly known as " _____ s". A single share of the _____ represents fractional ownership of the corporation in proportion to the total number of shares. This typically entitles the _____ holder to that fraction of the company's earnings, proceeds from liquidation of assets , or voting power, often dividing these up in proportion to the amount of money each _____ holder has invested. Not all _____ is necessarily equal, as certain classes of _____ may be issued for example without voting rights, with enhanced voting rights, or with a certain priority to receive profits or liquidation proceeds before or after other classes of shareholders.

Exam Probability: **Medium**

12. *Answer choices:*
(see index for correct answer)

- a. Immediate or cancel
- b. Stock transfer
- c. NewConnect
- d. Direct participation program

Guidance: level 1

:: Project management ::

Contemporary business and science treat as a _____ any undertaking, carried out individually or collaboratively and possibly involving research or design, that is carefully planned to achieve a particular aim.

Exam Probability: **Low**

13. *Answer choices:*
(see index for correct answer)

- a. Total project control
- b. Project initiation document
- c. Project
- d. Sequence step algorithm

Guidance: level 1

:: Economic globalization ::

_____ is an agreement in which one company hires another company to be responsible for a planned or existing activity that is or could be done internally,and sometimes involves transferring employees and assets from one firm to another.

Exam Probability: **Medium**

14. *Answer choices:*
(see index for correct answer)

- a. Outsourcing
- b. reshoring

Guidance: level 1

:: E-commerce ::

_____ is the activity of buying or selling of products on online services or over the Internet. Electronic commerce draws on technologies such as mobile commerce, electronic funds transfer, supply chain management, Internet marketing, online transaction processing, electronic data interchange , inventory management systems, and automated data collection systems.

Exam Probability: **Medium**

15. *Answer choices:*
(see index for correct answer)

- a. Onbuy
- b. Eurocheque
- c. The iBridge Network
- d. E-commerce

Guidance: level 1

:: Costs ::

In microeconomic theory, the _____ , or alternative cost, of making a particular choice is the value of the most valuable choice out of those that were not taken. In other words, opportunity that will require sacrifices.

Exam Probability: **Low**

16. *Answer choices:*
(see index for correct answer)

- a. Cost of poor quality
- b. Total cost
- c. Opportunity cost
- d. Further processing cost

Guidance: level 1

:: Legal terms ::

An _____ is an action which is inaccurate or incorrect. In some usages, an _____ is synonymous with a mistake. In statistics, " _____ " refers to the difference between the value which has been computed and the correct value. An _____ could result in failure or in a deviation from the intended performance or behaviour.

Exam Probability: **High**

17. *Answer choices:*
(see index for correct answer)

- a. Original jurisdiction
- b. Legal transplant
- c. Error
- d. Collective redress

Guidance: level 1

:: Materials ::

A _____ , also known as a feedstock, unprocessed material, or primary commodity, is a basic material that is used to produce goods, finished products, energy, or intermediate materials which are feedstock for future finished products. As feedstock, the term connotes these materials are bottleneck assets and are highly important with regard to producing other products. An example of this is crude oil, which is a _____ and a feedstock used in the production of industrial chemicals, fuels, plastics, and pharmaceutical goods; lumber is a _____ used to produce a variety of products including all types of furniture. The term " _____ " denotes materials in minimally processed or unprocessed in states; e.g., raw latex, crude oil, cotton, coal, raw biomass, iron ore, air, logs, or water i.e. "...any product of agriculture, forestry, fishing and any other mineral that is in its natural form or which has undergone the transformation required to prepare it for internationally marketing in substantial volumes."

Exam Probability: **Medium**

18. *Answer choices:*
(see index for correct answer)

- a. Orthotropic material
- b. Agricultural lime
- c. Salisbury screen

- d. Richlite

Guidance: level 1

:: Stock market ::

_____ is a form of stock which may have any combination of features not possessed by common stock including properties of both an equity and a debt instrument, and is generally considered a hybrid instrument. _____ s are senior to common stock, but subordinate to bonds in terms of claim and may have priority over common stock in the payment of dividends and upon liquidation. Terms of the _____ are described in the issuing company's articles of association or articles of incorporation.

Exam Probability: **Low**

19. *Answer choices:*
(see index for correct answer)

- a. Tech Buzz
- b. Secondary shares
- c. Microcap
- d. Central securities depository

Guidance: level 1

:: Information science ::

A _____ is a written, drawn, presented, or memorialized representation of thought. a _____ is a form, or written piece that trains a line of thought or as in history, a significant event. The word originates from the Latin _____ um, which denotes a "teaching" or "lesson": the verb doceo denotes "to teach". In the past, the word was usually used to denote a written proof useful as evidence of a truth or fact. In the computer age, " _____ " usually denotes a primarily textual computer file, including its structure and format, e.g. fonts, colors, and images. Contemporarily, " _____ " is not defined by its transmission medium, e.g., paper, given the existence of electronic _____ s. " _____ ation" is distinct because it has more denotations than " _____ ". _____ s are also distinguished from "realia", which are three-dimensional objects that would otherwise satisfy the definition of " _____ " because they memorialize or represent thought; _____ s are considered more as 2 dimensional representations. While _____ s are able to have large varieties of customization, all _____ s are able to be shared freely, and have the right to do so, creativity can be represented by _____ s, also. History, events, examples, opinion, etc. all can be expressed in _____ s.

Exam Probability: **High**

20. *Answer choices:*
(see index for correct answer)

- a. Pearl growing
- b. Information and Computer Science
- c. Inherent vice
- d. User-subjective approach

Guidance: level 1

:: Workplace ::

_____ is asystematic determination of a subject's merit, worth and significance, using criteria governed by a set of standards. It can assist an organization, program, design, project or any other intervention or initiative to assess any aim, realisable concept/proposal, or any alternative, to help in decision-making; or to ascertain the degree of achievement or value in regard to the aim and objectives and results of any such action that has been completed. The primary purpose of _____ , in addition to gaining insight into prior or existing initiatives, is to enable reflection and assist in the identification of future change.

Exam Probability: **High**

21. *Answer choices:*
(see index for correct answer)

- a. Queen bee syndrome
- b. Workplace revenge
- c. Evaluation
- d. Micromanagement

Guidance: level 1

:: Market research ::

A _____ is a small, but demographically diverse group of people and whose reactions are studied especially in market research or political analysis in guided or open discussions about a new product or something else to determine the reactions that can be expected from a larger population. It is a form of qualitative research consisting of interviews in which a group of people are asked about their perceptions, opinions, beliefs, and attitudes towards a product, service, concept, advertisement, idea, or packaging. Questions are asked in an interactive group setting where participants are free to talk with other group members. During this process, the researcher either takes notes or records the vital points he or she is getting from the group. Researchers should select members of the _____ carefully for effective and authoritative responses.

Exam Probability: **High**

22. *Answer choices:*
(see index for correct answer)

- a. Media Technology Monitor
- b. Focus group
- c. Market research and opinion polling in China
- d. Competitive intelligence

Guidance: level 1

:: Interest rates ::

An _____ is the amount of interest due per period, as a proportion of the amount lent, deposited or borrowed . The total interest on an amount lent or borrowed depends on the principal sum, the _____ , the compounding frequency, and the length of time over which it is lent, deposited or borrowed.

Exam Probability: **Low**

23. *Answer choices:*
(see index for correct answer)

- a. Zero interest-rate policy
- b. Coupon leverage
- c. Interest rate
- d. Annual effective discount rate

Guidance: level 1

:: Social security ::

_____ is "any government system that provides monetary assistance to people with an inadequate or no income." In the United States, this is usually called welfare or a social safety net, especially when talking about Canada and European countries.

Exam Probability: **Low**

24. *Answer choices:*
(see index for correct answer)

- a. Gosselin v. Quebec
- b. Bituah Leumi
- c. National Social Assistance Scheme
- d. Social security

Guidance: level 1

_____ is a legally enforceable claim for payment held by a business for goods supplied and/or services rendered that customers/clients have ordered but not paid for. These are generally in the form of invoices raised by a business and delivered to the customer for payment within an agreed time frame.

_____ is shown in a balance sheet as an asset. It is one of a series of accounting transactions dealing with the billing of a customer for goods and services that the customer has ordered. These may be distinguished from notes receivable, which are debts created through formal legal instruments called promissory notes.

Exam Probability: **Low**

25. *Answer choices:*
(see index for correct answer)

- a. double-entry bookkeeping
- b. General ledger
- c. Accounts receivable
- d. Capital expenditure

Guidance: level 1

In business and finance, _____ is a system of organizations, people, activities, information, and resources involved inmoving a product or service from supplier to customer. _____ activities involve the transformation of natural resources, raw materials, and components into a finished product that is delivered to the end customer. In sophisticated _____ systems, used products may re-enter the _____ at any point where residual value is recyclable. _____ s link value chains.

Exam Probability: **Medium**

26. *Answer choices:*
(see index for correct answer)

- a. Supply chain
- b. Supply-chain management
- c. Consumables
- d. Most valuable customers

:: Business ::

_____ is a trade policy that does not restrict imports or exports; it can also be understood as the free market idea applied to international trade. In government, _____ is predominantly advocated by political parties that hold liberal economic positions while economically left-wing and nationalist political parties generally support protectionism, the opposite of _____ .

Exam Probability: **High**

27. *Answer choices:*
(see index for correct answer)

- a. Business
- b. Operating subsidiary
- c. Business agility
- d. Door-to-door

:: Stock market ::

A _____ , equity market or share market is the aggregation of buyers and sellers of stocks , which represent ownership claims on businesses; these may include securities listed on a public stock exchange, as well as stock that is only traded privately. Examples of the latter include shares of private companies which are sold to investors through equity crowdfunding platforms. Stock exchanges list shares of common equity as well as other security types, e.g. corporate bonds and convertible bonds.

Exam Probability: **High**

28. *Answer choices:*
(see index for correct answer)

- a. Stock market
- b. Intermarket sweep order
- c. Street name securities
- d. Delivery versus payment

_____ refers to a business or organization attempting to acquire goods or services to accomplish its goals. Although there are several organizations that attempt to set standards in the _____ process, processes can vary greatly between organizations. Typically the word " _____ " is not used interchangeably with the word "procurement", since procurement typically includes expediting, supplier quality, and transportation and logistics in addition to _____ .

Exam Probability: **High**

29. *Answer choices:*
(see index for correct answer)

- a. surface-level diversity
- b. process perspective
- c. Purchasing
- d. similarity-attraction theory

Guidance: level 1

:: Graphic design ::

An _____ is an artifact that depicts visual perception, such as a photograph or other two-dimensional picture, that resembles a subject—usually a physical object—and thus provides a depiction of it. In the context of signal processing, an _____ is a distributed amplitude of color.

Exam Probability: **Medium**

30. *Answer choices:*
(see index for correct answer)

- a. Graphic charter
- b. Rich black
- c. Image
- d. Centerfold

Guidance: level 1

:: Business terms ::

A _____ is a short statement of why an organization exists, what its overall goal is, identifying the goal of its operations: what kind of product or service it provides, its primary customers or market, and its geographical region of operation. It may include a short statement of such fundamental matters as the organization's values or philosophies, a business's main competitive advantages, or a desired future state—the "vision".

Exam Probability: **High**

31. *Answer choices:*
(see index for correct answer)

- a. granular
- b. churn rate
- c. Mission statement
- d. Personal selling

Guidance: level 1

:: Competition (economics) ::

_____ arises whenever at least two parties strive for a goal which cannot be shared: where one's gain is the other's loss .

Exam Probability: **Low**

32. *Answer choices:*
(see index for correct answer)

- a. Tax competition
- b. Self-competition
- c. Category killer
- d. Economic forces

Guidance: level 1

:: Foreign direct investment ::

A _____ is an investment in the form of a controlling ownership in a business in one country by an entity based in another country. It is thus distinguished from a foreign portfolio investment by a notion of direct control.

33. *Answer choices:*

(see index for correct answer)

- a. Foreign direct investment in Romania
- b. Expropriation
- c. Foreign ownership
- d. International Centre for Settlement of Investment Disputes

Guidance: level 1

:: Generally Accepted Accounting Principles ::

An _____ or profit and loss account is one of the financial statements of a company and shows the company's revenues and expenses during a particular period.

Exam Probability: **Low**

34. *Answer choices:*

(see index for correct answer)

- a. Management accounting principles
- b. Net profit
- c. Matching principle
- d. Operating income

Guidance: level 1

:: Bribery ::

_____ is the act of giving or receiving something of value in exchange for some kind of influence or action in return, that the recipient would otherwise not offer. _____ is defined by Black's Law Dictionary as the offering, giving, receiving, or soliciting of any item of value to influence the actions of an official or other person in charge of a public or legal duty. Essentially, _____ is offering to do something for someone for the expressed purpose of receiving something in exchange. Gifts of money or other items of value which are otherwise available to everyone on an equivalent basis, and not for dishonest purposes, is not _____ . Offering a discount or a refund to all purchasers is a legal rebate and is not _____ . For example, it is legal for an employee of a Public Utilities Commission involved in electric rate regulation to accept a rebate on electric service that reduces their cost for electricity, when the rebate is available to other residential electric customers. Giving the rebate to influence them to look favorably on the electric utility's rate increase applications, however, would be considered _____ .

Exam Probability: **High**

35. *Answer choices:*
(see index for correct answer)

- a. English football bribery scandal
- b. Holyland Case
- c. Katta Subramanya Naidu
- d. Bribery

Guidance: level 1

:: Management occupations ::

_____ ship is the process of designing, launching and running a new business, which is often initially a small business. The people who create these businesses are called _____ s.

Exam Probability: **Medium**

36. *Answer choices:*
(see index for correct answer)

- a. Chief business development officer
- b. Vorstandsassistent
- c. Entrepreneur

- d. Functional manager

Guidance: level 1

:: ::

Competition arises whenever at least two parties strive for a goal which cannot be shared: where one's gain is the other's loss .

Exam Probability: **High**

37. *Answer choices:*
(see index for correct answer)

- a. similarity-attraction theory
- b. process perspective
- c. surface-level diversity
- d. cultural

Guidance: level 1

:: Management ::

A _____ is when two or more people come together to discuss one or more topics, often in a formal or business setting, but _____ s also occur in a variety of other environments. Many various types of _____ s exist.

Exam Probability: **Low**

38. *Answer choices:*
(see index for correct answer)

- a. Product life-cycle management
- b. Management by exception
- c. Meeting
- d. Economic order quantity

Guidance: level 1

:: Electronic feedback ::

_____ occurs when outputs of a system are routed back as inputs as part of a chain of cause-and-effect that forms a circuit or loop. The system can then be said to feed back into itself. The notion of cause-and-effect has to be handled carefully when applied to _____ systems.

Exam Probability: **Low**

39. *Answer choices:*
(see index for correct answer)

- a. Feedback
- b. Positive feedback

Guidance: level 1

:: Organizational behavior ::

_____ is the state or fact of exclusive rights and control over property, which may be an object, land/real estate or intellectual property. _____ involves multiple rights, collectively referred to as title, which may be separated and held by different parties.

Exam Probability: **Medium**

40. *Answer choices:*
(see index for correct answer)

- a. Ownership
- b. Satisficing
- c. Nut Island effect
- d. Managerial grid model

Guidance: level 1

:: Evaluation ::

_____ solving consists of using generic or ad hoc methods in an orderly manner to find solutions to _____ s. Some of the _____ -solving techniques developed and used in philosophy, artificial intelligence, computer science, engineering, mathematics, or medicine are related to mental _____ -solving techniques studied in psychology.

41. *Answer choices:*

(see index for correct answer)

- a. Continuous assessment
- b. Goddard College
- c. Immanent evaluation
- d. Narrative evaluation

Guidance: level 1

:: Stock market ::

A _____ , securities exchange or bourse, is a facility where stock brokers and traders can buy and sell securities, such as shares of stock and bonds and other financial instruments. _____ s may also provide for facilities the issue and redemption of such securities and instruments and capital events including the payment of income and dividends. Securities traded on a _____ include stock issued by listed companies, unit trusts, derivatives, pooled investment products and bonds. _____ s often function as "continuous auction" markets with buyers and sellers consummating transactions via open outcry at a central location such as the floor of the exchange or by using an electronic trading platform.

42. *Answer choices:*

(see index for correct answer)

- a. Shadow stock
- b. H share
- c. End of day
- d. Microcap

Guidance: level 1

:: ::

_____ is the collection of mechanisms, processes and relations by which corporations are controlled and operated. Governance structures and principles identify the distribution of rights and responsibilities among different participants in the corporation and include the rules and procedures for making decisions in corporate affairs. _____ is necessary because of the possibility of conflicts of interests between stakeholders, primarily between shareholders and upper management or among shareholders.

Exam Probability: **High**

43. *Answer choices:*
(see index for correct answer)

- a. personal values
- b. co-culture
- c. Sarbanes-Oxley act of 2002
- d. Corporate governance

Guidance: level 1

:: Business ::

The seller, or the provider of the goods or services, completes a sale in response to an acquisition, appropriation, requisition or a direct interaction with the buyer at the point of sale. There is a passing of title of the item, and the settlement of a price, in which agreement is reached on a price for which transfer of ownership of the item will occur. The seller, not the purchaser typically executes the sale and it may be completed prior to the obligation of payment. In the case of indirect interaction, a person who sells goods or service on behalf of the owner is known as a _____ man or _____ woman or _____ person, but this often refers to someone selling goods in a store/shop, in which case other terms are also common, including _____ clerk, shop assistant, and retail clerk.

Exam Probability: **Medium**

44. *Answer choices:*
(see index for correct answer)

- a. Service recovery
- b. Free trade
- c. Sales
- d. Door-to-door

:: Critical thinking ::

In psychology, _____ is regarded as the cognitive process resulting in the selection of a belief or a course of action among several alternative possibilities. Every _____ process produces a final choice, which may or may not prompt action.

Exam Probability: **Low**

45. *Answer choices:*
(see index for correct answer)

- a. Argumentation theory
- b. Evidence
- c. Topical logic
- d. Decision-making

:: Budgets ::

A _____ is a financial plan for a defined period, often one year. It may also include planned sales volumes and revenues, resource quantities, costs and expenses, assets, liabilities and cash flows. Companies, governments, families and other organizations use it to express strategic plans of activities or events in measurable terms.

Exam Probability: **Low**

46. *Answer choices:*
(see index for correct answer)

- a. Film budgeting
- b. Budget constraint
- c. Budgeted cost of work scheduled
- d. Link budget

:: Majority–minority relations ::

_____ , also known as reservation in India and Nepal, positive discrimination / action in the United Kingdom, and employment equity in Canada and South Africa, is the policy of promoting the education and employment of members of groups that are known to have previously suffered from discrimination. Historically and internationally, support for _____ has sought to achieve goals such as bridging inequalities in employment and pay, increasing access to education, promoting diversity, and redressing apparent past wrongs, harms, or hindrances.

Exam Probability: **Medium**

47. *Answer choices:*
(see index for correct answer)

- a. cultural dissonance
- b. Affirmative action
- c. cultural Relativism

Guidance: level 1

:: Management ::

In business, a _____ is the attribute that allows an organization to outperform its competitors. A _____ may include access to natural resources, such as high-grade ores or a low-cost power source, highly skilled labor, geographic location, high entry barriers, and access to new technology.

Exam Probability: **Low**

48. *Answer choices:*
(see index for correct answer)

- a. Community management
- b. Cross ownership
- c. Competitive advantage
- d. Product breakdown structure

Guidance: level 1

:: Macroeconomics ::

A foreign _____ is an investment in the form of a controlling ownership in a business in one country by an entity based in another country. It is thus distinguished from a foreign portfolio investment by a notion of direct control.

Exam Probability: **Low**

49. *Answer choices:*
(see index for correct answer)

- a. Direct investment
- b. Factor shares
- c. Consensus forecast
- d. Crisis theory

Guidance: level 1

:: ::

In regulatory jurisdictions that provide for it , _____ is a group of laws and organizations designed to ensure the rights of consumers as well as fair trade, competition and accurate information in the marketplace. The laws are designed to prevent the businesses that engage in fraud or specified unfair practices from gaining an advantage over competitors. They may also provides additional protection for those most vulnerable in society. _____ laws are a form of government regulation that aim to protect the rights of consumers. For example, a government may require businesses to disclose detailed information about products—particularly in areas where safety or public health is an issue, such as food.

Exam Probability: **High**

50. *Answer choices:*
(see index for correct answer)

- a. surface-level diversity
- b. functional perspective
- c. cultural
- d. similarity-attraction theory

Guidance: level 1

:: Management ::

_____ is the process of thinking about the activities required to achieve a desired goal. It is the first and foremost activity to achieve desired results. It involves the creation and maintenance of a plan, such as psychological aspects that require conceptual skills. There are even a couple of tests to measure someone's capability of _____ well. As such, _____ is a fundamental property of intelligent behavior. An important further meaning, often just called " _____ " is the legal context of permitted building developments.

Exam Probability: **Low**

51. *Answer choices:*
(see index for correct answer)

- a. Nonconformity
- b. Value migration
- c. Logistics support analysis
- d. Planning

Guidance: level 1

:: Business law ::

A _____ is a group of people who jointly supervise the activities of an organization, which can be either a for-profit business, nonprofit organization, or a government agency. Such a board's powers, duties, and responsibilities are determined by government regulations and the organization's own constitution and bylaws. These authorities may specify the number of members of the board, how they are to be chosen, and how often they are to meet.

Exam Probability: **High**

52. *Answer choices:*
(see index for correct answer)

- a. Articles of partnership
- b. Board of directors
- c. Business license
- d. Chattel mortgage

Guidance: level 1

:: Management ::

A _____ describes the rationale of how an organization creates, delivers, and captures value, in economic, social, cultural or other contexts. The process of _____ construction and modification is also called _____ innovation and forms a part of business strategy.

Exam Probability: **High**

53. *Answer choices:*
(see index for correct answer)

- a. Business model
- b. Project team builder
- c. Plan
- d. Management Week

Guidance: level 1

:: Systems theory ::

A _____ is a group of interacting or interrelated entities that form a unified whole. A _____ is delineated by its spatial and temporal boundaries, surrounded and influenced by its environment, described by its structure and purpose and expressed in its functioning.

Exam Probability: **Low**

54. *Answer choices:*
(see index for correct answer)

- a. subsystem
- b. System
- c. management system
- d. decentralized system

Guidance: level 1

:: Strategic management ::

_____ is a strategic planning technique used to help a person or organization identify strengths, weaknesses, opportunities, and threats related to business competition or project planning. It is intended to specify the objectives of the business venture or project and identify the internal and external factors that are favorable and unfavorable to achieving those objectives. Users of a _____ often ask and answer questions to generate meaningful information for each category to make the tool useful and identify their competitive advantage. SWOT has been described as the tried-and-true tool of strategic analysis.

Exam Probability: **High**

55. *Answer choices:*
(see index for correct answer)

- a. Value shop
- b. International business strategy
- c. Zaibatsu
- d. SWOT analysis

Guidance: level 1

:: Organizational structure ::

An _____ defines how activities such as task allocation, coordination, and supervision are directed toward the achievement of organizational aims.

Exam Probability: **High**

56. *Answer choices:*
(see index for correct answer)

- a. The Starfish and the Spider
- b. Organizational structure
- c. Automated Bureaucracy
- d. Blessed Unrest

Guidance: level 1

:: ::

A _____ is an organization, usually a group of people or a company, authorized to act as a single entity and recognized as such in law. Early incorporated entities were established by charter . Most jurisdictions now allow the creation of new _____ s through registration.

Exam Probability: **Medium**

57. *Answer choices:*
(see index for correct answer)

- a. deep-level diversity
- b. interpersonal communication
- c. personal values
- d. Corporation

Guidance: level 1

:: Financial markets ::

A _____ is a financial market in which long-term debt or equity-backed securities are bought and sold. _____ s channel the wealth of savers to those who can put it to long-term productive use, such as companies or governments making long-term investments. Financial regulators like the Bank of England and the U.S. Securities and Exchange Commission oversee _____ s to protect investors against fraud, among other duties.

Exam Probability: **Medium**

58. *Answer choices:*
(see index for correct answer)

- a. Fundamentally based indexes
- b. Commodity Exchange Act
- c. Round lot
- d. Forward market

Guidance: level 1

:: Critical thinking ::

An _____ is a set of statements usually constructed to describe a set of facts which clarifies the causes, context, and consequences of those facts. This description of the facts et cetera may establish rules or laws, and may clarify the existing rules or laws in relation to any objects, or phenomena examined. The components of an _____ can be implicit, and interwoven with one another.

Exam Probability: **Low**

59. *Answer choices:*

- a. Proof
- b. Explanation
- c. Argumentation theory
- d. Prudence

Guidance: level 1

Management

Management is the administration of an organization, whether it is a
business, a not-for-profit organization, or government body. Management
includes the activities of setting the strategy of an organization and
coordinating the efforts of its employees (or of volunteers) to accomplish its
objectives through the application of available resources, such as financial,
natural, technological, and human resources.

:: ::

_____ is the collection of mechanisms, processes and relations by which corporations are controlled and operated. Governance structures and principles identify the distribution of rights and responsibilities among different participants in the corporation and include the rules and procedures for making decisions in corporate affairs. _____ is necessary because of the possibility of conflicts of interests between stakeholders, primarily between shareholders and upper management or among shareholders.

Exam Probability: **Medium**

1. *Answer choices:*

(see index for correct answer)

- a. levels of analysis
- b. hierarchical
- c. Character
- d. Corporate governance

Guidance: level 1

:: Logistics ::

_____ is generally the detailed organization and implementation of a complex operation. In a general business sense, _____ is the management of the flow of things between the point of origin and the point of consumption in order to meet requirements of customers or corporations. The resources managed in _____ may include tangible goods such as materials, equipment, and supplies, as well as food and other consumable items. The _____ of physical items usually involves the integration of information flow, materials handling, production, packaging, inventory, transportation, warehousing, and often security.

Exam Probability: **High**

2. *Answer choices:*
(see index for correct answer)

- a. Ground Parachute Extraction System
- b. Logistics in World War I
- c. Tracking number
- d. Logistics

Guidance: level 1

:: Life skills ::

_____ , emotional leadership , emotional quotient and _____ quotient , is the capability of individuals to recognize their own emotions and those of others, discern between different feelings and label them appropriately, use emotional information to guide thinking and behavior, and manage and/or adjust emotions to adapt to environments or achieve one's goal.

Exam Probability: **Medium**

3. *Answer choices:*
(see index for correct answer)

- a. emotion work
- b. Emotional intelligence
- c. coping mechanism
- d. multiple intelligence

Guidance: level 1

:: Organizational theory ::

_____ refers to both a body of non-elective government officials and an administrative policy-making group. Historically, a _____ was a government administration managed by departments staffed with non-elected officials. Today, _____ is the administrative system governing any large institution, whether publicly owned or privately owned. The public administration in many countries is an example of a _____ , but so is the centralized hierarchical structure of a business firm.

Exam Probability: **Medium**

4. *Answer choices:*
(see index for correct answer)

- a. Mimetic isomorphism
- b. Bureaucracy
- c. Interaction value analysis
- d. Staff augmentation

Guidance: level 1

:: Management ::

A _____ is an idea of the future or desired result that a person or a group of people envisions, plans and commits to achieve. People endeavor to reach _____ s within a finite time by setting deadlines.

Exam Probability: **Medium**

5. *Answer choices:*
(see index for correct answer)

- a. Business chess
- b. Management styles
- c. DMSMS
- d. Goal

Guidance: level 1

:: Human resource management ::

_____ , also known as management by results , was first popularized by Peter Drucker in his 1954 book The Practice of Management. _____ is the process of defining specific objectives within an organization that management can convey to organization members, then deciding on how to achieve each objective in sequence. This process allows managers to take work that needs to be done one step at a time to allow for a calm, yet productive work environment. This process also helps organization members to see their accomplishments as they achieve each objective, which reinforces a positive work environment and a sense of achievement. An important part of MBO is the measurement and comparison of an employee's actual performance with the standards set. Ideally, when employees themselves have been involved with the goal-setting and choosing the course of action to be followed by them, they are more likely to fulfill their responsibilities.According to George S. Odiorne, the system of _____ can be described as a process whereby the superior and subordinate jointly identify common goals, define each individual's major areas of responsibility in terms of the results expected of him or her, and use these measures as guides for operating the unit and assessing the contribution of each of its members.

Exam Probability: **Medium**

6. *Answer choices:*
(see index for correct answer)

- a. Multiculturalism
- b. Management by objectives
- c. Vendor management system
- d. Illness rate

Guidance: level 1

:: Management ::

In organizational studies, _____ is the efficient and effective development of an organization's resources when they are needed. Such resources may include financial resources, inventory, human skills, production resources, or information technology and natural resources.

Exam Probability: **Low**

7. *Answer choices:*
(see index for correct answer)

- a. Resource management
- b. Management by exception
- c. Management entrenchment
- d. Decentralized decision-making

Guidance: level 1

:: Product design ::

_____ as a verb is to create a new product to be sold by a business to its customers. A very broad coefficient and effective generation and development of ideas through a process that leads to new products. Thus, it is a major aspect of new product development.

Exam Probability: **Low**

8. *Answer choices:*
(see index for correct answer)

- a. Product design
- b. Beta Tank
- c. Studio Job
- d. Rodney Fitch

Guidance: level 1

:: Budgets ::

A _____ is a financial plan for a defined period, often one year. It may also include planned sales volumes and revenues, resource quantities, costs and expenses, assets, liabilities and cash flows. Companies, governments, families and other organizations use it to express strategic plans of activities or events in measurable terms.

Exam Probability: **Medium**

9. *Answer choices:*
(see index for correct answer)

- a. Budgeted cost of work scheduled
- b. Operating budget
- c. Budget
- d. Envelope system

Guidance: level 1

A _____ is an individual or institution that legally owns one or more shares of stock in a public or private corporation. _____ s may be referred to as members of a corporation. Legally, a person is not a _____ in a corporation until their name and other details are entered in the corporation's register of _____ s or members.

Exam Probability: **Low**

10. *Answer choices:*
(see index for correct answer)

- a. Shareholder
- b. cultural
- c. imperative
- d. surface-level diversity

Guidance: level 1

_____ , known in Europe as research and technological development , refers to innovative activities undertaken by corporations or governments in developing new services or products, or improving existing services or products. _____ constitutes the first stage of development of a potential new service or the production process.

Exam Probability: **High**

11. *Answer choices:*
(see index for correct answer)

- a. co-culture
- b. information systems assessment
- c. Research and development
- d. deep-level diversity

Guidance: level 1

:: Teams ::

A _____ usually refers to a group of individuals who work together from different geographic locations and rely on communication technology such as email, FAX, and video or voice conferencing services in order to collaborate. The term can also refer to groups or teams that work together asynchronously or across organizational levels. Powell, Piccoli and Ives define _____ s as "groups of geographically, organizationally and/or time dispersed workers brought together by information and telecommunication technologies to accomplish one or more organizational tasks." According to Ale Ebrahim et. al. , _____ s can also be defined as "small temporary groups of geographically, organizationally and/or time dispersed knowledge workers who coordinate their work predominantly with electronic information and communication technologies in order to accomplish one or more organization tasks."

Exam Probability: **Medium**

12. *Answer choices:*
(see index for correct answer)

- a. Virtual team
- b. Team-building

Guidance: level 1

:: Production economics ::

_____ is the joint use of a resource or space. It is also the process of dividing and distributing. In its narrow sense, it refers to joint or alternating use of inherently finite goods, such as a common pasture or a shared residence. Still more loosely, " _____ " can actually mean giving something as an outright gift: for example, to "share" one`s food really means to give some of it as a gift. _____ is a basic component of human interaction, and is responsible for strengthening social ties and ensuring a person`s well-being.

Exam Probability: **High**

13. *Answer choices:*
(see index for correct answer)

- a. Factor price
- b. Sharing

- c. Constant elasticity of transformation
- d. Diminishing returns

Guidance: level 1

:: Business ethics ::

_____ is a type of harassment technique that relates to a sexual nature and the unwelcome or inappropriate promise of rewards in exchange for sexual favors. _____ includes a range of actions from mild transgressions to sexual abuse or assault. Harassment can occur in many different social settings such as the workplace, the home, school, churches, etc. Harassers or victims may be of any gender.

Exam Probability: **Low**

14. *Answer choices:*
(see index for correct answer)

- a. Sexual harassment
- b. Foreign official
- c. Moral hazard
- d. Minecode

Guidance: level 1

:: ::

Business is the activity of making one's living or making money by producing or buying and selling products . Simply put, it is "any activity or enterprise entered into for profit. It does not mean it is a company, a corporation, partnership, or have any such formal organization, but it can range from a street peddler to General Motors."

Exam Probability: **High**

15. *Answer choices:*
(see index for correct answer)

- a. Firm
- b. functional perspective
- c. co-culture
- d. similarity-attraction theory

Guidance: level 1

_____ is the amount of time someone works beyond normal working hours. The term is also used for the pay received for this time. Normal hours may be determined in several ways.

Exam Probability: **High**

16. *Answer choices:*
(see index for correct answer)

- a. corporate values
- b. hierarchical perspective
- c. Overtime
- d. open system

Guidance: level 1

:: Industrial agreements ::

_____ is a process of negotiation between employers and a group of employees aimed at agreements to regulate working salaries, working conditions, benefits, and other aspects of workers' compensation and rights for workers. The interests of the employees are commonly presented by representatives of a trade union to which the employees belong. The collective agreements reached by these negotiations usually set out wage scales, working hours, training, health and safety, overtime, grievance mechanisms, and rights to participate in workplace or company affairs.

Exam Probability: **Medium**

17. *Answer choices:*
(see index for correct answer)

- a. Federal Labor Relations Act
- b. Pattern bargaining
- c. Mutual gains bargaining
- d. Common rule awards

Guidance: level 1

:: Business ::

The seller, or the provider of the goods or services, completes a sale in response to an acquisition, appropriation, requisition or a direct interaction with the buyer at the point of sale. There is a passing of title of the item, and the settlement of a price, in which agreement is reached on a price for which transfer of ownership of the item will occur. The seller, not the purchaser typically executes the sale and it may be completed prior to the obligation of payment. In the case of indirect interaction, a person who sells goods or service on behalf of the owner is known as a _____ man or _____ woman or _____ person, but this often refers to someone selling goods in a store/shop, in which case other terms are also common, including _____ clerk, shop assistant, and retail clerk.

18. *Answer choices:*

(see index for correct answer)

- a. Kingdomality
- b. Corporate social media
- c. Ansoff Matrix
- d. Sales

Guidance: level 1

:: Statistical terminology ::

_____ is the ability to avoid wasting materials, energy, efforts, money, and time in doing something or in producing a desired result. In a more general sense, it is the ability to do things well, successfully, and without waste. In more mathematical or scientific terms, it is a measure of the extent to which input is well used for an intended task or function . It often specifically comprises the capability of a specific application of effort to produce a specific outcome with a minimum amount or quantity of waste, expense, or unnecessary effort. _____ refers to very different inputs and outputs in different fields and industries.

19. *Answer choices:*

(see index for correct answer)

- a. Percentile rank
- b. Trend stationary

- c. Efficiency
- d. Standardised mortality rate

Guidance: level 1

:: Statistical terminology ::

_____ is the magnitude or dimensions of a thing. _____ can be measured as length, width, height, diameter, perimeter, area, volume, or mass.

Exam Probability: **High**

20. *Answer choices:*
(see index for correct answer)

- a. Size
- b. Gompertz function
- c. Trend stationary
- d. Kurtosis risk

Guidance: level 1

:: Decision theory ::

Within economics the concept of _____ is used to model worth or value, but its usage has evolved significantly over time. The term was introduced initially as a measure of pleasure or satisfaction within the theory of utilitarianism by moral philosophers such as Jeremy Bentham and John Stuart Mill. But the term has been adapted and reapplied within neoclassical economics, which dominates modern economic theory, as a _____ function that represents a consumer's preference ordering over a choice set. As such, it is devoid of its original interpretation as a measurement of the pleasure or satisfaction obtained by the consumer from that choice.

Exam Probability: **Low**

21. *Answer choices:*
(see index for correct answer)

- a. Expected value of perfect information
- b. Regret
- c. Utility
- d. ELECTRE

Guidance: level 1

_____ , a form of alternative dispute resolution , is a way to resolve disputes outside the courts. The dispute will be decided by one or more persons , which renders the " _____ award". An _____ award is legally binding on both sides and enforceable in the courts.

Exam Probability: **Medium**

22. *Answer choices:*
(see index for correct answer)

- a. Arbitration
- b. Punitive damages
- c. Colour of right
- d. Person of interest

Guidance: level 1

_____ es can be learned implicitly within cultural contexts. People may develop _____ es toward or against an individual, an ethnic group, a sexual or gender identity, a nation, a religion, a social class, a political party, theoretical paradigms and ideologies within academic domains, or a species. _____ ed means one-sided, lacking a neutral viewpoint, or not having an open mind. _____ can come in many forms and is related to prejudice and intuition.

Exam Probability: **Low**

23. *Answer choices:*
(see index for correct answer)

- a. Percentage point
- b. Statistical epidemiology
- c. Bias
- d. Statistical genetics

Guidance: level 1

_____ is a chemical element with symbol Pb and atomic number 82. It is a heavy metal that is denser than most common materials. _____ is soft and malleable, and also has a relatively low melting point. When freshly cut, _____ is silvery with a hint of blue; it tarnishes to a dull gray color when exposed to air. _____ has the highest atomic number of any stable element and three of its isotopes are endpoints of major nuclear decay chains of heavier elements.

Exam Probability: **Medium**

24. *Answer choices:*
(see index for correct answer)

- a. Lead
- b. Alice Hamilton
- c. Carbonless copy paper
- d. Risk Information Exchange

Guidance: level 1

:: Employment discrimination ::

A _____ is a metaphor used to represent an invisible barrier that keeps a given demographic from rising beyond a certain level in a hierarchy.

Exam Probability: **Low**

25. *Answer choices:*
(see index for correct answer)

- a. Glass ceiling
- b. Marriage bars
- c. LGBT employment discrimination in the United States
- d. Glass cliff

Guidance: level 1

:: Social networks ::

_____ broadly refers to those factors of effectively functioning social groups that include such things as interpersonal relationships, a shared sense of identity, a shared understanding, shared norms, shared values, trust, cooperation, and reciprocity. However, the many views of this complex subject make a single definition difficult.

Exam Probability: **Low**

26. *Answer choices:*
(see index for correct answer)

- a. Social network aggregation
- b. Wish Upon A Hero
- c. Crowd computing
- d. Online learning community

Guidance: level 1

:: Organizational theory ::

Decentralisation is the process by which the activities of an organization, particularly those regarding planning and decision making, are distributed or delegated away from a central, authoritative location or group. Concepts of _____ have been applied to group dynamics and management science in private businesses and organizations, political science, law and public administration, economics, money and technology.

Exam Probability: **Medium**

27. *Answer choices:*
(see index for correct answer)

- a. Organizational learning
- b. Contingency theory
- c. Organizational engineering
- d. Team leader

Guidance: level 1

:: Information science ::

_____ is the resolution of uncertainty; it is that which answers the question of "what an entity is" and thus defines both its essence and nature of its characteristics. _____ relates to both data and knowledge, as data is meaningful _____ representing values attributed to parameters, and knowledge signifies understanding of a concept. _____ is uncoupled from an observer, which is an entity that can access _____ and thus discern what it specifies; _____ exists beyond an event horizon for example. In the case of knowledge, the _____ itself requires a cognitive observer to be obtained.

Exam Probability: **Medium**

28. *Answer choices:*
(see index for correct answer)

- a. Findability
- b. Cultural informatics
- c. Subject indexing
- d. Data drilling

Guidance: level 1

:: Business law ::

A _____ is a business entity created by two or more parties, generally characterized by shared ownership, shared returns and risks, and shared governance. Companies typically pursue _____ s for one of four reasons: to access a new market, particularly emerging markets; to gain scale efficiencies by combining assets and operations; to share risk for major investments or projects; or to access skills and capabilities.

Exam Probability: **Low**

29. *Answer choices:*
(see index for correct answer)

- a. Output contract
- b. Undervalue transaction
- c. General assignment
- d. Joint venture

Guidance: level 1

_____ , executive management, upper management, or a management team is generally a team of individuals at the highest level of management of an organization who have the day-to-day tasks of managing that organization — sometimes a company or a corporation.

Exam Probability: **Low**

30. *Answer choices:*
(see index for correct answer)

- a. Fresh tracks
- b. ABC Consultants
- c. Skills management
- d. Senior management

Guidance: level 1

:: ::

According to Torrington, a _____ is usually developed by conducting a job analysis, which includes examining the tasks and sequences of tasks necessary to perform the job. The analysis considers the areas of knowledge and skills needed for the job. A job usually includes several roles. According to Hall, the _____ might be broadened to form a person specification or may be known as "terms of reference". The person/job specification can be presented as a stand-alone document, but in practice it is usually included within the _____ . A _____ is often used by employers in the recruitment process.

Exam Probability: **High**

31. *Answer choices:*
(see index for correct answer)

- a. Sarbanes-Oxley act of 2002
- b. Job description
- c. information systems assessment
- d. corporate values

Guidance: level 1

:: Product management ::

_____ s, also known as Shewhart charts or process-behavior charts, are a statistical process control tool used to determine if a manufacturing or business process is in a state of control.

Exam Probability: **Medium**

32. *Answer choices:*
(see index for correct answer)

- a. Trademark look
- b. Control chart
- c. Technology acceptance model
- d. business name

Guidance: level 1

:: Marketing ::

_____ , in marketing, manufacturing, call centres and management, is the use of flexible computer-aided manufacturing systems to produce custom output. Such systems combine the low unit costs of mass production processes with the flexibility of individual customization.

Exam Probability: **Medium**

33. *Answer choices:*
(see index for correct answer)

- a. Book of business
- b. Meta marketing
- c. Mass customization
- d. Global Center for Health Innovation

Guidance: level 1

:: Monopoly (economics) ::

_____ is a category of property that includes intangible creations of the human intellect. _____ encompasses two types of rights: industrial property rights and copyright. It was not until the 19th century that the term " _____ " began to be used, and not until the late 20th century that it became commonplace in the majority of the world.

34. *Answer choices:*
(see index for correct answer)

- a. Public utility
- b. Intellectual property
- c. Privatization
- d. Monopoly

Guidance: level 1

:: Production and manufacturing ::

_____ is a set of techniques and tools for process improvement. Though as a shortened form it may be found written as 6S, it should not be confused with the methodology known as 6S .

Exam Probability: **Medium**

35. *Answer choices:*
(see index for correct answer)

- a. Changeover
- b. Engineering validation test
- c. Six Sigma
- d. Report generator

Guidance: level 1

:: ::

_____ consists of using generic or ad hoc methods in an orderly manner to find solutions to problems. Some of the problem-solving techniques developed and used in philosophy, artificial intelligence, computer science, engineering, mathematics, or medicine are related to mental problem-solving techniques studied in psychology.

Exam Probability: **High**

36. *Answer choices:*
(see index for correct answer)

- a. interpersonal communication
- b. hierarchical
- c. Problem solving

- d. deep-level diversity

:: Employment ::

The _____ is an individual's metaphorical "journey" through learning, work and other aspects of life. There are a number of ways to define _____ and the term is used in a variety of ways.

Exam Probability: **Low**

37. *Answer choices:*
(see index for correct answer)

- a. Externship
- b. Numerary
- c. Encore career
- d. Career

:: ::

In organizational behavior and industrial/organizational psychology, proactivity or _____ behavior by individuals refers to anticipatory, change-oriented and self-initiated behavior in situations. _____ behavior involves acting in advance of a future situation, rather than just reacting. It means taking control and making things happen rather than just adjusting to a situation or waiting for something to happen. _____ employees generally do not need to be asked to act, nor do they require detailed instructions.

Exam Probability: **Low**

38. *Answer choices:*
(see index for correct answer)

- a. Proactive
- b. surface-level diversity
- c. Character
- d. open system

_____ is an organized effort to gather information about target markets or customers. It is a very important component of business strategy. The term is commonly interchanged with marketing research; however, expert practictioners may wish to draw a distinction, in that marketing research is concerned specifically about marketing processes, while _____ is concerned specifically with markets.

Exam Probability: **Medium**

39. *Answer choices:*
(see index for correct answer)

- a. Market research
- b. Nonprobability sampling
- c. Mode effect
- d. DigitalMR

Guidance: level 1

:: Human resource management ::

_____ is a core function of human resource management and it is related to the specification of contents, methods and relationship of jobs in order to satisfy technological and organizational requirements as well as the social and personal requirements of the job holder or the employee. Its principles are geared towards how the nature of a person's job affects their attitudes and behavior at work, particularly relating to characteristics such as skill variety and autonomy. The aim of a _____ is to improve job satisfaction, to improve through-put, to improve quality and to reduce employee problems .

Exam Probability: **Low**

40. *Answer choices:*
(see index for correct answer)

- a. Employee value proposition
- b. Joint Personnel Administration
- c. Organizational chart
- d. Sham peer review

Guidance: level 1

An _____ is a person temporarily or permanently residing in a country other than their native country. In common usage, the term often refers to professionals, skilled workers, or artists taking positions outside their home country, either independently or sent abroad by their employers, who can be companies, universities, governments, or non-governmental organisations. Effectively migrant workers, they usually earn more than they would at home, and less than local employees. However, the term ` _____ ` is also used for retirees and others who have chosen to live outside their native country. Historically, it has also referred to exiles.

Exam Probability: **High**

41. *Answer choices:*
(see index for correct answer)

- a. hierarchical perspective
- b. surface-level diversity
- c. deep-level diversity
- d. process perspective

Guidance: level 1

:: Scientific method ::

In the social sciences and life sciences, a _____ is a research method involving an up-close, in-depth, and detailed examination of a subject of study , as well as its related contextual conditions.

Exam Probability: **Medium**

42. *Answer choices:*
(see index for correct answer)

- a. Causal research
- b. explanatory research
- c. Preference test
- d. Case study

Guidance: level 1

:: Business law ::

A _____ is an arrangement where parties, known as partners, agree to cooperate to advance their mutual interests. The partners in a _____ may be individuals, businesses, interest-based organizations, schools, governments or combinations. Organizations may partner to increase the likelihood of each achieving their mission and to amplify their reach. A _____ may result in issuing and holding equity or may be only governed by a contract.

Exam Probability: **Low**

43. *Answer choices:*
(see index for correct answer)

- a. Copyright transfer agreement
- b. De facto corporation and corporation by estoppel
- c. Partnership
- d. Whitewash waiver

Guidance: level 1

:: Analysis ::

_____ is the process of breaking a complex topic or substance into smaller parts in order to gain a better understanding of it. The technique has been applied in the study of mathematics and logic since before Aristotle , though _____ as a formal concept is a relatively recent development.

Exam Probability: **Medium**

44. *Answer choices:*
(see index for correct answer)

- a. Situational analysis
- b. Analysis
- c. Rational analysis
- d. Deviation analysis

Guidance: level 1

:: Management ::

_____ is the identification, evaluation, and prioritization of risks followed by coordinated and economical application of resources to minimize, monitor, and control the probability or impact of unfortunate events or to maximize the realization of opportunities.

Exam Probability: **Low**

45. *Answer choices:*
(see index for correct answer)

- a. Risk management
- b. Mission critical
- c. Virtual customer environment
- d. Preventive action

Guidance: level 1

:: Quality management ::

A _____ or quality control circle is a group of workers who do the same or similar work, who meet regularly to identify, analyze and solve work-related problems. Normally small in size, the group is usually led by a supervisor or manager and presents its solutions to management; where possible, workers implement the solutions themselves in order to improve the performance of the organization and motivate employees. _____ s were at their most popular during the 1980s, but continue to exist in the form of Kaizen groups and similar worker participation schemes.

Exam Probability: **Low**

46. *Answer choices:*
(see index for correct answer)

- a. Indian Register Quality Systems
- b. Informal Methods
- c. Det Norske Veritas
- d. Bureau Veritas

Guidance: level 1

:: ::

_____ is the process of two or more people or organizations working together to complete a task or achieve a goal. _____ is similar to cooperation. Most _____ requires leadership, although the form of leadership can be social within a decentralized and egalitarian group. Teams that work collaboratively often access greater resources, recognition and rewards when facing competition for finite resources.

Exam Probability: **Medium**

47. *Answer choices:*

(see index for correct answer)

- a. empathy
- b. Sarbanes-Oxley act of 2002
- c. interpersonal communication
- d. information systems assessment

Guidance: level 1

:: Labor ::

The workforce or labour force is the labour pool in employment. It is generally used to describe those working for a single company or industry, but can also apply to a geographic region like a city, state, or country. Within a company, its value can be labelled as its "Workforce in Place". The workforce of a country includes both the employed and the unemployed. The labour force participation rate, LFPR , is the ratio between the labour force and the overall size of their cohort . The term generally excludes the employers or management, and can imply those involved in manual labour. It may also mean all those who are available for work.

Exam Probability: **Medium**

48. *Answer choices:*

(see index for correct answer)

- a. Labor force
- b. Side letter
- c. New Unionism
- d. Shreni

Guidance: level 1

Systems theory is the interdisciplinary study of systems. A system is a cohesive conglomeration of interrelated and interdependent parts that is either natural or man-made. Every system is delineated by its spatial and temporal boundaries, surrounded and influenced by its environment, described by its structure and purpose or nature and expressed in its functioning. In terms of its effects, a system can be more than the sum of its parts if it expresses synergy or emergent behavior. Changing one part of the system usually affects other parts and the whole system, with predictable patterns of behavior. For systems that are self-learning and self-adapting, the positive growth and adaptation depend upon how well the system is adjusted with its environment. Some systems function mainly to support other systems by aiding in the maintenance of the other system to prevent failure. The goal of systems theory is systematically discovering a system's dynamics, constraints, conditions and elucidating principles that can be discerned and applied to systems at every level of nesting, and in every field for achieving optimized equifinality.

Exam Probability: **Medium**

49. *Answer choices:*
(see index for correct answer)

- a. Interdependence
- b. Ray Hammond
- c. Scenario analysis
- d. Business continuity planning

Guidance: level 1

:: Management ::

The _____ is a strategy performance management tool – a semi-standard structured report, that can be used by managers to keep track of the execution of activities by the staff within their control and to monitor the consequences arising from these actions.

Exam Probability: **Low**

50. *Answer choices:*
(see index for correct answer)

- a. Balanced scorecard

- b. Porter five forces analysis
- c. Stovepipe
- d. middle manager

Guidance: level 1

:: Human resource management ::

_____ expands the capacity of individuals to perform in leadership roles within organizations. Leadership roles are those that facilitate execution of a company's strategy through building alignment, winning mindshare and growing the capabilities of others. Leadership roles may be formal, with the corresponding authority to make decisions and take responsibility, or they may be informal roles with little official authority .

Exam Probability: **High**

51. *Answer choices:*
(see index for correct answer)

- a. Dr. Marri Channa Reddy Human Resource Development Institute of Andhra Pradesh
- b. Contractor management
- c. Leadership development
- d. Simultaneous recruiting of new graduates

Guidance: level 1

:: Management ::

In business, a _____ is the attribute that allows an organization to outperform its competitors. A _____ may include access to natural resources, such as high-grade ores or a low-cost power source, highly skilled labor, geographic location, high entry barriers, and access to new technology.

Exam Probability: **High**

52. *Answer choices:*
(see index for correct answer)

- a. U-procedure and Theory U
- b. Opera management
- c. Competitive advantage
- d. Stewardship theory

Guidance: level 1

In political science, an _____ is a means by which a petition signed by a certain minimum number of registered voters can force a government to choose to either enact a law or hold a public vote in parliament in what is called indirect _____ , or under direct _____ , the proposition is immediately put to a plebiscite or referendum, in what is called a Popular initiated Referendum or citizen-initiated referendum).

Exam Probability: **Medium**

53. *Answer choices:*
(see index for correct answer)

- a. The Transformation Project
- b. Task
- c. Initiative
- d. Fast-track construction

Guidance: level 1

_____ are the people who make up the workforce of an organization, business sector, or economy. "Human capital" is sometimes used synonymously with " _____ ", although human capital typically refers to a narrower effect . Likewise, other terms sometimes used include manpower, talent, labor, personnel, or simply people.

Exam Probability: **Low**

54. *Answer choices:*
(see index for correct answer)

- a. Employee value proposition
- b. Workforce modeling
- c. Job enrichment
- d. Human resources

Guidance: level 1

_____ is the process of designing, launching and running a new business, which is often initially a small business. The people who create these businesses are called entrepreneurs.

Exam Probability: **Medium**

55. *Answer choices:*
(see index for correct answer)

- a. General partner
- b. Entrepreneurship
- c. City manager
- d. Chief diversity officer

Guidance: level 1

:: Marketing ::

_____ is based on a marketing concept which can be adopted by an organization as a strategy for business expansion. Where implemented, a franchisor licenses its know-how, procedures, intellectual property, use of its business model, brand, and rights to sell its branded products and services to a franchisee. In return the franchisee pays certain fees and agrees to comply with certain obligations, typically set out in a Franchise Agreement.

Exam Probability: **Low**

56. *Answer choices:*
(see index for correct answer)

- a. Franchising
- b. Franchise disclosure document
- c. Mass market
- d. Meta marketing

Guidance: level 1

:: Production economics ::

In microeconomics, _____ are the cost advantages that enterprises obtain due to their scale of operation , with cost per unit of output decreasing with increasing scale.

57. *Answer choices:*

(see index for correct answer)

- a. Factor price
- b. short run
- c. Productivity world
- d. Economies of scale

Guidance: level 1

:: Supply chain management ::

_____ is the process of finding and agreeing to terms, and acquiring goods, services, or works from an external source, often via a tendering or competitive bidding process. _____ is used to ensure the buyer receives goods, services, or works at the best possible price when aspects such as quality, quantity, time, and location are compared. Corporations and public bodies often define processes intended to promote fair and open competition for their business while minimizing risks such as exposure to fraud and collusion.

Exam Probability: **Low**

58. *Answer choices:*

(see index for correct answer)

- a. National Centre for Cold-chain Development
- b. Procurement
- c. ClearOrbit
- d. Vendor-managed inventory

Guidance: level 1

:: Occupations ::

An _____ is a person who has a position of authority in a hierarchical organization. The term derives from the late Latin from officiarius, meaning "official".

Exam Probability: **Low**

59. *Answer choices:*

(see index for correct answer)

- a. Miner
- b. Elevator operator
- c. Manciple
- d. Biologist

Guidance: level 1

Business law

Corporate law (also known as business law) is the body of law governing the rights, relations, and conduct of persons, companies, organizations and businesses. It refers to the legal practice relating to, or the theory of corporations. Corporate law often describes the law relating to matters which derive directly from the life-cycle of a corporation. It thus encompasses the formation, funding, governance, and death of a corporation.

:: ::

_____ s and acquisitions are transactions in which the ownership of companies, other business organizations, or their operating units are transferred or consolidated with other entities. As an aspect of strategic management, M&A can allow enterprises to grow or downsize, and change the nature of their business or competitive position.

Exam Probability: **Low**

1. *Answer choices:*
(see index for correct answer)

- a. cultural
- b. Merger
- c. open system
- d. corporate values

Guidance: level 1

:: ::

_____ , also referred to as orthostasis, is a human position in which the body is held in an upright position and supported only by the feet.

Exam Probability: **Low**

2. *Answer choices:*
(see index for correct answer)

- a. Character
- b. Standing
- c. process perspective
- d. cultural

Guidance: level 1

:: ::

_____ is a process whereby a person assumes the parenting of another, usually a child, from that person's biological or legal parent or parents. Legal _____ s permanently transfers all rights and responsibilities, along with filiation, from the biological parent or parents.

Exam Probability: **High**

3. *Answer choices:*
(see index for correct answer)

- a. imperative
- b. surface-level diversity
- c. empathy
- d. levels of analysis

Guidance: level 1

:: Contract law ::

_____ is a legal cause of action and a type of civil wrong, in which a binding agreement or bargained-for exchange is not honored by one or more of the parties to the contract by non-performance or interference with the other party's performance. Breach occurs when a party to a contract fails to fulfill its obligation as described in the contract, or communicates an intent to fail the obligation or otherwise appears not to be able to perform its obligation under the contract. Where there is _____ , the resulting damages will have to be paid by the party breaching the contract to the aggrieved party.

Exam Probability: **Low**

4. *Answer choices:*
(see index for correct answer)

- a. Duress
- b. Breach of contract
- c. South African contract law

- d. Recording contract

Guidance: level 1

:: International relations ::

_____ is double mindedness or double heartedness in duplicity, fraud, or deception. It may involve intentional deceit of others, or self-deception.

Exam Probability: **Medium**

5. *Answer choices:*
(see index for correct answer)

- a. Bad faith
- b. Global Alliance for Peace and Prosperity
- c. Neoclassical realism
- d. Conflict early warning

Guidance: level 1

:: Commercial item transport and distribution ::

_____ s may be negotiable or non-negotiable. Negotiable _____ s allow transfer of ownership of that commodity without having to deliver the physical commodity. See Delivery order.

Exam Probability: **Low**

6. *Answer choices:*
(see index for correct answer)

- a. Warehouse receipt
- b. Courier software
- c. Container ship
- d. Freight quality partnerships

Guidance: level 1

:: Personal property law ::

Bailment describes a legal relationship in common law where physical possession of personal property, or a chattel, is transferred from one person to another person who subsequently has possession of the property. It arises when a person gives property to someone else for safekeeping, and is a cause of action independent of contract or tort.

Exam Probability: **Medium**

7. *Answer choices:*
(see index for correct answer)

- a. Bailee
- b. bailment

Guidance: level 1

:: Legal terms ::

_____ , or exemplary damages, are damages assessed in order to punish the defendant for outrageous conduct and/or to reform or deter the defendant and others from engaging in conduct similar to that which formed the basis of the lawsuit. Although the purpose of _____ is not to compensate the plaintiff, the plaintiff will receive all or some of the _____ award.

Exam Probability: **Medium**

8. *Answer choices:*
(see index for correct answer)

- a. Gross negligence
- b. Punitive damages
- c. Prejudice
- d. Forfeiture

Guidance: level 1

:: ::

The U.S. _____ is an independent agency of the United States federal government. The SEC holds primary responsibility for enforcing the federal securities laws, proposing securities rules, and regulating the securities industry, the nation's stock and options exchanges, and other activities and organizations, including the electronic securities markets in the United States.

Exam Probability: **Medium**

9. *Answer choices:*
(see index for correct answer)

- a. co-culture
- b. hierarchical perspective
- c. corporate values
- d. information systems assessment

Guidance: level 1

:: Actuarial science ::

_____ is the possibility of losing something of value. Values can be gained or lost when taking _____ resulting from a given action or inaction, foreseen or unforeseen . _____ can also be defined as the intentional interaction with uncertainty. Uncertainty is a potential, unpredictable, and uncontrollable outcome; _____ is a consequence of action taken in spite of uncertainty.

Exam Probability: **Medium**

10. *Answer choices:*
(see index for correct answer)

- a. John Graunt
- b. Risk
- c. Asset allocation
- d. Maximum life span

Guidance: level 1

:: ::

The Sherman Antitrust Act of 1890 was a United States antitrust law that regulates competition among enterprises, which was passed by Congress under the presidency of Benjamin Harrison.

Exam Probability: **Low**

11. *Answer choices:*

(see index for correct answer)

- a. process perspective
- b. Sherman Act
- c. interpersonal communication
- d. levels of analysis

Guidance: level 1

:: Debt ::

A _____ is a party that has a claim on the services of a second party. It is a person or institution to whom money is owed. The first party, in general, has provided some property or service to the second party under the assumption that the second party will return an equivalent property and service. The second party is frequently called a debtor or borrower. The first party is called the _____ , which is the lender of property, service, or money.

Exam Probability: **High**

12. *Answer choices:*

(see index for correct answer)

- a. Financial assistance
- b. Borrowing base
- c. Extendible bond
- d. Creditor

Guidance: level 1

:: ::

The _____ of 1933, also known as the 1933 Act, the _____ , the Truth in _____ , the Federal _____ , and the `33 Act, was enacted by the United States Congress on May 27, 1933, during the Great Depression, after the stock market crash of 1929. Legislated pursuant to the Interstate Commerce Clause of the Constitution, it requires every offer or sale of securities that uses the means and instrumentalities of interstate commerce to be registered with the SEC pursuant to the 1933 Act, unless an exemption from registration exists under the law. The term "means and instrumentalities of interstate commerce" is extremely broad and it is virtually impossible to avoid the operation of the statute by attempting to offer or sell a security without using an "instrumentality" of interstate commerce. Any use of a telephone, for example, or the mails would probably be enough to subject the transaction to the statute.

Exam Probability: **High**

13. *Answer choices:*

(see index for correct answer)

- a. imperative
- b. deep-level diversity
- c. similarity-attraction theory
- d. corporate values

Guidance: level 1

:: Generally Accepted Accounting Principles ::

In accounting, _____ is the income that a business have from its normal business activities, usually from the sale of goods and services to customers. _____ is also referred to as sales or turnover.Some companies receive _____ from interest, royalties, or other fees. _____ may refer to business income in general, or it may refer to the amount, in a monetary unit, earned during a period of time, as in "Last year, Company X had _____ of $42 million". Profits or net income generally imply total _____ minus total expenses in a given period. In accounting, in the balance statement it is a subsection of the Equity section and _____ increases equity, it is often referred to as the "top line" due to its position on the income statement at the very top. This is to be contrasted with the "bottom line" which denotes net income .

14. *Answer choices:*
(see index for correct answer)

- a. Revenue
- b. Cost principle
- c. Management accounting principles
- d. Deferred income

Guidance: level 1

:: ::

_____ refers to a business or organization attempting to acquire goods or services to accomplish its goals. Although there are several organizations that attempt to set standards in the _____ process, processes can vary greatly between organizations. Typically the word " _____ " is not used interchangeably with the word "procurement", since procurement typically includes expediting, supplier quality, and transportation and logistics in addition to _____ .

15. *Answer choices:*
(see index for correct answer)

- a. deep-level diversity
- b. personal values
- c. information systems assessment
- d. Purchasing

Guidance: level 1

:: ::

An _____ is a formal or official change made to a law, contract, constitution, or other legal document. It is based on the verb to amend, which means to change for better. _____ s can add, remove, or update parts of these agreements. They are often used when it is better to change the document than to write a new one.

16. *Answer choices:*

- a. Amendment
- b. information systems assessment
- c. levels of analysis
- d. open system

Guidance: level 1

:: ::

The _____ to the United States Constitution prevents the government from making laws which respect an establishment of religion, prohibit the free exercise of religion, or abridge the freedom of speech, the freedom of the press, the right to peaceably assemble, or the right to petition the government for redress of grievances. It was adopted on December 15, 1791, as one of the ten amendments that constitute the Bill of Rights.

Exam Probability: **Low**

17. *Answer choices:*

- a. First Amendment
- b. interpersonal communication
- c. cultural
- d. functional perspective

Guidance: level 1

:: Competition law ::

In competition law, a _____ is a market in which a particular product or service is sold. It is the intersection of a relevant product market and a relevant geographic market. The European Commission defines a _____ and its product and geographic components as follows.

Exam Probability: **Low**

18. *Answer choices:*

- a. Relevant market
- b. Orange-Book-Standard
- c. Illegal per se

- d. Essential facilities doctrine

Guidance: level 1

:: Utilitarianism ::

_____ is a family of consequentialist ethical theories that promotes actions that maximize happiness and well-being for the majority of a population. Although different varieties of _____ admit different characterizations, the basic idea behind all of them is to in some sense maximize utility, which is often defined in terms of well-being or related concepts. For instance, Jeremy Bentham, the founder of _____ , described utility as

Exam Probability: **Medium**

19. *Answer choices:*
(see index for correct answer)

- a. The Collected Works of Jeremy Bentham
- b. Utilitarianism
- c. Paradox of hedonism
- d. Telishment

Guidance: level 1

:: Equity (law) ::

An assignment is a legal term used in the context of the law of contract and of property. In both instances, assignment is the process whereby a person, the assignor, transfers rights or benefits to another, the _____ . An assignment may not transfer a duty, burden or detriment without the express agreement of the _____ . The right or benefit being assigned may be a gift or it may be paid for with a contractual consideration such as money.

Exam Probability: **High**

20. *Answer choices:*
(see index for correct answer)

- a. assignor
- b. Equitable conversion

Guidance: level 1

A contract is a legally-binding agreement which recognises and governs the rights and duties of the parties to the agreement. A contract is legally enforceable because it meets the requirements and approval of the law. An agreement typically involves the exchange of goods, services, money, or promises of any of those. In the event of breach of contract, the law awards the injured party access to legal remedies such as damages and cancellation.

Exam Probability: **High**

21. *Answer choices:*

(see index for correct answer)

- a. similarity-attraction theory
- b. Contract law
- c. imperative
- d. empathy

Guidance: level 1

:: Business ethics ::

_____ is a type of harassment technique that relates to a sexual nature and the unwelcome or inappropriate promise of rewards in exchange for sexual favors. _____ includes a range of actions from mild transgressions to sexual abuse or assault. Harassment can occur in many different social settings such as the workplace, the home, school, churches, etc. Harassers or victims may be of any gender.

Exam Probability: **Low**

22. *Answer choices:*

(see index for correct answer)

- a. Earnings quality
- b. Sexual harassment
- c. Accounting ethics
- d. Resource Conservation and Recovery Act

Guidance: level 1

_____ is the practice of protecting the natural environment by individuals, organizations and governments. Its objectives are to conserve natural resources and the existing natural environment and, where possible, to repair damage and reverse trends.

Exam Probability: **Low**

23. *Answer choices:*
(see index for correct answer)

- a. levels of analysis
- b. open system
- c. co-culture
- d. Environmental Protection

Guidance: level 1

:: ::

_____ is the practical authority granted to a legal body to administer justice within a defined field of responsibility, e.g., Michigan tax law. In federations like the United States, areas of _____ apply to local, state, and federal levels; e.g. the court has _____ to apply federal law.

Exam Probability: **Low**

24. *Answer choices:*
(see index for correct answer)

- a. cultural
- b. open system
- c. Jurisdiction
- d. functional perspective

Guidance: level 1

:: ::

A _____ is an individual or institution that legally owns one or more shares of stock in a public or private corporation. _____ s may be referred to as members of a corporation. Legally, a person is not a _____ in a corporation until their name and other details are entered in the corporation's register of _____ s or members.

Exam Probability: **High**

25. *Answer choices:*
(see index for correct answer)

- a. functional perspective
- b. surface-level diversity
- c. imperative
- d. Character

Guidance: level 1

:: Sexual harassment in the United States ::

In law, a _____, reasonable man, or the man on the Clapham omnibus is a hypothetical person of legal fiction crafted by the courts and communicated through case law and jury instructions.

Exam Probability: **Low**

26. *Answer choices:*
(see index for correct answer)

- a. Alexander v. Yale
- b. War Zone
- c. Blakey v. Continental Airlines
- d. Reasonable person

Guidance: level 1

:: Business models ::

A _____ is "an autonomous association of persons united voluntarily to meet their common economic, social, and cultural needs and aspirations through a jointly-owned and democratically-controlled enterprise". _____ s may include.

27. *Answer choices:*
(see index for correct answer)

- a. InnovationXchange
- b. Volatility, uncertainty, complexity and ambiguity
- c. Cooperative
- d. The Community Company

Guidance: level 1

:: Asset ::

In financial accounting, an _____ is any resource owned by the business. Anything tangible or intangible that can be owned or controlled to produce value and that is held by a company to produce positive economic value is an _____ . Simply stated, _____ s represent value of ownership that can be converted into cash . The balance sheet of a firm records the monetary value of the _____ s owned by that firm. It covers money and other valuables belonging to an individual or to a business.

28. *Answer choices:*
(see index for correct answer)

- a. Fixed asset
- b. Current asset

Guidance: level 1

:: Shareholders ::

A _____ is a payment made by a corporation to its shareholders, usually as a distribution of profits. When a corporation earns a profit or surplus, the corporation is able to re-invest the profit in the business and pay a proportion of the profit as a _____ to shareholders. Distribution to shareholders may be in cash or, if the corporation has a _____ reinvestment plan, the amount can be paid by the issue of further shares or share repurchase. When _____ s are paid, shareholders typically must pay income taxes, and the corporation does not receive a corporate income tax deduction for the _____ payments.

29. *Answer choices:*

- a. Shareholder Executive
- b. Majority interest
- c. Dividend
- d. Shotgun clause

Guidance: level 1

:: Legal reasoning ::

_____ is a Latin expression meaning on its first encounter or at first sight. The literal translation would be "at first face" or "at first appearance", from the feminine forms of primus and facies , both in the ablative case. In modern, colloquial and conversational English, a common translation would be "on the face of it". The term _____ is used in modern legal English to signify that upon initial examination, sufficient corroborating evidence appears to exist to support a case. In common law jurisdictions, _____ denotes evidence that, unless rebutted, would be sufficient to prove a particular proposition or fact. The term is used similarly in academic philosophy. Most legal proceedings, in most jurisdictions, require a _____ case to exist, following which proceedings may then commence to test it, and create a ruling.

30. *Answer choices:*

- a. Reasonable man
- b. Probable cause
- c. deliberation

Guidance: level 1

:: ::

In legal terminology, a _____ is any formal legal document that sets out the facts and legal reasons that the filing party or parties believes are sufficient to support a claim against the party or parties against whom the claim is brought that entitles the plaintiff to a remedy . For example, the Federal Rules of Civil Procedure that govern civil litigation in United States courts provide that a civil action is commenced with the filing or service of a pleading called a _____ . Civil court rules in states that have incorporated the Federal Rules of Civil Procedure use the same term for the same pleading.

Exam Probability: **High**

31. *Answer choices:*
(see index for correct answer)

- a. information systems assessment
- b. Sarbanes-Oxley act of 2002
- c. empathy
- d. Complaint

Guidance: level 1

:: Debt ::

_____ is the trust which allows one party to provide money or resources to another party wherein the second party does not reimburse the first party immediately , but promises either to repay or return those resources at a later date. In other words, _____ is a method of making reciprocity formal, legally enforceable, and extensible to a large group of unrelated people.

Exam Probability: **Medium**

32. *Answer choices:*
(see index for correct answer)

- a. Student debt
- b. Crown debt
- c. Credit
- d. Cessio bonorum

Guidance: level 1

In everyday language, _____ refers to exaggerated or false praise. In law, _____ is a promotional statement or claim that expresses subjective rather than objective views, which no "reasonable person" would take literally. _____ serves to "puff up" an exaggerated image of what is being described and is especially featured in testimonials.

Exam Probability: **Medium**

33. *Answer choices:*
(see index for correct answer)

- a. Co-branding
- b. Puffery
- c. Trade promotion
- d. Pressbook

Guidance: level 1

_____ or statute law is written law set down by a body of legislature or by a singular legislator . This is as opposed to oral or customary law; or regulatory law promulgated by the executive or common law of the judiciary. Statutes may originate with national, state legislatures or local municipalities.

Exam Probability: **Medium**

34. *Answer choices:*
(see index for correct answer)

- a. ratification
- b. Statutory Law
- c. Statute of repose
- d. statute law

Guidance: level 1

A _____ is a source or supply from which a benefit is produced and it has some utility. _____ s can broadly be classified upon their availability—they are classified into renewable and non-renewable _____ s.Examples of non renewable _____ s are coal ,crude oil natural gas nuclear energy etc. Examples of renewable _____ s are air,water,wind,solar energy etc. They can also be classified as actual and potential on the basis of level of development and use, on the basis of origin they can be classified as biotic and abiotic, and on the basis of their distribution, as ubiquitous and localized . An item becomes a _____ with time and developing technology. Typically, _____ s are materials, energy, services, staff, knowledge, or other assets that are transformed to produce benefit and in the process may be consumed or made unavailable. Benefits of _____ utilization may include increased wealth, proper functioning of a system, or enhanced well-being. From a human perspective a natural _____ is anything obtained from the environment to satisfy human needs and wants. From a broader biological or ecological perspective a _____ satisfies the needs of a living organism .

35. *Answer choices:*
(see index for correct answer)

- a. The Practice Standard for Scheduling
- b. Cost-benefit
- c. Terms of reference
- d. Resource

Guidance: level 1

:: ::

_____ , in United States trademark law, is a statutory cause of action that permits a party to petition the Trademark Trial and Appeal Board of the Patent and Trademark Office to cancel a trademark registration that "may disparage or falsely suggest a connection with persons, living or dead, institutions, beliefs, or national symbols, or bring them into contempt or disrepute." Unlike claims regarding the validity of the mark, a _____ claim can be brought "at any time," subject to equitable defenses such as laches.

36. *Answer choices:*
(see index for correct answer)

- a. cultural
- b. interpersonal communication
- c. surface-level diversity
- d. Disparagement

Guidance: level 1

:: Law ::

_____ is a body of law which defines the role, powers, and structure of different entities within a state, namely, the executive, the parliament or legislature, and the judiciary; as well as the basic rights of citizens and, in federal countries such as the United States and Canada, the relationship between the central government and state, provincial, or territorial governments.

Exam Probability: **High**

37. *Answer choices:*
(see index for correct answer)

- a. Comparative law
- b. Constitutional law

Guidance: level 1

:: Business law ::

In the United States, the United Kingdom, Australia, Canada and South Africa, _____ relates to the doctrines of the law of agency. It is relevant particularly in corporate law and constitutional law. _____ refers to a situation where a reasonable third party would understand that an agent had authority to act. This means a principal is bound by the agent's actions, even if the agent had no actual authority, whether express or implied. It raises an estoppel because the third party is given an assurance, which he relies on and would be inequitable for the principal to deny the authority given. _____ can legally be found, even if actual authority has not been given.

Exam Probability: **Medium**

- a. Administration
- b. Economic torts
- c. Apparent authority
- d. Company mortgage

Guidance: level 1

:: Business ::

An _____ is a key document used by limited liability companies to outline the business' financial and functional decisions including rules, regulations and provisions. The purpose of the document is to govern the internal operations of the business in a way that suits the specific needs of the business owners. Once the document is signed by the members of the limited liability company, it acts as an official contract binding them to its terms. _____ is mandatory as per laws only in 5 states - California, Delaware, Maine, Missouri, and New York LLCs operating without an _____ are governed by the state's default rules contained in the relevant statute and developed through state court decisions. An _____ is similar in function to corporate by-laws, or analogous to a partnership agreement in multi-member LLCs. In single-member LLCs, an _____ is a declaration of the structure that the member has chosen for the company and sometimes used to prove in court that the LLC structure is separate from that of the individual owner and thus necessary so that the owner has documentation to prove that he or she is indeed separate from the entity itself.

Exam Probability: **Low**

- a. Legal governance, risk management, and compliance
- b. Corporate services
- c. Operating agreement
- d. EPG Model

Guidance: level 1

:: Euthenics ::

_____ is an ethical framework and suggests that an entity, be it an organization or individual, has an obligation to act for the benefit of society at large. _____ is a duty every individual has to perform so as to maintain a balance between the economy and the ecosystems. A trade-off may exist between economic development, in the material sense, and the welfare of the society and environment, though this has been challenged by many reports over the past decade. _____ means sustaining the equilibrium between the two. It pertains not only to business organizations but also to everyone whose any action impacts the environment. This responsibility can be passive, by avoiding engaging in socially harmful acts, or active, by performing activities that directly advance social goals. _____ must be intergenerational since the actions of one generation have consequences on those following.

Exam Probability: **High**

40. *Answer choices:*
(see index for correct answer)

- a. Home economics
- b. Euthenics
- c. Minnie Cumnock Blodgett
- d. Social responsibility

Guidance: level 1

:: Contract law ::

An _____ , or simply option, is defined as "a promise which meets the requirements for the formation of a contract and limits the promisor's power to revoke an offer."

Exam Probability: **Low**

41. *Answer choices:*
(see index for correct answer)

- a. Exceptio non adimpleti contractus
- b. Subcontractor
- c. Condition precedent
- d. Contract lifecycle management

Guidance: level 1

:: Criminal law ::

_____ is the body of law that relates to crime. It proscribes conduct perceived as threatening, harmful, or otherwise endangering to the property, health, safety, and moral welfare of people inclusive of one's self. Most _____ is established by statute, which is to say that the laws are enacted by a legislature. _____ includes the punishment and rehabilitation of people who violate such laws. _____ varies according to jurisdiction, and differs from civil law, where emphasis is more on dispute resolution and victim compensation, rather than on punishment or rehabilitation. Criminal procedure is a formalized official activity that authenticates the fact of commission of a crime and authorizes punitive or rehabilitative treatment of the offender.

Exam Probability: **High**

42. *Answer choices:*
(see index for correct answer)

- a. Self-incrimination
- b. Mala prohibita
- c. Mala in se
- d. complicit

Guidance: level 1

:: Ethically disputed business practices ::

_____ is the trading of a public company's stock or other securities by individuals with access to nonpublic information about the company. In various countries, some kinds of trading based on insider information is illegal. This is because it is seen as unfair to other investors who do not have access to the information, as the investor with insider information could potentially make larger profits than a typical investor could make. The rules governing _____ are complex and vary significantly from country to country. The extent of enforcement also varies from one country to another. The definition of insider in one jurisdiction can be broad, and may cover not only insiders themselves but also any persons related to them, such as brokers, associates and even family members. A person who becomes aware of non-public information and trades on that basis may be guilty of a crime.

Exam Probability: **High**

43. *Answer choices:*

- a. Insider trading
- b. Repo 105
- c. Suicide bidding
- d. Operation Red Spider

Guidance: level 1

:: Business law ::

A _____ is an arrangement where parties, known as partners, agree to cooperate to advance their mutual interests. The partners in a _____ may be individuals, businesses, interest-based organizations, schools, governments or combinations. Organizations may partner to increase the likelihood of each achieving their mission and to amplify their reach. A _____ may result in issuing and holding equity or may be only governed by a contract.

Exam Probability: **High**

44. *Answer choices:*

- a. Security interest
- b. Free agent
- c. Finance lease
- d. Agency in English law

Guidance: level 1

:: Jurisdiction ::

In United States law, _____ jurisdiction is the subject-matter jurisdiction of United States federal courts to hear a civil case because the plaintiff has alleged a violation of the United States Constitution, federal law, or a treaty to which the United States is a party.

Exam Probability: **Low**

45. *Answer choices:*

- a. Removal jurisdiction
- b. Federal question jurisdiction
- c. Federal question

- d. Jurisdiction in rem

Guidance: level 1

:: Legal doctrines and principles ::

In the common law of torts, _____ loquitur is a doctrine that infers negligence from the very nature of an accident or injury in the absence of direct evidence on how any defendant behaved. Although modern formulations differ by jurisdiction, common law originally stated that the accident must satisfy the necessary elements of negligence: duty, breach of duty, causation, and injury. In _____ loquitur, the elements of duty of care, breach, and causation are inferred from an injury that does not ordinarily occur without negligence.

Exam Probability: **Low**

46. *Answer choices:*
(see index for correct answer)

- a. Exclusionary rule
- b. Res ipsa loquitur
- c. Assumption of risk
- d. Acquiescence

Guidance: level 1

:: ::

In logic and philosophy, an _____ is a series of statements , called the premises or premisses , intended to determine the degree of truth of another statement, the conclusion. The logical form of an _____ in a natural language can be represented in a symbolic formal language, and independently of natural language formally defined " _____ s" can be made in math and computer science.

Exam Probability: **Low**

47. *Answer choices:*
(see index for correct answer)

- a. interpersonal communication
- b. corporate values
- c. imperative

- d. Argument

Guidance: level 1

:: Contract law ::

_____ is a doctrine in contract law that describes terms that are so extremely unjust, or overwhelmingly one-sided in favor of the party who has the superior bargaining power, that they are contrary to good conscience. Typically, an unconscionable contract is held to be unenforceable because no reasonable or informed person would otherwise agree to it. The perpetrator of the conduct is not allowed to benefit, because the consideration offered is lacking, or is so obviously inadequate, that to enforce the contract would be unfair to the party seeking to escape the contract.

Exam Probability: **Low**

48. *Answer choices:*
(see index for correct answer)

- a. Unconscionability
- b. Condition precedent
- c. Doctrine of concurrent delay
- d. Principles of International Commercial Contracts

Guidance: level 1

:: ::

An _____ is a criminal accusation that a person has committed a crime. In jurisdictions that use the concept of felonies, the most serious criminal offence is a felony; jurisdictions that do not use the felonies concept often use that of an indictable offence, an offence that requires an _____ .

Exam Probability: **Medium**

49. *Answer choices:*
(see index for correct answer)

- a. cultural
- b. personal values
- c. Indictment
- d. deep-level diversity

Guidance: level 1

_____ or accountancy is the measurement, processing, and communication of financial information about economic entities such as businesses and corporations. The modern field was established by the Italian mathematician Luca Pacioli in 1494. _____ , which has been called the "language of business", measures the results of an organization's economic activities and conveys this information to a variety of users, including investors, creditors, management, and regulators. Practitioners of _____ are known as accountants. The terms "_____" and "financial reporting" are often used as synonyms.

Exam Probability: **Low**

50. *Answer choices:*
(see index for correct answer)

- a. open system
- b. cultural
- c. empathy
- d. Accounting

Guidance: level 1

A lawsuit is a proceeding by a party or parties against another in the civil court of law. The archaic term "suit in law" is found in only a small number of laws still in effect today. The term "lawsuit" is used in reference to a civil action brought in a court of law in which a plaintiff, a party who claims to have incurred loss as a result of a defendant's actions, demands a legal or equitable remedy. The defendant is required to respond to the plaintiff's complaint. If the plaintiff is successful, judgment is in the plaintiff's favor, and a variety of court orders may be issued to enforce a right, award damages, or impose a temporary or permanent injunction to prevent an act or compel an act. A declaratory judgment may be issued to prevent future legal disputes.

Exam Probability: **Medium**

51. *Answer choices:*
(see index for correct answer)

- a. similarity-attraction theory
- b. information systems assessment
- c. Litigation
- d. Character

Guidance: level 1

:: Contract law ::

A _____ is a contract in which one party agrees to supply as much of a good or service as is required by the other party, and in exchange the other party expressly or implicitly promises that it will obtain its goods or services exclusively from the first party. For example, a grocery store might enter into a contract with the farmer who grows oranges under which the farmer would supply the grocery store with as many oranges as the store could sell. The farmer could sue for breach of contract if the store were thereafter to purchase oranges for this purpose from any other party. The converse of this situation is an output contract, in which one buyer agrees to purchase however much of a good or service the seller is able to produce.

Exam Probability: **Low**

52. *Answer choices:*
(see index for correct answer)

- a. Formal contract
- b. Requirements contract
- c. Severability
- d. Contractual term

Guidance: level 1

:: Psychometrics ::

_____ is a dynamic, structured, interactive process where a neutral third party assists disputing parties in resolving conflict through the use of specialized communication and negotiation techniques. All participants in _____ are encouraged to actively participate in the process. _____ is a "party-centered" process in that it is focused primarily upon the needs, rights, and interests of the parties. The mediator uses a wide variety of techniques to guide the process in a constructive direction and to help the parties find their optimal solution. A mediator is facilitative in that she/he manages the interaction between parties and facilitates open communication. _____ is also evaluative in that the mediator analyzes issues and relevant norms , while refraining from providing prescriptive advice to the parties .

Exam Probability: **Low**

53. *Answer choices:*
(see index for correct answer)

- a. Bipolar spectrum diagnostic scale
- b. Mediation
- c. Online assessment
- d. Multidimensional scaling

Guidance: level 1

:: ::

_____ is the assignment of any responsibility or authority to another person to carry out specific activities. It is one of the core concepts of management leadership. However, the person who delegated the work remains accountable for the outcome of the delegated work. _____ empowers a subordinate to make decisions, i.e. it is a shifting of decision-making authority from one organizational level to a lower one. _____ , if properly done, is not fabrication. The opposite of effective _____ is micromanagement, where a manager provides too much input, direction, and review of delegated work. In general, _____ is good and can save money and time, help in building skills, and motivate people. On the other hand, poor _____ might cause frustration and confusion to all the involved parties. Some agents, however, do not favour a _____ and consider the power of making a decision rather burdensome.

Exam Probability: **Low**

54. *Answer choices:*
(see index for correct answer)

- a. Sarbanes-Oxley act of 2002
- b. functional perspective
- c. hierarchical
- d. Delegation

Guidance: level 1

:: Investment ::

In finance, the benefit from an _____ is called a return. The return may consist of a gain realised from the sale of property or an _____, unrealised capital appreciation, or _____ income such as dividends, interest, rental income etc., or a combination of capital gain and income. The return may also include currency gains or losses due to changes in foreign currency exchange rates.

Exam Probability: **Medium**

55. *Answer choices:*
(see index for correct answer)

- a. Master-feeder
- b. Binary option
- c. VISTA
- d. Investment

Guidance: level 1

:: Commercial crimes ::

_____ is the act of withholding assets for the purpose of conversion of such assets, by one or more persons to whom the assets were entrusted, either to be held or to be used for specific purposes. _____ is a type of financial fraud. For example, a lawyer might embezzle funds from the trust accounts of their clients; a financial advisor might embezzle the funds of investors; and a husband or a wife might embezzle funds from a bank account jointly held with the spouse.

Exam Probability: **Medium**

56. *Answer choices:*

- a. Price fixing
- b. Monopolization
- c. Embezzlement
- d. Offshore leaks

Guidance: level 1

:: Auctioneering ::

An _____ is a process of buying and selling goods or services by offering them up for bid, taking bids, and then selling the item to the highest bidder. The open ascending price _____ is arguably the most common form of _____ in use today. Participants bid openly against one another, with each subsequent bid required to be higher than the previous bid. An _____ eer may announce prices, bidders may call out their bids themselves , or bids may be submitted electronically with the highest current bid publicly displayed. In a Dutch _____ , the _____ eer begins with a high asking price for some quantity of like items; the price is lowered until a participant is willing to accept the _____ eer's price for some quantity of the goods in the lot or until the seller's reserve price is met. While _____ s are most associated in the public imagination with the sale of antiques, paintings, rare collectibles and expensive wines , _____ s are also used for commodities, livestock, radio spectrum and used cars. In economic theory, an _____ may refer to any mechanism or set of trading rules for exchange.

Exam Probability: **High**

57. *Answer choices:*

- a. Art auction
- b. How Much Wood Would a Woodchuck Chuck
- c. Calor licitantis
- d. Demsetz auction

Guidance: level 1

:: Legal terms ::

An _____ is a legal and equitable remedy in the form of a special court order that compels a party to do or refrain from specific acts. "When a court employs the extraordinary remedy of _____ , it directs the conduct of a party, and does so with the backing of its full coercive powers." A party that fails to comply with an _____ faces criminal or civil penalties, including possible monetary sanctions and even imprisonment. They can also be charged with contempt of court. Counter _____ s are _____ s that stop or reverse the enforcement of another _____ .

Exam Probability: **Medium**

58. *Answer choices:*
(see index for correct answer)

- a. Adverse
- b. Judicial estoppel
- c. Injunction
- d. Immediately upon arrival

Guidance: level 1

:: Contract law ::

A _____ , unlike a void contract, is a valid contract which may be either affirmed or rejected at the option of one of the parties. At most, one party to the contract is bound. The unbound party may repudiate the contract, at which time the contract becomes void.

Exam Probability: **Low**

59. *Answer choices:*
(see index for correct answer)

- a. Implied authority
- b. United States contract law
- c. Performance Based Contracting
- d. Voidable contract

Guidance: level 1

Finance

Finance is a field that is concerned with the allocation (investment) of assets and liabilities over space and time, often under conditions of risk or uncertainty. Finance can also be defined as the science of money management. Participants in the market aim to price assets based on their risk level, fundamental value, and their expected rate of return. Finance can be split into three sub-categories: public finance, corporate finance and personal finance.

:: Business law ::

A _____ is an arrangement where parties, known as partners, agree to cooperate to advance their mutual interests. The partners in a _____ may be individuals, businesses, interest-based organizations, schools, governments or combinations. Organizations may partner to increase the likelihood of each achieving their mission and to amplify their reach. A _____ may result in issuing and holding equity or may be only governed by a contract.

Exam Probability: **Low**

1. *Answer choices:*
(see index for correct answer)

- a. Operating lease
- b. Partnership
- c. Ease of doing business index
- d. Trading while insolvent

Guidance: level 1

:: Management accounting ::

In economics, _____ s, indirect costs or overheads are business expenses that are not dependent on the level of goods or services produced by the business. They tend to be time-related, such as interest or rents being paid per month, and are often referred to as overhead costs. This is in contrast to variable costs, which are volume-related and unknown at the beginning of the accounting year. For a simple example, such as a bakery, the monthly rent for the baking facilities, and the monthly payments for the security system and basic phone line are _____ s, as they do not change according to how much bread the bakery produces and sells. On the other hand, the wage costs of the bakery are variable, as the bakery will have to hire more workers if the production of bread increases. Economists reckon _____ as a entry barrier for new entrepreneurs.

Exam Probability: **Low**

2. *Answer choices:*
(see index for correct answer)

- a. Extended cost
- b. Direct material total variance
- c. Fixed cost
- d. Dual overhead rate

Guidance: level 1

:: Generally Accepted Accounting Principles ::

The _____ principle is a cornerstone of accrual accounting together with the matching principle. They both determine the accounting period in which revenues and expenses are recognized. According to the principle, revenues are recognized when they are realized or realizable, and are earned , no matter when cash is received. In cash accounting – in contrast – revenues are recognized when cash is received no matter when goods or services are sold.

Exam Probability: **Low**

3. *Answer choices:*
(see index for correct answer)

- a. Deferred income
- b. net realisable value
- c. Consolidation
- d. Earnings before interest, taxes and depreciation

:: Finance ::

_____ , in finance and accounting, means stated value or face value. From this come the expressions at par , over par and under par .

Exam Probability: **High**

4. *Answer choices:*

(see index for correct answer)

- a. Rate of profit
- b. Yield
- c. Net interest margin
- d. Par value

:: ::

_____ is a concept of English common law and is a necessity for simple contracts but not for special contracts . The concept has been adopted by other common law jurisdictions, including the US.

Exam Probability: **High**

5. *Answer choices:*

(see index for correct answer)

- a. surface-level diversity
- b. Character
- c. co-culture
- d. cultural

:: Leasing ::

A finance lease is a type of lease in which a finance company is typically the legal owner of the asset for the duration of the lease, while the lessee not only has operating control over the asset, but also has a some share of the economic risks and returns from the change in the valuation of the underlying asset.

Exam Probability: **Medium**

6. *Answer choices:*
(see index for correct answer)

- a. Farmout agreement
- b. Synthetic lease

Guidance: level 1

:: Basel II ::

All businesses take risks based on two factors: the probability an adverse circumstance will come about and the cost of such adverse circumstance.Risk management is the study of how to control risks and balance the possibility of gains.

Exam Probability: **Medium**

7. *Answer choices:*
(see index for correct answer)

- a. Market risk
- b. Basic indicator approach
- c. Advanced measurement approach
- d. Standardized approach

Guidance: level 1

:: Investment ::

_____ , and investment appraisal, is the planning process used to determine whether an organization's long term investments such as new machinery, replacement of machinery, new plants, new products, and research development projects are worth the funding of cash through the firm's capitalization structure . It is the process of allocating resources for major capital, or investment, expenditures. One of the primary goals of _____ investments is to increase the value of the firm to the shareholders.

Exam Probability: **High**

8. *Answer choices:*
(see index for correct answer)

- a. Asset price inflation
- b. Philatelic investment
- c. Capital budgeting
- d. Investment performance

Guidance: level 1

:: Monopoly (economics) ::

A _____ is a form of intellectual property that gives its owner the legal right to exclude others from making, using, selling, and importing an invention for a limited period of years, in exchange for publishing an enabling public disclosure of the invention. In most countries _____ rights fall under civil law and the _____ holder needs to sue someone infringing the _____ in order to enforce his or her rights. In some industries _____ s are an essential form of competitive advantage; in others they are irrelevant.

Exam Probability: **High**

9. *Answer choices:*
(see index for correct answer)

- a. Intellectual property
- b. Network effect
- c. Third-party access
- d. Patent

Guidance: level 1

:: Taxation ::

In a tax system, the _____ is the ratio at which a business or person is taxed. There are several methods used to present a _____ : statutory, average, marginal, and effective. These rates can also be presented using different definitions applied to a tax base: inclusive and exclusive.

Exam Probability: **Medium**

10. *Answer choices:*
(see index for correct answer)

- a. Cess
- b. Fiscal drag
- c. Taxpayer receipt
- d. Tax rate

Guidance: level 1

:: ::

_____ , often abbreviated as B/E in finance, is the point of balance making neither a profit nor a loss. The term originates in finance but the concept has been applied in other fields.

Exam Probability: **High**

11. *Answer choices:*
(see index for correct answer)

- a. Sarbanes-Oxley act of 2002
- b. Break-even
- c. deep-level diversity
- d. co-culture

Guidance: level 1

:: ::

A _____ is a fund into which a sum of money is added during an employee's employment years, and from which payments are drawn to support the person's retirement from work in the form of periodic payments. A _____ may be a "defined benefit plan" where a fixed sum is paid regularly to a person, or a "defined contribution plan" under which a fixed sum is invested and then becomes available at retirement age. _____ s should not be confused with severance pay; the former is usually paid in regular installments for life after retirement, while the latter is typically paid as a fixed amount after involuntary termination of employment prior to retirement.

Exam Probability: **High**

12. *Answer choices:*

(see index for correct answer)

- a. interpersonal communication
- b. information systems assessment
- c. personal values
- d. Sarbanes-Oxley act of 2002

Guidance: level 1

:: Expense ::

A company's _____ , or As a result, the computation of the _____ is considerably more complex. Tax law may provide for different treatment of items of income and expenses as a result of tax policy. The differences may be of permanent or temporary nature. Permanent items are in the form of non taxable income and non taxable expenses. Things such as expenses considered not deductible by taxing authorities , the range of tax rates applicable to various levels of income, different tax rates in different jurisdictions, multiple layers of tax on income, and other issues.

Exam Probability: **Low**

13. *Answer choices:*

(see index for correct answer)

- a. Tax expense
- b. Business overhead expense disability insurance
- c. Momentem
- d. Interest expense

Guidance: level 1

Cash and _____ s are the most liquid current assets found on a business's balance sheet. _____ s are short-term commitments "with temporarily idle cash and easily convertible into a known cash amount". An investment normally counts to be a _____ when it has a short maturity period of 90 days or less, and can be included in the cash and _____ s balance from the date of acquisition when it carries an insignificant risk of changes in the asset value; with more than 90 days maturity, the asset is not considered as cash and _____ s. Equity investments mostly are excluded from _____ s, unless they are essentially _____ s, for instance, if the preferred shares acquired within a short maturity period and with specified recovery date.

Exam Probability: **Medium**

14. *Answer choices:*
(see index for correct answer)

- a. Dam
- b. Allowance
- c. Spondulix
- d. Metallism

Guidance: level 1

:: ::

A _____ is an individual or institution that legally owns one or more shares of stock in a public or private corporation. _____ s may be referred to as members of a corporation. Legally, a person is not a _____ in a corporation until their name and other details are entered in the corporation's register of _____ s or members.

Exam Probability: **Low**

15. *Answer choices:*
(see index for correct answer)

- a. Shareholder
- b. open system
- c. hierarchical
- d. corporate values

:: Business ethics ::

In accounting and in most Schools of economic thought, _____ is a rational and unbiased estimate of the potential market price of a good, service, or asset. It takes into account such objectivity factors as.

Exam Probability: **High**

16. *Answer choices:*
(see index for correct answer)

- a. Fair value
- b. MBA Oath
- c. Contingent work
- d. Journal of Business Ethics

:: Hazard analysis ::

Broadly speaking, a _____ is the combined effort of 1. identifying and analyzing potential events that may negatively impact individuals, assets, and/or the environment ; and 2. making judgments "on the tolerability of the risk on the basis of a risk analysis" while considering influencing factors . Put in simpler terms, a _____ analyzes what can go wrong, how likely it is to happen, what the potential consequences are, and how tolerable the identified risk is. As part of this process, the resulting determination of risk may be expressed in a quantitative or qualitative fashion. The _____ is an inherent part of an overall risk management strategy, which attempts to, after a _____ , "introduce control measures to eliminate or reduce" any potential risk-related consequences.

Exam Probability: **High**

17. *Answer choices:*
(see index for correct answer)

- a. Risk assessment
- b. Hazard identification
- c. Swiss cheese model

:: Investment ::

The _____ is a measure of an investment's rate of return. The term internal refers to the fact that the calculation excludes external factors, such as the risk-free rate, inflation, the cost of capital, or various financial risks.

Exam Probability: **Low**

18. *Answer choices:*
(see index for correct answer)

- a. Media for equity
- b. Fed model
- c. Internal rate of return
- d. Alternative investment

Guidance: level 1

:: Generally Accepted Accounting Principles ::

_____ is the accounting classification of an account. It is part of double-entry book-keeping technique.

Exam Probability: **High**

19. *Answer choices:*
(see index for correct answer)

- a. Normal balance
- b. Access to finance
- c. Write-off
- d. Financial position of the United States

Guidance: level 1

:: Investment ::

In finance, the benefit from an _____ is called a return. The return may consist of a gain realised from the sale of property or an _____ , unrealised capital appreciation , or _____ income such as dividends, interest, rental income etc., or a combination of capital gain and income. The return may also include currency gains or losses due to changes in foreign currency exchange rates.

Exam Probability: **High**

20. *Answer choices:*
(see index for correct answer)

- a. Vulture capitalist
- b. Investment
- c. Acertus Market Sentiment Indicator
- d. Low Exercise Price Option

Guidance: level 1

:: E-commerce ::

A _____ is a plastic payment card that can be used instead of cash when making purchases. It is similar to a credit card, but unlike a credit card, the money is immediately transferred directly from the cardholder's bank account when performing a transaction.

Exam Probability: **Low**

21. *Answer choices:*
(see index for correct answer)

- a. Debit card
- b. Privalia
- c. Online savings account
- d. Online Shopping in Bangladesh

Guidance: level 1

:: Capital (economics) ::

In Economics and Accounting, the _____ is the cost of a company's funds , or, from an investor's point of view "the required rate of return on a portfolio company's existing securities". It is used to evaluate new projects of a company. It is the minimum return that investors expect for providing capital to the company, thus setting a benchmark that a new project has to meet.

Exam Probability: **Medium**

22. *Answer choices:*
(see index for correct answer)

- a. financial capital
- b. operating capital
- c. Cost of capital
- d. required rate of return

Guidance: level 1

:: Business economics ::

A _____ is a term used primarily in cost accounting to describe something to which costs are assigned. Common examples of _____ s are: product lines, geographic territories, customers, departments or anything else for which management would like to quantify cost.

Exam Probability: **High**

23. *Answer choices:*
(see index for correct answer)

- a. Wear and tear
- b. Cost object
- c. Corporate ecosystem
- d. Consumer economy

Guidance: level 1

:: Consumer theory ::

A _____ is a technical term in psychology, economics and philosophy usually used in relation to choosing between alternatives. For example, someone prefers A over B if they would rather choose A than B.

Exam Probability: **Medium**

24. *Answer choices:*

- a. Preference
- b. Consumption
- c. Snob effect
- d. Rational addiction

Guidance: level 1

:: Generally Accepted Accounting Principles ::

A _____ is a reduction of the recognized value of something. In accounting, this is a recognition of the reduced or zero value of an asset. In income tax statements, this is a reduction of taxable income, as a recognition of certain expenses required to produce the income.

Exam Probability: **Medium**

25. *Answer choices:*

- a. Gross profit
- b. Write-off
- c. Deprival value
- d. Gross sales

Guidance: level 1

:: Cash flow ::

_____ s are narrowly interconnected with the concepts of value, interest rate and liquidity. A _____ that shall happen on a future day tN can be transformed into a _____ of the same value in t0.

Exam Probability: **High**

26. *Answer choices:*
(see index for correct answer)

- a. Cash flow
- b. Discounted payback period
- c. Factoring
- d. Cash flow forecasting

Guidance: level 1

:: International taxation ::

_____ is the levying of tax by two or more jurisdictions on the same declared income , asset , or financial transaction . Double liability is mitigated in a number of ways, for example.

Exam Probability: **Low**

27. *Answer choices:*
(see index for correct answer)

- a. Destination principle
- b. Spahn tax
- c. Common Reporting Standard
- d. Double taxation

Guidance: level 1

:: Fixed income market ::

The _____ is a financial market where participants can issue new debt, known as the primary market, or buy and sell debt securities, known as the secondary market. This is usually in the form of bonds, but it may include notes, bills, and so on.

Exam Probability: **High**

28. *Answer choices:*
(see index for correct answer)

- a. Fixed-income attribution
- b. Fixed income
- c. Yield curve
- d. Bond market

Guidance: level 1

:: ::

MCI, Inc. was an American telecommunication corporation, currently a subsidiary of Verizon Communications, with its main office in Ashburn, Virginia. The corporation was formed originally as a result of the merger of _____ and MCI Communications corporations, and used the name MCI _____ , succeeded by _____ , before changing its name to the present version on April 12, 2003, as part of the corporation's ending of its bankruptcy status. The company traded on NASDAQ as WCOM and MCIP . The corporation was purchased by Verizon Communications with the deal finalizing on January 6, 2006, and is now identified as that company's Verizon Enterprise Solutions division with the local residential divisions being integrated slowly into local Verizon subsidiaries.

Exam Probability: **Medium**

29. *Answer choices:*
(see index for correct answer)

- a. interpersonal communication
- b. cultural
- c. personal values
- d. WorldCom

Guidance: level 1

:: ::

_____ focuses on ratios, equities and debts. It is useful for portfolio management,distribution of dividend,capital raising,hedging and looking after fluctuations in foreign currency and product cycles.Financial managers are the people who will do research and based on the research, decide what sort of capital to obtain in order to fund the company's assets as well as maximizing the value of the firm for all the stakeholders. It also refers to the efficient and effective management of money in such a manner as to accomplish the objectives of the organization. It is the specialized function directly associated with the top management. The significance of this function is not seen in the `Line` but also in the capacity of the `Staff` in overall of a company. It has been defined differently by different experts in the field.

Exam Probability: **High**

30. *Answer choices:*
(see index for correct answer)

- a. deep-level diversity
- b. interpersonal communication
- c. Financial management
- d. functional perspective

Guidance: level 1

:: Funds ::

_____ value is the value of an entity's assets minus the value of its liabilities, often in relation to open-end or mutual funds, since shares of such funds registered with the U.S. Securities and Exchange Commission are redeemed at their _____ value. It is also a key figure with regard to hedge funds and venture capital funds when calculating the value of the underlying investments in these funds by investors. This may also be the same as the book value or the equity value of a business. _____ value may represent the value of the total equity, or it may be divided by the number of shares outstanding held by investors, thereby representing the _____ value per share.

Exam Probability: **High**

31. *Answer choices:*
(see index for correct answer)

- a. IberoAmerican Federation of Mutual Funds
- b. Social Enterprise Investment Fund
- c. Net asset
- d. Indie Fund

Guidance: level 1

:: Mathematical finance ::

_____ is the value of an asset at a specific date. It measures the nominal future sum of money that a given sum of money is "worth" at a specified time in the future assuming a certain interest rate, or more generally, rate of return; it is the present value multiplied by the accumulation function. The value does not include corrections for inflation or other factors that affect the true value of money in the future. This is used in time value of money calculations.

Exam Probability: **Low**

32. *Answer choices:*
(see index for correct answer)

- a. Future value
- b. Trinomial tree
- c. Perpetuity
- d. Exotic option

Guidance: level 1

:: ::

_____ is the study and management of exchange relationships. _____ is the business process of creating relationships with and satisfying customers. With its focus on the customer, _____ is one of the premier components of business management.

Exam Probability: **Medium**

33. *Answer choices:*
(see index for correct answer)

- a. cultural
- b. similarity-attraction theory
- c. deep-level diversity
- d. corporate values

Guidance: level 1

:: Fixed income market ::

In finance, the _____ is a curve showing several yields or interest rates across different contract lengths for a similar debt contract. The curve shows the relation between the interest rate and the time to maturity, known as the "term", of the debt for a given borrower in a given currency. For example, the U.S. dollar interest rates paid on U.S. Treasury securities for various maturities are closely watched by many traders, and are commonly plotted on a graph such as the one on the right which is informally called "the _____". More formal mathematical descriptions of this relation are often called the term structure of interest rates.

Exam Probability: **High**

34. *Answer choices:*
(see index for correct answer)

- a. Fixed-income attribution
- b. Bond market
- c. Inter-dealer broker
- d. credit market

Guidance: level 1

:: Income taxes ::

An _____ is a tax imposed on individuals or entities that varies with respective income or profits . _____ generally is computed as the product of a tax rate times taxable income. Taxation rates may vary by type or characteristics of the taxpayer.

Exam Probability: **Low**

35. *Answer choices:*
(see index for correct answer)

- a. Income tax
- b. Hall income tax
- c. Income Tax Act 1842
- d. Illinois Fair Tax

Guidance: level 1

:: Markets (customer bases) ::

In economics, _____ is the economic price for which a good or service is offered in the marketplace. It is of interest mainly in the study of microeconomics. Market value and _____ are equal only under conditions of market efficiency, equilibrium, and rational expectations.

Exam Probability: **Medium**

36. *Answer choices:*
(see index for correct answer)

- a. Marketization
- b. nonmarket
- c. Market price
- d. Parity product

Guidance: level 1

:: Business economics ::

In finance, _____ is the risk of losses caused by interest rate changes. The prices of most financial instruments, such as stocks and bonds move inversely with interest rates, so investors are subject to capital loss when rates rise.

Exam Probability: **Low**

37. *Answer choices:*
(see index for correct answer)

- a. Service innovation
- b. Incremental operating margin
- c. Rate risk
- d. Disclosed fees

Guidance: level 1

:: Financial risk ::

_____ is the risk that arises for bond owners from fluctuating interest rates. How much _____ a bond has depends on how sensitive its price is to interest rate changes in the market. The sensitivity depends on two things, the bond's time to maturity, and the coupon rate of the bond.

38. *Answer choices:*
(see index for correct answer)

- a. Dividend policy
- b. Interest rate risk
- c. Government risk
- d. Solvency cone

Guidance: level 1

:: Inventory ::

It requires a detailed physical count, so that the company knows exactly how many of each goods brought on specific dates remained at year end inventory. When this information is found, the amount of goods are multiplied by their purchase cost at their purchase date, to get a number for the ending inventory cost.

Exam Probability: **Medium**

39. *Answer choices:*
(see index for correct answer)

- a. Phantom inventory
- b. Inventory optimization
- c. Reorder point
- d. Specific identification

Guidance: level 1

:: Costs ::

In economics, _____ is the total economic cost of production and is made up of variable cost, which varies according to the quantity of a good produced and includes inputs such as labour and raw materials, plus fixed cost, which is independent of the quantity of a good produced and includes inputs that cannot be varied in the short term: fixed costs such as buildings and machinery, including sunk costs if any. Since cost is measured per unit of time, it is a flow variable.

Exam Probability: **High**

40. *Answer choices:*

- a. Prospective costs
- b. Cost reduction
- c. Total cost
- d. Cost of products sold

Guidance: level 1

:: Costs ::

In microeconomic theory, the _____ , or alternative cost, of making a particular choice is the value of the most valuable choice out of those that were not taken. In other words, opportunity that will require sacrifices.

Exam Probability: **High**

41. *Answer choices:*

- a. Repugnancy costs
- b. Sliding scale fees
- c. Cost reduction
- d. Manufacturing cost

Guidance: level 1

:: Mathematical finance ::

In economics and finance, _____ , also known as present discounted value, is the value of an expected income stream determined as of the date of valuation. The _____ is always less than or equal to the future value because money has interest-earning potential, a characteristic referred to as the time value of money, except during times of negative interest rates, when the _____ will be more than the future value. Time value can be described with the simplified phrase, "A dollar today is worth more than a dollar tomorrow". Here, `worth more` means that its value is greater. A dollar today is worth more than a dollar tomorrow because the dollar can be invested and earn a day's worth of interest, making the total accumulate to a value more than a dollar by tomorrow. Interest can be compared to rent. Just as rent is paid to a landlord by a tenant without the ownership of the asset being transferred, interest is paid to a lender by a borrower who gains access to the money for a time before paying it back. By letting the borrower have access to the money, the lender has sacrificed the exchange value of this money, and is compensated for it in the form of interest. The initial amount of the borrowed funds is less than the total amount of money paid to the lender.

Exam Probability: **Medium**

42. *Answer choices:*
(see index for correct answer)

- a. Econophysics
- b. No free lunch with vanishing risk
- c. Statistical arbitrage
- d. Quantitative investing

Guidance: level 1

:: bad_topic ::

_____ refers to systematic approach to the governance and realization of value from the things that a group or entity is responsible for, over their whole life cycles. It may apply both to tangible assets and to intangible assets . _____ is a systematic process of developing, operating, maintaining, upgrading, and disposing of assets in the most cost-effective manner .

Exam Probability: **High**

43. *Answer choices:*
(see index for correct answer)

- a. return period
- b. floating exchange
- c. Liquidation preference
- d. Asset management

Guidance: level 1

:: Accounting terminology ::

_____ or capital expense is the money a company spends to buy, maintain, or improve its fixed assets, such as buildings, vehicles, equipment, or land. It is considered a _____ when the asset is newly purchased or when money is used towards extending the useful life of an existing asset, such as repairing the roof.

Exam Probability: **High**

44. *Answer choices:*
(see index for correct answer)

- a. Accounts receivable
- b. Fair value accounting
- c. Record to report
- d. Statement of financial position

Guidance: level 1

:: Management accounting ::

_____ are costs that are not directly accountable to a cost object . _____ may be either fixed or variable. _____ include administration, personnel and security costs. These are those costs which are not directly related to production. Some _____ may be overhead. But some overhead costs can be directly attributed to a project and are direct costs.

Exam Probability: **Medium**

45. *Answer choices:*
(see index for correct answer)

- a. Average per-bit delivery cost
- b. Fixed assets management

- c. Process costing
- d. Indirect costs

Guidance: level 1

:: Free accounting software ::

A _____ is the principal book or computer file for recording and totaling economic transactions measured in terms of a monetary unit of account by account type, with debits and credits in separate columns and a beginning monetary balance and ending monetary balance for each account.

Exam Probability: **Low**

46. *Answer choices:*
(see index for correct answer)

- a. SQL-Ledger
- b. JGnash
- c. TurboCASH
- d. Ledger

Guidance: level 1

:: Financial accounting ::

_____ is the value of all the non-financial and financial assets owned by an institutional unit or sector minus the value of all its outstanding liabilities. Since financial assets minus outstanding liabilities equal net financial assets, _____ can also be conveniently expressed as non-financial assets plus net financial assets. _____ can apply to companies, individuals, governments or economic sectors such as the sector of financial corporations or to entire countries.

Exam Probability: **Low**

47. *Answer choices:*
(see index for correct answer)

- a. Exit rate
- b. Net worth
- c. Hidden asset
- d. Holding gains

Guidance: level 1

:: Expense ::

_____ relates to the cost of borrowing money. It is the price that a lender charges a borrower for the use of the lender's money. On the income statement, _____ can represent the cost of borrowing money from banks, bond investors, and other sources. _____ is different from operating expense and CAPEX, for it relates to the capital structure of a company, and it is usually tax-deductible.

Exam Probability: **High**

48. *Answer choices:*
(see index for correct answer)

- a. Stock option expensing
- b. Expense account
- c. expenditure
- d. Corporate travel

Guidance: level 1

:: Marketing ::

_____ or stock is the goods and materials that a business holds for the ultimate goal of resale .

Exam Probability: **Low**

49. *Answer choices:*
(see index for correct answer)

- a. Field research
- b. Inventory
- c. Email production
- d. Pitching engine

Guidance: level 1

:: Generally Accepted Accounting Principles ::

_____ , or non-current liabilities, are liabilities that are due beyond a year or the normal operation period of the company. The normal operation period is the amount of time it takes for a company to turn inventory into cash. On a classified balance sheet, liabilities are separated between current and _____ to help users assess the company's financial standing in short-term and long-term periods. _____ give users more information about the long-term prosperity of the company, while current liabilities inform the user of debt that the company owes in the current period. On a balance sheet, accounts are listed in order of liquidity, so _____ come after current liabilities. In addition, the specific long-term liability accounts are listed on the balance sheet in order of liquidity. Therefore, an account due within eighteen months would be listed before an account due within twenty-four months. Examples of _____ are bonds payable, long-term loans, capital leases, pension liabilities, post-retirement healthcare liabilities, deferred compensation, deferred revenues, deferred income taxes, and derivative liabilities.

Exam Probability: **Medium**

50. *Answer choices:*

(see index for correct answer)

- a. Long-term liabilities
- b. Completed-contract method
- c. Cost principle
- d. Earnings before interest, taxes, depreciation, and amortization

Guidance: level 1

:: ::

The _____ of a function of a real variable measures the sensitivity to change of the function value with respect to a change in its argument . _____ s are a fundamental tool of calculus. For example, the _____ of the position of a moving object with respect to time is the object's velocity: this measures how quickly the position of the object changes when time advances.

Exam Probability: **Low**

51. *Answer choices:*

(see index for correct answer)

- a. empathy
- b. personal values
- c. Derivative
- d. imperative

Guidance: level 1

:: ::

In business, economics or investment, market _____ is a market's feature whereby an individual or firm can quickly purchase or sell an asset without causing a drastic change in the asset's price. _____ is about how big the trade-off is between the speed of the sale and the price it can be sold for. In a liquid market, the trade-off is mild: selling quickly will not reduce the price much. In a relatively illiquid market, selling it quickly will require cutting its price by some amount.

Exam Probability: **Low**

52. *Answer choices:*

(see index for correct answer)

- a. deep-level diversity
- b. Liquidity
- c. empathy
- d. hierarchical

Guidance: level 1

:: ::

_____ is a marketing communication that employs an openly sponsored, non-personal message to promote or sell a product, service or idea. Sponsors of _____ are typically businesses wishing to promote their products or services. _____ is differentiated from public relations in that an advertiser pays for and has control over the message. It differs from personal selling in that the message is non-personal, i.e., not directed to a particular individual. _____ is communicated through various mass media, including traditional media such as newspapers, magazines, television, radio, outdoor _____ or direct mail; and new media such as search results, blogs, social media, websites or text messages. The actual presentation of the message in a medium is referred to as an advertisement, or "ad" or advert for short.

53. *Answer choices:*

- a. Advertising
- b. cultural
- c. Sarbanes-Oxley act of 2002
- d. functional perspective

Guidance: level 1

:: Management accounting ::

_____ s are costs that change as the quantity of the good or service that a business produces changes. _____ s are the sum of marginal costs over all units produced. They can also be considered normal costs. Fixed costs and _____ s make up the two components of total cost. Direct costs are costs that can easily be associated with a particular cost object. However, not all _____ s are direct costs. For example, variable manufacturing overhead costs are _____ s that are indirect costs, not direct costs. _____ s are sometimes called unit-level costs as they vary with the number of units produced.

54. *Answer choices:*

- a. Variable cost
- b. Certified Management Accountants of Canada
- c. RCA open-source application
- d. Backflush accounting

Guidance: level 1

:: Valuation (finance) ::

_____ refers to an assessment of the viability, stability, and profitability of a business, sub-business or project.

55. *Answer choices:*

- a. Post-money valuation
- b. Chepakovich valuation model
- c. Financial analysis
- d. Appraisal value

Guidance: level 1

:: Project management ::

Some scenarios associate "this kind of planning" with learning "life skills". _____ s are necessary, or at least useful, in situations where individuals need to know what time they must be at a specific location to receive a specific service, and where people need to accomplish a set of goals within a set time period.

Exam Probability: **Low**

56. *Answer choices:*
(see index for correct answer)

- a. Advanced Integrated Practice
- b. Budgeted cost of work performed
- c. Schedule
- d. Aggregate planning

Guidance: level 1

:: Inventory ::

_____ is a system of inventory in which updates are made on a periodic basis. This differs from perpetual inventory systems, where updates are made as seen fit.

Exam Probability: **High**

57. *Answer choices:*
(see index for correct answer)

- a. Periodic inventory
- b. Decomposition
- c. Stock control
- d. Perpetual inventory

Guidance: level 1

In finance, a put or _____ is a stock market device which gives the owner the right, but not the obligation, to sell an asset , at a specified price , by a predetermined date to a given party . The purchase of a _____ is interpreted as a negative sentiment about the future value of theunderlying stock. The term "put" comes from the fact that the owner has the right to "put up for sale" the stock or index.

Exam Probability: **Low**

58. *Answer choices:*
(see index for correct answer)

- a. Credit default option
- b. Chicago Options Associates
- c. Put option
- d. Mountain range

Guidance: level 1

In finance, return is a profit on an investment. It comprises any change in value of the investment, and/or cash flows which the investor receives from the investment, such as interest payments or dividends. It may be measured either in absolute terms or as a percentage of the amount invested. The latter is also called the holding period return.

Exam Probability: **Medium**

59. *Answer choices:*
(see index for correct answer)

- a. Rate of return
- b. imperative
- c. personal values
- d. similarity-attraction theory

Guidance: level 1

Human resource management

Human resource (HR) management is the strategic approach to the effective management of organization workers so that they help the business gain a competitive advantage. It is designed to maximize employee performance in service of an employer's strategic objectives. HR is primarily concerned with the management of people within organizations, focusing on policies and on systems. HR departments are responsible for overseeing employee-benefits design, employee recruitment, training and development, performance appraisal, and rewarding (e.g., managing pay and benefit systems). HR also concerns itself with organizational change and industrial relations, that is, the balancing of organizational practices with requirements arising from collective bargaining and from governmental laws.

:: Labor terms ::

_____ , often called DI or disability income insurance, or income protection, is a form of insurance that insures the beneficiary`s earned income against the risk that a disability creates a barrier for a worker to complete the core functions of their work. For example, the worker may suffer from an inability to maintain composure in the case of psychological disorders or an injury, illness or condition that causes physical impairment or incapacity to work. It encompasses paid sick leave, short-term disability benefits , and long-term disability benefits . Statistics show that in the US a disabling accident occurs, on average, once every second. In fact, nearly 18.5% of Americans are currently living with a disability, and 1 out of every 4 persons in the US workforce will suffer a disabling injury before retirement.

Exam Probability: **Low**

1. *Answer choices:*

(see index for correct answer)

- a. Disability insurance
- b. Benefit incidence
- c. Indexation of contracts
- d. Civilian workers

:: ::

_____ is the process of gathering and measuring information on targeted variables in an established system, which then enables one to answer relevant questions and evaluate outcomes. _____ is a component of research in all fields of study including physical and social sciences, humanities, and business. While methods vary by discipline, the emphasis on ensuring accurate and honest collection remains the same. The goal for all _____ is to capture quality evidence that allows analysis to lead to the formulation of convincing and credible answers to the questions that have been posed.

Exam Probability: **Low**

2. *Answer choices:*

(see index for correct answer)

- a. deep-level diversity
- b. empathy
- c. interpersonal communication
- d. cultural

:: Stress ::

_____ means beneficial stress—either psychological, physical , or biochemical/radiological .

Exam Probability: **Low**

3. *Answer choices:*

(see index for correct answer)

- a. Holmes and Rahe stress scale
- b. Abiotic stress
- c. Compassion fatigue
- d. Eustress

:: Asset ::

In financial accounting, an _____ is any resource owned by the business. Anything tangible or intangible that can be owned or controlled to produce value and that is held by a company to produce positive economic value is an _____ . Simply stated, _____ s represent value of ownership that can be converted into cash . The balance sheet of a firm records the monetary value of the _____ s owned by that firm. It covers money and other valuables belonging to an individual or to a business.

Exam Probability: **High**

4. *Answer choices:*

(see index for correct answer)

- a. Asset
- b. Current asset

Guidance: level 1

:: ::

_____ is overt or covert, often harmful, social interaction with the intention of inflicting damage or other unpleasantness upon another individual. It may occur either reactively or without provocation. In humans, frustration due to blocked goals can cause _____ . Human _____ can be classified into direct and indirect _____ ; whilst the former is characterized by physical or verbal behavior intended to cause harm to someone, the latter is characterized by behavior intended to harm the social relations of an individual or group.

Exam Probability: **Low**

5. *Answer choices:*

(see index for correct answer)

- a. levels of analysis
- b. hierarchical
- c. empathy
- d. process perspective

Guidance: level 1

:: ::

_____ is the stock of habits, knowledge, social and personality attributes embodied in the ability to perform labor so as to produce economic value.

Exam Probability: **High**

6. *Answer choices:*
(see index for correct answer)

- a. Human capital
- b. process perspective
- c. information systems assessment
- d. Sarbanes-Oxley act of 2002

Guidance: level 1

:: Labour relations ::

A _____ , also known as a post-entry closed shop, is a form of a union security clause. Under this, the employer agrees to either only hire labor union members or to require that any new employees who are not already union members become members within a certain amount of time. Use of the _____ varies widely from nation to nation, depending on the level of protection given trade unions in general.

Exam Probability: **High**

7. *Answer choices:*
(see index for correct answer)

- a. Featherbedding
- b. Acas
- c. Broad left
- d. Work Order Act

Guidance: level 1

:: ::

_____ is a method for employees to organize into a labor union in which a majority of employees in a bargaining unit sign authorization forms, or "cards", stating they wish to be represented by the union. Since the National Labor Relations Act became law in 1935, _____ has been an alternative to the National Labor Relations Board's election process. _____ and election are both overseen by the National Labor Relations Board. The difference is that with card sign-up, employees sign authorization cards stating they want a union, the cards are submitted to the NLRB and if more than 50% of the employees submitted cards, the NLRB requires the employer to recognize the union. The NLRA election process is an additional step with the NLRB conducting a secret ballot election after authorization cards are submitted. In both cases the employer never sees the authorization cards or any information that would disclose how individual employees voted.

Exam Probability: **Medium**

8. *Answer choices:*
(see index for correct answer)

- a. process perspective
- b. Card check
- c. Sarbanes-Oxley act of 2002
- d. hierarchical

Guidance: level 1

:: Offshoring ::

A _____ is the temporary suspension or permanent termination of employment of an employee or, more commonly, a group of employees for business reasons, such as personnel management or downsizing an organization. Originally, _____ referred exclusively to a temporary interruption in work, or employment but this has evolved to a permanent elimination of a position in both British and US English, requiring the addition of "temporary" to specify the original meaning of the word. A _____ is not to be confused with wrongful termination. Laid off workers or displaced workers are workers who have lost or left their jobs because their employer has closed or moved, there was insufficient work for them to do, or their position or shift was abolished . Downsizing in a company is defined to involve the reduction of employees in a workforce. Downsizing in companies became a popular practice in the 1980s and early 1990s as it was seen as a way to deliver better shareholder value as it helps to reduce the costs of employers . Indeed, recent research on downsizing in the U.S., UK, and Japan suggests that downsizing is being regarded by management as one of the preferred routes to help declining organizations, cutting unnecessary costs, and improve organizational performance. Usually a _____ occurs as a cost cutting measure.

Exam Probability: **High**

9. *Answer choices:*
(see index for correct answer)

- a. Offshoring Research Network
- b. Advanced Contact Solutions
- c. Offshore company
- d. Layoff

Guidance: level 1

:: Social psychology ::

In social psychology, _____ is the phenomenon of a person exerting less effort to achieve a goal when he or she works in a group than when working alone. This is seen as one of the main reasons groups are sometimes less productive than the combined performance of their members working as individuals, but should be distinguished from the accidental coordination problems that groups sometimes experience.

Exam Probability: **High**

10. *Answer choices:*
(see index for correct answer)

- a. Mind control
- b. brainwriting
- c. Social loafing
- d. coercive persuasion

Guidance: level 1

:: Behavioral and social facets of systemic risk ::

_____ is the difficulty in understanding an issue and effectively making decisions when one has too much information about that issue. Generally, the term is associated with the excessive quantity of daily information. _____ most likely originated from information theory, which are studies in the storage, preservation, communication, compression, and extraction of information. The term, _____ , was first used in Bertram Gross' 1964 book, The Managing of Organizations, and it was further popularized by Alvin Toffler in his bestselling 1970 book Future Shock. Speier et al. stated.

Exam Probability: **Medium**

11. *Answer choices:*
(see index for correct answer)

- a. Gatekeeping
- b. Herd behavior
- c. vicious cycle
- d. Information overload

Guidance: level 1

:: Labor rights ::

A _____ is a wrong or hardship suffered, real or supposed, which forms legitimate grounds of complaint. In the past, the word meant the infliction or cause of hardship.

Exam Probability: **Low**

12. *Answer choices:*
(see index for correct answer)

- a. Swift raids

- b. Labor rights
- c. The Hyatt 100
- d. China Labour Bulletin

Guidance: level 1

:: Corporate governance ::

An _____ is generally a person responsible for running an organization, although the exact nature of the role varies depending on the organization. In many militaries, an _____ , or "XO," is the second-in-command, reporting to the commanding officer. The XO is typically responsible for the management of day-to-day activities, freeing the commander to concentrate on strategy and planning the unit's next move.

Exam Probability: **Low**

13. *Answer choices:*
(see index for correct answer)

- a. Short swing
- b. Director of communications
- c. Executive officer
- d. Model Audit Rule 205

Guidance: level 1

:: United States federal labor legislation ::

The _____ of 1988 is a United States federal law that generally prevents employers from using polygraph tests, either for pre-employment screening or during the course of employment, with certain exemptions.

Exam Probability: **Medium**

14. *Answer choices:*
(see index for correct answer)

- a. Railway Labor Act
- b. Employee Polygraph Protection Act
- c. National Whistleblowers Center
- d. Age Discrimination in Employment Act

Guidance: level 1

_____ is an approach to problem solving. It involves taking action and reflecting upon the results. This helps improve the problem-solving process as well as simplify the solutions developed by the team.

Exam Probability: **Medium**

15. *Answer choices:*
(see index for correct answer)

- a. Audience response system
- b. double loop learning
- c. Collaborative learning
- d. Action learning

Guidance: level 1

:: ::

A _____ contract is a form of employment that carries fewer hours per week than a full-time job. They work in shifts. The shifts are often rotational. Workers are considered to be _____ if they commonly work fewer than 30 hours per week. According to the International Labour Organization, the number of _____ workers has increased from one-fourth to a half in the past 20 years in most developed countries, excluding the United States. There are many reasons for working _____, including the desire to do so, having one's hours cut back by an employer and being unable to find a full-time job. The International Labour Organisation Convention 175 requires that _____ workers be treated no less favourably than full-time workers.

Exam Probability: **Medium**

16. *Answer choices:*
(see index for correct answer)

- a. information systems assessment
- b. Part-time
- c. similarity-attraction theory
- d. imperative

Guidance: level 1

A _____ is monetary compensation paid by an employer to an employee in exchange for work done. Payment may be calculated as a fixed amount for each task completed , or at an hourly or daily rate , or based on an easily measured quantity of work done.

Exam Probability: **High**

17. *Answer choices:*
(see index for correct answer)

- a. interpersonal communication
- b. Sarbanes-Oxley act of 2002
- c. Wage
- d. Character

Guidance: level 1

A _____ is an occupation founded upon specialized educational training, the purpose of which is to supply disinterested objective counsel and service to others, for a direct and definite compensation, wholly apart from expectation of other business gain. The term is a truncation of the term "liberal _____ ", which is, in turn, an Anglicization of the French term " _____ libérale". Originally borrowed by English users in the 19th century, it has been re-borrowed by international users from the late 20th, though the class overtones of the term do not seem to survive retranslation: "liberal _____ s" are, according to the European Union's Directive on Recognition of _____ al Qualifications "those practiced on the basis of relevant _____ al qualifications in a personal, responsible and _____ ally independent capacity by those providing intellectual and conceptual services in the interest of the client and the public".

Exam Probability: **Medium**

18. *Answer choices:*
(see index for correct answer)

- a. Sarbanes-Oxley act of 2002
- b. hierarchical perspective
- c. Profession
- d. functional perspective

:: Training ::

_____ is the process of ensuring compliance with laws, regulations, rules, standards, or social norms. By enforcing laws and regulations, governments attempt to effectuate successful implementation of policies.

Exam Probability: **Medium**

19. *Answer choices:*
(see index for correct answer)

- a. Training
- b. Teletraining
- c. Enforcement
- d. Large Group Capacitation

:: Human resource management ::

A _____ is a group of people with different functional expertise working toward a common goal. It may include people from finance, marketing, operations, and human resources departments. Typically, it includes employees from all levels of an organization. Members may also come from outside an organization .

Exam Probability: **Low**

20. *Answer choices:*
(see index for correct answer)

- a. Onboarding
- b. Management development
- c. Cross-functional team
- d. Person specification

:: Management ::

_____ is the kind of knowledge that is difficult to transfer to another person by means of writing it down or verbalizing it. For example, that London is in the United Kingdom is a piece of explicit knowledge that can be written down, transmitted, and understood by a recipient. However, the ability to speak a language, ride a bicycle, knead dough, play a musical instrument, or design and use complex equipment requires all sorts of knowledge that is not always known explicitly, even by expert practitioners, and which is difficult or impossible to explicitly transfer to other people.

Exam Probability: **High**

21. *Answer choices:*
(see index for correct answer)

- a. Behavioral risk management
- b. Fall guy
- c. Defensive expenditures
- d. Tacit knowledge

Guidance: level 1

:: Business ethics ::

_____ is a persistent pattern of mistreatment from others in the workplace that causes either physical or emotional harm. It can include such tactics as verbal, nonverbal, psychological, physical abuse and humiliation. This type of workplace aggression is particularly difficult because, unlike the typical school bully, workplace bullies often operate within the established rules and policies of their organization and their society. In the majority of cases, bullying in the workplace is reported as having been by someone who has authority over their victim. However, bullies can also be peers, and occasionally subordinates. Research has also investigated the impact of the larger organizational context on bullying as well as the group-level processes that impact on the incidence and maintenance of bullying behaviour. Bullying can be covert or overt. It may be missed by superiors; it may be known by many throughout the organization. Negative effects are not limited to the targeted individuals, and may lead to a decline in employee morale and a change in organizational culture. It can also take place as overbearing supervision, constant criticism, and blocking promotions.

Exam Probability: **Low**

22. *Answer choices:*
(see index for correct answer)

- a. Society of Corporate Compliance and Ethics
- b. Workplace bullying
- c. Price discrimination
- d. Creative destruction

Guidance: level 1

:: ::

_____ is the administration of an organization, whether it is a business, a not-for-profit organization, or government body. _____ includes the activities of setting the strategy of an organization and coordinating the efforts of its employees to accomplish its objectives through the application of available resources, such as financial, natural, technological, and human resources. The term " _____ " may also refer to those people who manage an organization.

Exam Probability: **Medium**

23. *Answer choices:*
(see index for correct answer)

- a. co-culture
- b. levels of analysis
- c. interpersonal communication
- d. Management

Guidance: level 1

:: Teams ::

A _____ usually refers to a group of individuals who work together from different geographic locations and rely on communication technology such as email, FAX, and video or voice conferencing services in order to collaborate. The term can also refer to groups or teams that work together asynchronously or across organizational levels. Powell, Piccoli and Ives define _____ s as "groups of geographically, organizationally and/or time dispersed workers brought together by information and telecommunication technologies to accomplish one or more organizational tasks." According to Ale Ebrahim et. al., _____ s can also be defined as "small temporary groups of geographically, organizationally and/or time dispersed knowledge workers who coordinate their work predominantly with electronic information and communication technologies in order to accomplish one or more organization tasks."

Exam Probability: **Medium**

24. *Answer choices:*
(see index for correct answer)

- a. Team-building
- b. team composition

Guidance: level 1

:: Human resource management ::

_____ involves improving the effectiveness of organizations and the individuals and teams within them. Training may be viewed as related to immediate changes in organizational effectiveness via organized instruction, while development is related to the progress of longer-term organizational and employee goals. While _____ technically have differing definitions, the two are oftentimes used interchangeably and/or together. _____ has historically been a topic within applied psychology but has within the last two decades become closely associated with human resources management, talent management, human resources development, instructional design, human factors, and knowledge management.

Exam Probability: **High**

25. *Answer choices:*
(see index for correct answer)

- a. Lego Serious Play
- b. Training and development
- c. Service record
- d. Contractor management

Guidance: level 1

:: Unemployment ::

In economics, a _____ is a business cycle contraction when there is a general decline in economic activity. Macroeconomic indicators such as GDP, investment spending, capacity utilization, household income, business profits, and inflation fall, while bankruptcies and the unemployment rate rise. In the United Kingdom, it is defined as a negative economic growth for two consecutive quarters.

Exam Probability: **Medium**

26. *Answer choices:*
(see index for correct answer)

- a. Reserve army of labour
- b. JobBridge
- c. Unemployment Provision Convention, 1934
- d. Employment Promotion and Protection against Unemployment Convention, 1988

Guidance: level 1

:: ::

The _____ or labour force is the labour pool in employment. It is generally used to describe those working for a single company or industry, but can also apply to a geographic region like a city, state, or country. Within a company, its value can be labelled as its " _____ in Place". The _____ of a country includes both the employed and the unemployed. The labour force participation rate, LFPR, is the ratio between the labour force and the overall size of their cohort. The term generally excludes the employers or management, and can imply those involved in manual labour. It may also mean all those who are available for work.

Exam Probability: **Low**

27. *Answer choices:*

(see index for correct answer)

- a. Workforce
- b. hierarchical
- c. personal values
- d. open system

Guidance: level 1

:: Workplace ::

_____ or occupational violence refers to violence, usually in the form of physical abuse or threat, that creates a risk to the health and safety of an employee or multiple employees. The National Institute for Occupational Safety and Health defines worker on worker, personal relationship, customer/client, and criminal intent all as categories of violence in the workplace. These four categories are further broken down into three levels: Level one displays early warning signs of violence, Level two is slightly more violent, and level three is significantly violent. Many workplaces have initiated programs and protocols to protect their workers as the Occupational Health Act of 1970 states that employers must provide an environment in which employees are free of harm or harmful conditions.

Exam Probability: **Low**

28. *Answer choices:*
(see index for correct answer)

- a. Discrimination based on hair texture
- b. Workplace violence
- c. Workplace phobia
- d. Occupational stress

Guidance: level 1

:: Management ::

The term _____ refers to measures designed to increase the degree of autonomy and self-determination in people and in communities in order to enable them to represent their interests in a responsible and self-determined way, acting on their own authority. It is the process of becoming stronger and more confident, especially in controlling one's life and claiming one's rights. _____ as action refers both to the process of self- _____ and to professional support of people, which enables them to overcome their sense of powerlessness and lack of influence, and to recognize and use their resources. To do work with power.

Exam Probability: **High**

29. *Answer choices:*
(see index for correct answer)

- a. Iterative and incremental development
- b. Corporate recovery
- c. Dominant design
- d. Empowerment

Guidance: level 1

:: ::

_____ is a belief that hard work and diligence have a moral benefit and an inherent ability, virtue or value to strengthen character and individual abilities. It is a set of values centered on importance of work and manifested by determination or desire to work hard. Social ingrainment of this value is considered to enhance character through hard work that is respective to an individual's field of work.

Exam Probability: **High**

30. *Answer choices:*
(see index for correct answer)

- a. Sarbanes-Oxley act of 2002
- b. Work ethic
- c. hierarchical perspective
- d. surface-level diversity

Guidance: level 1

:: Human resource management ::

_____ is a process for identifying and developing new leaders who can replace old leaders when they leave, retire or die. _____ increases the availability of experienced and capable employees that are prepared to assume these roles as they become available. Taken narrowly, "replacement planning" for key roles is the heart of _____ .

Exam Probability: **High**

31. *Answer choices:*
(see index for correct answer)

- a. Illness rate
- b. Succession planning
- c. Parallel running
- d. Focal Point Review

Guidance: level 1

:: Employment compensation ::

A _____ is an agreement between a company and an employee specifying that the employee will receive certain significant benefits if employment is terminated. Most definitions specify the employment termination is as a result of a merger or takeover, also known as "Change-in-control benefits", but more recently the term has been used to describe perceived excessive CEO severance packages unrelated to change in ownership . The benefits may include severance pay, cash bonuses, stock options, or other benefits.

Exam Probability: **High**

32. *Answer choices:*
(see index for correct answer)

- a. Basic income
- b. Seasonal bonuses
- c. Golden parachute
- d. Total Reward

Guidance: level 1

:: Employment compensation ::

A _____ is pay and benefits employees receive when they leave employment at a company unwillfully. In addition to their remaining regular pay, it may include some of the following.

Exam Probability: **Medium**

33. *Answer choices:*
(see index for correct answer)

- a. Wages for housework
- b. Severance package
- c. Corporate child care
- d. Living wage

Guidance: level 1

:: ::

A _____ is a research instrument consisting of a series of questions for the purpose of gathering information from respondents. The _____ was invented by the Statistical Society of London in 1838.

Exam Probability: **Medium**

34. *Answer choices:*
(see index for correct answer)

- a. Character
- b. Questionnaire
- c. open system
- d. co-culture

Guidance: level 1

:: Minimum wage ::

A _____ is the lowest remuneration that employers can legally pay their workers—the price floor below which workers may not sell their labor. Most countries had introduced _____ legislation by the end of the 20th century.

Exam Probability: **High**

:: Psychometrics ::

A _____ is a set of categories designed to elicit information about a quantitative or a qualitative attribute. In the social sciences, particularly psychology, common examples are the Likert response scale and 1-10 _____ s in which a person selects the number which is considered to reflect the perceived quality of a product.

Exam Probability: **Medium**

:: Management ::

A _____ is when two or more people come together to discuss one or more topics, often in a formal or business setting, but _____ s also occur in a variety of other environments. Many various types of _____ s exist.

Exam Probability: **Low**

:: Employment ::

_____ is measuring the output of a particular business process or procedure, then modifying the process or procedure to increase the output, increase efficiency, or increase the effectiveness of the process or procedure. _____ can be applied to either individual performance such as an athlete or organizational performance such as a racing team or a commercial business.

Exam Probability: **Medium**

38. *Answer choices:*
(see index for correct answer)

- a. Attendance allowance
- b. Performance improvement
- c. Social VAT
- d. Local hiring

:: Industrial relations ::

_____ or employee satisfaction is a measure of workers' contentedness with their job, whether or not they like the job or individual aspects or facets of jobs, such as nature of work or supervision. _____ can be measured in cognitive , affective , and behavioral components. Researchers have also noted that _____ measures vary in the extent to which they measure feelings about the job , or cognitions about the job .

Exam Probability: **Low**

39. *Answer choices:*
(see index for correct answer)

- a. European Journal of Industrial Relations
- b. Workforce Investment Board
- c. Industrial violence
- d. Job satisfaction

:: Production and manufacturing ::

_____ is a theory of management that analyzes and synthesizes workflows. Its main objective is improving economic efficiency, especially labor productivity. It was one of the earliest attempts to apply science to the engineering of processes and to management. _____ is sometimes known as Taylorism after its founder, Frederick Winslow Taylor.

Exam Probability: **Low**

40. *Answer choices:*
(see index for correct answer)

- a. Value-added agriculture
- b. Mockup
- c. Scientific management
- d. Miniaturization

Guidance: level 1

:: Labor relations in the United States ::

In the context of U.S. labor politics, " _____ s" refers to state laws that prohibit union security agreements between companies and labor unions. Under these laws, employees in unionized workplaces are banned from negotiating contracts which require all members who benefit from the union contract to contribute to the costs of union representation.

Exam Probability: **Medium**

41. *Answer choices:*
(see index for correct answer)

- a. Strong Economy for All Coalition
- b. Right-to-work law
- c. Taylor Law
- d. Jobs with Justice

Guidance: level 1

:: ::

_____ is the withdrawal from one's position or occupation or from one's active working life. A person may also semi-retire by reducing work hours.

42. *Answer choices:*
(see index for correct answer)

- a. Retirement
- b. personal values
- c. surface-level diversity
- d. information systems assessment

Guidance: level 1

:: Business law ::

An _____ is a natural person, business, or corporation that provides goods or services to another entity under terms specified in a contract or within a verbal agreement. Unlike an employee, an _____ does not work regularly for an employer but works as and when required, during which time they may be subject to law of agency. _____ s are usually paid on a freelance basis. Contractors often work through a limited company or franchise, which they themselves own, or may work through an umbrella company.

Exam Probability: **High**

43. *Answer choices:*
(see index for correct answer)

- a. Apparent authority
- b. Independent contractor
- c. Rules of origin
- d. Limited liability

Guidance: level 1

:: Organizational theory ::

Decentralisation is the process by which the activities of an organization, particularly those regarding planning and decision making, are distributed or delegated away from a central, authoritative location or group. Concepts of _____ have been applied to group dynamics and management science in private businesses and organizations, political science, law and public administration, economics, money and technology.

Exam Probability: **Low**

44. *Answer choices:*
(see index for correct answer)

- a. Requisite organization
- b. Decentralization
- c. Mutual aid
- d. Organizational engineering

Guidance: level 1

:: Labour law ::

A _____ is a legal contract that is meant to limit the liability of an employer whose employees are romantically involved. An employer may choose to require a _____ when a romantic relationship within the company becomes known, in order to indemnify the company in case the employees' romantic relationship fails, primarily so that one party can't bring a sexual harassment lawsuit against the company. To that end, the _____ states that the relationship is consensual, and both parties of the relationship must sign it. The _____ may also stipulate rules for acceptable romantic behavior in the workplace.

Exam Probability: **High**

45. *Answer choices:*
(see index for correct answer)

- a. Non-disclosure agreement
- b. Love contract
- c. Undue hardship
- d. Bharat Forge Co Ltd v Uttam Manohar Nakate

Guidance: level 1

:: Management ::

A _____ is a method or technique that has been generally accepted as superior to any alternatives because it produces results that are superior to those achieved by other means or because it has become a standard way of doing things, e.g., a standard way of complying with legal or ethical requirements.

Exam Probability: **High**

46. *Answer choices:*

- a. Defensive expenditures
- b. Backsourcing
- c. Place management
- d. Best practice

Guidance: level 1

:: Labor ::

_____ refers to the process of grouping activities into departments. Division of labour creates specialists who need coordination. This coordination is facilitated by grouping specialists together in departments.

Exam Probability: **Medium**

47. *Answer choices:*

- a. Departmentalization
- b. Bought priesthood
- c. Wage compression
- d. Labor pool

Guidance: level 1

:: Validity (statistics) ::

In psychometrics, _____ is the extent to which a score on a scale or test predicts scores on some criterion measure.

Exam Probability: **Medium**

48. *Answer choices:*

- a. Criterion validity
- b. Statistical conclusion
- c. Validation
- d. Predictive validity

Guidance: level 1

:: Free market ::

Piece work is any type of employment in which a worker is paid a fixed _____ for each unit produced or action performed regardless of time.

Exam Probability: **High**

49. *Answer choices:*
(see index for correct answer)

- a. Regulated market
- b. Free market

Guidance: level 1

:: Survey methodology ::

An _____ is a conversation where questions are asked and answers are given. In common parlance, the word " _____ " refers to a one-on-one conversation between an _____ er and an _____ ee. The _____ er asks questions to which the _____ ee responds, usually so information may be transferred from _____ ee to _____ er . Sometimes, information can be transferred in both directions. It is a communication, unlike a speech, which produces a one-way flow of information.

Exam Probability: **Medium**

50. *Answer choices:*
(see index for correct answer)

- a. World Association for Public Opinion Research
- b. Total survey error
- c. Census
- d. Survey sampling

Guidance: level 1

:: ::

In production, research, retail, and accounting, a _____ is the value of money that has been used up to produce something or deliver a service, and hence is not available for use anymore. In business, the _____ may be one of acquisition, in which case the amount of money expended to acquire it is counted as _____ . In this case, money is the input that is gone in order to acquire the thing. This acquisition _____ may be the sum of the _____ of production as incurred by the original producer, and further _____ s of transaction as incurred by the acquirer over and above the price paid to the producer. Usually, the price also includes a mark-up for profit over the _____ of production.

Exam Probability: **Medium**

51. *Answer choices:*
(see index for correct answer)

- a. hierarchical
- b. empathy
- c. imperative
- d. surface-level diversity

Guidance: level 1

:: Income ::

A _____ is a unit in systems of monetary compensation for employment. It is commonly used in public service, both civil and military, but also for companies of the private sector. _____ s facilitate the employment process by providing a fixed framework of salary ranges, as opposed to a free negotiation. Typically, _____ s encompass two dimensions: a "vertical" range where each level corresponds to the responsibility of, and requirements needed for a certain position; and a "horizontal" range within this scale to allow for monetary incentives rewarding the employee's quality of performance or length of service. Thus, an employee progresses within the horizontal and vertical ranges upon achieving positive appraisal on a regular basis. In most cases, evaluation is done annually and encompasses more than one method.

Exam Probability: **Low**

52. *Answer choices:*
(see index for correct answer)

- a. Creative real estate investing
- b. Pay grade
- c. Mandatory tipping
- d. Imputed income

Guidance: level 1

:: ::

A _____ seeks to further a particular profession, the interests of individuals engaged in that profession and the public interest. In the United States, such an association is typically a nonprofit organization for tax purposes.

Exam Probability: **High**

53. *Answer choices:*
(see index for correct answer)

- a. Character
- b. Professional association
- c. corporate values
- d. hierarchical perspective

Guidance: level 1

:: Offshoring ::

Outsourcing is an agreement in which one company hires another company to be responsible for a planned or existing activity that is or could be done internally,and sometimes involves transferring employees and assets from one firm to another.

Exam Probability: **Medium**

54. *Answer choices:*
(see index for correct answer)

- a. Offshore company
- b. Offshoring Research Network
- c. Offshore custom software development
- d. Offshore outsourcing

Guidance: level 1

In educational development, _____ provides a person, often a student, focus for selecting a career or subject to undertake in the future. Often educational institutions provide career counsellors to assist students with their educational development.

Exam Probability: **High**

55. *Answer choices:*

- a. cultural
- b. Career development
- c. co-culture
- d. deep-level diversity

Guidance: level 1

:: Nepotism ::

_____ is the granting of favour to relatives in various fields, including business, politics, entertainment, sports, religion and other activities. The term originated with the assignment of nephews to important positions by Catholic popes and bishops. Trading parliamentary employment for favors is a modern-day example of _____ . Criticism of _____ , however, can be found in ancient Indian texts such as the Kural literature.

Exam Probability: **High**

56. *Answer choices:*

- a. Cardinal-nephew
- b. Wasta
- c. Crachach
- d. Nepotism

Guidance: level 1

:: ::

_____ is defined by sociologist John R. Schermerhorn as the "...degree to which the people affected by decision are treated by dignity and respect. The theory focuses on the interpersonal treatment people receive when procedures are implemented.

Exam Probability: **Low**

57. *Answer choices:*
(see index for correct answer)

- a. Interactional justice
- b. hierarchical perspective
- c. Sarbanes-Oxley act of 2002
- d. personal values

Guidance: level 1

:: Validity (statistics) ::

_____ is "the degree to which a test measures what it claims, or purports, to be measuring." In the classical model of test validity, _____ is one of three main types of validity evidence, alongside content validity and criterion validity. Modern validity theory defines _____ as the overarching concern of validity research, subsuming all other types of validity evidence.

Exam Probability: **Medium**

58. *Answer choices:*
(see index for correct answer)

- a. Incremental validity
- b. Construct validity
- c. Face validity
- d. Content validity

Guidance: level 1

:: Organizational theory ::

_____ is the process of creating, retaining, and transferring knowledge within an organization. An organization improves over time as it gains experience. From this experience, it is able to create knowledge. This knowledge is broad, covering any topic that could better an organization. Examples may include ways to increase production efficiency or to develop beneficial investor relations. Knowledge is created at four different units: individual, group, organizational, and inter organizational.

Exam Probability: **Low**

59. *Answer choices:*

- a. Proactivity
- b. Organizational learning
- c. Smart city
- d. Swift trust

Guidance: level 1

Information systems

Information systems (IS) are formal, sociotechnical, organizational systems designed to collect, process, store, and distribute information. In a sociotechnical perspective Information Systems are composed by four components: technology, process, people and organizational structure.

:: Distribution, retailing, and wholesaling ::

_____ measures the performance of a system. Certain goals are defined and the _____ gives the percentage to which those goals should be achieved. Fill rate is different from _____ .

Exam Probability: **Medium**

1. *Answer choices:*
(see index for correct answer)

- a. Balance of contract
- b. Service level
- c. CGC Japan
- d. 350 West Mart Center

Guidance: level 1

:: Internet advertising ::

_____ , according to the United States federal law known as the Anti _____ Consumer Protection Act, is registering, trafficking in, or using an Internet domain name with bad faith intent to profit from the goodwill of a trademark belonging to someone else. The cybersquatter then offers to sell the domain to the person or company who owns a trademark contained within the name at an inflated price.

2. *Answer choices:*

- a. Conversion optimization
- b. Domain drop catching
- c. Boltblue
- d. Premium Rich Media

Guidance: level 1

:: Data quality ::

_____ is the maintenance of, and the assurance of the accuracy and consistency of, data over its entire life-cycle, and is a critical aspect to the design, implementation and usage of any system which stores, processes, or retrieves data. The term is broad in scope and may have widely different meanings depending on the specific context even under the same general umbrella of computing. It is at times used as a proxy term for data quality, while data validation is a pre-requisite for _____ . _____ is the opposite of data corruption. The overall intent of any _____ technique is the same: ensure data is recorded exactly as intended and upon later retrieval, ensure the data is the same as it was when it was originally recorded. In short, _____ aims to prevent unintentional changes to information. _____ is not to be confused with data security, the discipline of protecting data from unauthorized parties.

3. *Answer choices:*

- a. One-for-one checking
- b. Information quality
- c. Referential integrity
- d. Input mask

Guidance: level 1

:: Data security ::

_____ , sometimes shortened to InfoSec, is the practice of preventing unauthorized access, use, disclosure, disruption, modification, inspection, recording or destruction of information. The information or data may take any form, e.g. electronic or physical. _____ `s primary focus is the balanced protection of the confidentiality, integrity and availability of data while maintaining a focus on efficient policy implementation, all without hampering organization productivity. This is largely achieved through a multi-step risk management process that identifies assets, threat sources, vulnerabilities, potential impacts, and possible controls, followed by assessment of the effectiveness of the risk management plan.

Exam Probability: **Low**

4. *Answer choices:*
(see index for correct answer)

- a. Certified Information Systems Auditor
- b. Information security
- c. Misuse detection
- d. Backup sync share

Guidance: level 1

:: Outsourcing ::

A service-level agreement is a commitment between a service provider and a client. Particular aspects of the service – quality, availability, responsibilities – are agreed between the service provider and the service user. The most common component of SLA is that the services should be provided to the customer as agreed upon in the contract. As an example, Internet service providers and telcos will commonly include _____ s within the terms of their contracts with customers to define the level of service being sold in plain language terms. In this case the SLA will typically have a technical definition in mean time between failures , mean time to repair or mean time to recovery ; identifying which party is responsible for reporting faults or paying fees; responsibility for various data rates; throughput; jitter; or similar measurable details.

Exam Probability: **Medium**

5. *Answer choices:*
(see index for correct answer)

- a. Request for proposal
- b. Sourcing agent
- c. Service level agreement
- d. Print and mail outsourcing

Guidance: level 1

:: Internet marketing ::

_____ is the measurement, collection, analysis and reporting of web data for purposes of understanding and optimizing web usage. However, _____ is not just a process for measuring web traffic but can be used as a tool for business and market research, and to assess and improve the effectiveness of a website. _____ applications can also help companies measure the results of traditional print or broadcast advertising campaigns. It helps one to estimate how traffic to a website changes after the launch of a new advertising campaign. _____ provides information about the number of visitors to a website and the number of page views. It helps gauge traffic and popularity trends which is useful for market research.

Exam Probability: **High**

6. *Answer choices:*
(see index for correct answer)

- a. Internet presence management
- b. SocialFlow
- c. Personalized retargeting
- d. Negative keyword

Guidance: level 1

:: Management ::

_____ is the identification of an organization's assets, followed by the development, documentation, and implementation of policies and procedures for protecting these assets.

Exam Probability: **Low**

7. *Answer choices:*
(see index for correct answer)

- a. Concept of the Corporation

- b. Extended enterprise
- c. Knowledge ecosystem
- d. Security management

Guidance: level 1

:: Cloud storage ::

_____ was an online backup service for both Windows and macOS users. Linux support was made available in Q3, 2014. In 2007 _____ was acquired by EMC, and in 2013 _____ was included in the EMC Backup Recovery Systems division's product list.On September 7, 2016, Dell Inc. acquired EMC Corporation to form Dell Technologies, restructuring the original Dell Inc. as a subsidiary of Dell Technologies.. On March 19, 2018 Carbonite acquired _____ from Dell for $148.5 million in cash and in 2019 shut down the service, incorporating _____'s clients into its own online backup service programs.

Exam Probability: **Low**

8. *Answer choices:*
(see index for correct answer)

- a. Mozy
- b. Rackspace Cloud
- c. Memonic
- d. Zadara Storage

Guidance: level 1

:: ::

A _____ is server software, or hardware dedicated to running said software, that can satisfy World Wide Web client requests. A _____ can, in general, contain one or more websites. A _____ processes incoming network requests over HTTP and several other related protocols.

Exam Probability: **Medium**

9. *Answer choices:*
(see index for correct answer)

- a. Web server
- b. surface-level diversity

- c. hierarchical perspective
- d. process perspective

Guidance: level 1

:: Big data ::

_____ refers to the skills, technologies, practices for continuous iterative exploration and investigation of past business performance to gain insight and drive business planning. _____ focuses on developing new insights and understanding of business performance based on data and statistical methods. In contrast, business intelligence traditionally focuses on using a consistent set of metrics to both measure past performance and guide business planning, which is also based on data and statistical methods.

Exam Probability: **High**

10. *Answer choices:*
(see index for correct answer)

- a. Oracle Big Data Appliance
- b. Industrial Internet
- c. Platfora
- d. Sense Networks

Guidance: level 1

:: Industrial automation ::

_____ is the technology by which a process or procedure is performed with minimal human assistance. _____ or automatic control is the use of various control systems for operating equipment such as machinery, processes in factories, boilers and heat treating ovens, switching on telephone networks, steering and stabilization of ships, aircraft and other applications and vehicles with minimal or reduced human intervention.

Exam Probability: **High**

11. *Answer choices:*
(see index for correct answer)

- a. Collaborative process automation systems
- b. CODESYS
- c. PLCopen

- d. Automation

Guidance: level 1

:: Payment systems ::

A _____ is any system used to settle financial transactions through the transfer of monetary value. This includes the institutions, instruments, people, rules, procedures, standards, and technologies that make it exchange possible. A common type of _____ is called an operational network that links bank accounts and provides for monetary exchange using bank deposits. Some _____ s also include credit mechanisms, which are essentially a different aspect of payment.

Exam Probability: **High**

12. *Answer choices:*
(see index for correct answer)

- a. PayPoint
- b. Payment system
- c. Google Wallet
- d. Bankgiro

Guidance: level 1

:: Marketing ::

_____ is a business model in which consumers create value and businesses consume that value. For example, when a consumer writes reviews or when a consumer gives a useful idea for new product development then that consumer is creating value for the business if the business adopts the input. In the C2B model, a reverse auction or demand collection model, enables buyers to name or demand their own price, which is often binding, for a specific good or service. Inside of a consumer to business market the roles involved in the transaction must be established and the consumer must offer something of value to the business.

Exam Probability: **Medium**

13. *Answer choices:*
(see index for correct answer)

- a. Price on application
- b. Adobe Analytics
- c. Accreditation in Public Relations
- d. Consumer-to-business

Guidance: level 1

:: Virtual reality ::

_____ is an experience taking place within simulated and immersive environments that can be similar to or completely different from the real world. Applications of _____ can include entertainment and educational purposes . Other, distinct types of VR style technology include augmented reality and mixed reality.

Exam Probability: **Medium**

14. *Answer choices:*
(see index for correct answer)

- a. Free look
- b. Virtual cocoon
- c. Virtual reality
- d. Photosynth

Guidance: level 1

:: Data management ::

_____ involves combining data residing in different sources and providing users with a unified view of them. This process becomes significant in a variety of situations, which include both commercial and scientific domains. _____ appears with increasing frequency as the volume and the need to share existing data explodes. It has become the focus of extensive theoretical work, and numerous open problems remain unsolved. _____ encourages collaboration between internal as well as external users

Exam Probability: **Low**

15. *Answer choices:*
(see index for correct answer)

- a. Data integration
- b. Distributed data store
- c. XLDB

- d. SQL programming tool

:: Satellite navigation systems ::

_____ Galilei was an Italian astronomer, physicist and engineer, sometimes described as a polymath. _____ has been called the "father of observational astronomy", the "father of modern physics", the "father of the scientific method", and the "father of modern science".

Exam Probability: **Medium**

16. *Answer choices:*

- a. European Satellite Services Provider
- b. Galileo
- c. Satellite navigation
- d. Quasi-Zenith Satellite System

:: Network architecture ::

An _____ is a controlled private network that allows access to partners, vendors and suppliers or an authorized set of customers – normally to a subset of the information accessible from an organization's intranet. An _____ is similar to a DMZ in that it provides access to needed services for authorized parties, without granting access to an organization's entire network. An _____ is a private network organization.

Exam Probability: **Medium**

17. *Answer choices:*

- a. client-server
- b. Extranet

:: Information science ::

The United States National Forum on _____ defines _____ as "... the hyper ability to know when there is a need for information, to be able to identify, locate, evaluate, and effectively use that information for the issue or problem at hand." The American Library Association defines "_____" as a set of abilities requiring individuals to "recognize when information is needed and have the ability to locate, evaluate, and use effectively the needed information. Other definitions incorporate aspects of "skepticism, judgement, free thinking, questioning, and understanding..." or incorporate competencies that an informed citizen of an information society ought to possess to participate intelligently and actively in that society.

Exam Probability: **Low**

18. *Answer choices:*
(see index for correct answer)

- a. Jason Farradane
- b. International Coalition for GeoInformatics
- c. Information literacy
- d. Evolutionary informatics

Guidance: level 1

:: Security compliance ::

_____ refers to the inability to withstand the effects of a hostile environment. A window of _____ is a time frame within which defensive measures are diminished, compromised or lacking.

Exam Probability: **Low**

19. *Answer choices:*
(see index for correct answer)

- a. Threat
- b. North American Electric Reliability Corporation
- c. Information assurance vulnerability alert
- d. 201 CMR 17.00

Guidance: level 1

:: Data security ::

_____ are safeguards or countermeasures to avoid, detect, counteract, or minimize security risks to physical property, information, computer systems, or other assets.

Exam Probability: **Low**

20. *Answer choices:*
(see index for correct answer)

- a. Crypto cloud computing
- b. Cyber Insider Threat
- c. Security controls
- d. Blancco

Guidance: level 1

:: Virtual reality ::

An _____ , a concept in Hinduism that means "descent", refers to the material appearance or incarnation of a deity on earth. The relative verb to "alight, to make one's appearance" is sometimes used to refer to any guru or revered human being.

Exam Probability: **Low**

21. *Answer choices:*
(see index for correct answer)

- a. Endocentric environment
- b. Avatar
- c. Web3D Consortium
- d. International Stereoscopic Union

Guidance: level 1

:: Data management ::

_____ represents the business objects that contain the most valuable, agreed upon information shared across an organization. It can cover relatively static reference data, transactional, unstructured, analytical, hierarchical and metadata. It is the primary focus of the information technology discipline of _____ management .

22. *Answer choices:*
(see index for correct answer)

- a. CommVault Systems
- b. HyperLogLog
- c. Master data
- d. Metadata

Guidance: level 1

:: Commercial item transport and distribution ::

In commerce, supply-chain management , the management of the flow of goods and services, involves the movement and storage of raw materials, of work-in-process inventory, and of finished goods from point of origin to point of consumption. Interconnected or interlinked networks, channels and node businesses combine in the provision of products and services required by end customers in a supply chain. Supply-chain management has been defined as the "design, planning, execution, control, and monitoring of supply-chain activities with the objective of creating net value, building a competitive infrastructure, leveraging worldwide logistics, synchronizing supply with demand and measuring performance globally."SCM practice draws heavily from the areas of industrial engineering, systems engineering, operations management, logistics, procurement, information technology, and marketing and strives for an integrated approach. Marketing channels play an important role in supply-chain management. Current research in supply-chain management is concerned with topics related to sustainability and risk management, among others. Some suggest that the "people dimension" of SCM, ethical issues, internal integration, transparency/visibility, and human capital/talent management are topics that have, so far, been underrepresented on the research agenda.

23. *Answer choices:*
(see index for correct answer)

- a. Freight exchange
- b. Bulk cargo
- c. Supply chain management
- d. Skid mount

Guidance: level 1

:: Confidence tricks ::

_____ is the fraudulent attempt to obtain sensitive information such as usernames, passwords and credit card details by disguising oneself as a trustworthy entity in an electronic communication. Typically carried out by email spoofing or instant messaging, it often directs users to enter personal information at a fake website which matches the look and feel of the legitimate site.

Exam Probability: **Medium**

24. *Answer choices:*
(see index for correct answer)

- a. Cackle-bladder
- b. Television Preview
- c. Phishing
- d. Scams in intellectual property

Guidance: level 1

:: Types of marketing ::

In microeconomics and management, _____ is an arrangement in which the supply chain of a company is owned by that company. Usually each member of the supply chain produces a different product or service, and the products combine to satisfy a common need. It is contrasted with horizontal integration, wherein a company produces several items which are related to one another. _____ has also described management styles that bring large portions of the supply chain not only under a common ownership, but also into one corporation .

Exam Probability: **Low**

25. *Answer choices:*
(see index for correct answer)

- a. Close Range Marketing
- b. Vertical integration
- c. Social pull marketing
- d. Ambush marketing

Guidance: level 1

:: Knowledge engineering ::

The _____ is an extension of the World Wide Web through standards by the World Wide Web Consortium . The standards promote common data formats and exchange protocols on the Web, most fundamentally the Resource Description Framework . According to the W3C, "The _____ provides a common framework that allows data to be shared and reused across application, enterprise, and community boundaries". The _____ is therefore regarded as an integrator across different content, information applications and systems.

Exam Probability: **High**

26. *Answer choices:*

(see index for correct answer)

- a. Knowledge level modeling
- b. Knowledge Acquisition and Documentation Structuring
- c. Semantic Web
- d. Knowledge engineer

Guidance: level 1

:: Service-oriented (business computing) ::

_____ is a style of software design where services are provided to the other components by application components, through a communication protocol over a network. The basic principles of _____ are independent of vendors, products and technologies.A service is a discrete unit of functionality that can be accessed remotely and acted upon and updated independently, such as retrieving a credit card statement online.

Exam Probability: **High**

27. *Answer choices:*

(see index for correct answer)

- a. Service reusability principle
- b. Event-driven architecture
- c. TOA Technologies
- d. Service-oriented architecture

Guidance: level 1

:: Computer data ::

In computer science, _____ is the ability to access an arbitrary element of a sequence in equal time or any datum from a population of addressable elements roughly as easily and efficiently as any other, no matter how many elements may be in the set. It is typically contrasted to sequential access.

Exam Probability: **Low**

28. *Answer choices:*

- a. Seed loading
- b. Random access
- c. Attribute
- d. Data efficiency

Guidance: level 1

:: Management ::

The _____ is a strategy performance management tool – a semi-standard structured report, that can be used by managers to keep track of the execution of activities by the staff within their control and to monitor the consequences arising from these actions.

Exam Probability: **High**

29. *Answer choices:*

- a. Product breakdown structure
- b. Meeting
- c. Behavioral risk management
- d. Goals Breakdown Structure

Guidance: level 1

:: Information systems ::

A _____ is an information system used for decision-making, and for the coordination, control, analysis, and visualization of information in an organization; especially in a company.

30. *Answer choices:*
(see index for correct answer)

- a. Hybrid positioning system
- b. Disparate system
- c. Joint Interface Control Officer
- d. Data infrastructure

Guidance: level 1

:: Data transmission ::

In telecommunications and computing, _____ is the number of bits that are conveyed or processed per unit of time.

Exam Probability: **Medium**

31. *Answer choices:*
(see index for correct answer)

- a. Low bit
- b. Frame slip
- c. Gillham code
- d. Bit rate

Guidance: level 1

:: Data collection ::

_____ is information that either does not have a pre-defined data model or is not organized in a pre-defined manner. Unstructured information is typically text-heavy, but may contain data such as dates, numbers, and facts as well. This results in irregularities and ambiguities that make it difficult to understand using traditional programs as compared to data stored in fielded form in databases or annotated in documents.

Exam Probability: **Low**

32. *Answer choices:*
(see index for correct answer)

- a. Data farming
- b. Unstructured data
- c. Data scraping

- d. Natural experiment

Guidance: level 1

:: E-commerce ::

Electronic governance or e-governance is the application of information and communication technology for delivering government services, exchange of information, communication transactions, integration of various stand-alone systems and services between government-to-citizen , government-to-business , _____ , government-to-employees as well as back-office processes and interactions within the entire government framework. Through e-governance, government services are made available to citizens in a convenient, efficient, and transparent manner. The three main target groups that can be distinguished in governance concepts are government, citizens, andbusinesses/interest groups. In e-governance, there are no distinct boundaries.

Exam Probability: **Low**

33. *Answer choices:*
(see index for correct answer)

- a. Government-to-government
- b. IDEAL
- c. Computer reservations system
- d. AbleCommerce

Guidance: level 1

:: Remote administration software ::

_____ is a protocol used on the Internet or local area network to provide a bidirectional interactive text-oriented communication facility using a virtual terminal connection. User data is interspersed in-band with _____ control information in an 8-bit byte oriented data connection over the Transmission Control Protocol .

Exam Probability: **High**

34. *Answer choices:*
(see index for correct answer)

- a. Telnet
- b. Web-based SSH

- c. Proxy Networks, Inc.
- d. Systancia

Guidance: level 1

:: Critical thinking ::

In psychology, _____ is regarded as the cognitive process resulting in the selection of a belief or a course of action among several alternative possibilities. Every _____ process produces a final choice, which may or may not prompt action.

Exam Probability: **Low**

35. *Answer choices:*
(see index for correct answer)

- a. Attacking Faulty Reasoning
- b. Explanatory power
- c. Decidophobia
- d. Source credibility

Guidance: level 1

:: ::

A _____ is a knowledge base website on which users collaboratively modify content and structure directly from the web browser. In a typical _____ , text is written using a simplified markup language and often edited with the help of a rich-text editor.

Exam Probability: **Medium**

36. *Answer choices:*
(see index for correct answer)

- a. Wiki
- b. Character
- c. open system
- d. information systems assessment

Guidance: level 1

:: Data management ::

_____ is a set of processes and technologies that supports the collection, managing, and publishing of information in any form or medium. When stored and accessed via computers, this information may be more specifically referred to as digital content, or simply as content.

Exam Probability: **Medium**

37. *Answer choices:*
(see index for correct answer)

- a. Network transparency
- b. Database server
- c. Content management
- d. Holos

Guidance: level 1

:: Consumer behaviour ::

_____ is the ratio of users who click on a specific link to the number of total users who view a page, email, or advertisement. It is commonly used to measure the success of an online advertising campaign for a particular website as well as the effectiveness of email campaigns.

Exam Probability: **High**

38. *Answer choices:*
(see index for correct answer)

- a. Shopping
- b. Customer analytics
- c. Diderot effect
- d. Cash mob

Guidance: level 1

:: Reputation management ::

_____ refers to the influencing and controlling of an individual's or group's reputation. Originally a public relations term, the growth of the internet and social media, along with _____ companies, have made search results a core part of an individual's or group's reputation. Online _____ , sometimes abbreviated as ORM, focuses on the management of product and service search website results. Ethical grey areas include mug shot removal sites, astroturfing customer review sites, censoring negative complaints, and using search engine optimization tactics to influence results.

Exam Probability: **Medium**

39. *Answer choices:*
(see index for correct answer)

- a. Distrust
- b. Lithium Technologies
- c. Reputation management
- d. EigenTrust

Guidance: level 1

:: Product testing ::

_____ is a characteristic of a product or system, whose interfaces are completely understood, to work with other products or systems, at present or in the future, in either implementation or access, without any restrictions.

Exam Probability: **High**

40. *Answer choices:*
(see index for correct answer)

- a. Sensory analysis
- b. Wine tasting
- c. Whisky tasting
- d. Beer tasting

Guidance: level 1

:: World Wide Web Consortium standards ::

_____ is a markup language that defines a set of rules for encoding documents in a format that is both human-readable and machine-readable. The W3C's XML 1.0 Specification and several other related specifications—all of them free open standards—define XML.

Exam Probability: **Low**

41. *Answer choices:*
(see index for correct answer)

- a. Hyper Text Markup Language
- b. Extensible Markup Language

Guidance: level 1

:: Telecommunication theory ::

In reliability theory and reliability engineering, the term _____ has the following meanings.

Exam Probability: **Medium**

42. *Answer choices:*
(see index for correct answer)

- a. Attenuation-to-crosstalk ratio
- b. Availability
- c. Frequency mixer
- d. Field strength in free space

Guidance: level 1

:: Data management ::

In business, _____ is a method used to define and manage the critical data of an organization to provide, with data integration, a single point of reference. The data that is mastered may include reference data- the set of permissible values, and the analytical data that supports decision making.

Exam Probability: **Medium**

43. *Answer choices:*
(see index for correct answer)

- a. Virtual directory
- b. Change data capture
- c. Database-centric architecture
- d. Operational database

:: ::

A _____ is a control panel usually located directly ahead of a vehicle's driver, displaying instrumentation and controls for the vehicle's operation.

Exam Probability: **Medium**

44. *Answer choices:*
(see index for correct answer)

- a. levels of analysis
- b. surface-level diversity
- c. interpersonal communication
- d. Dashboard

:: Data ::

_____ is a branch of mathematics working with data collection, organization, analysis, interpretation and presentation. In applying _____ to, for example, a scientific, industrial, or social problem, it is conventional to begin with a statistical population or a statistical model process to be studied. Populations can be diverse topics such as "all people living in a country" or "every atom composing a crystal". _____ deals with every aspect of data, including the planning of data collection in terms of the design of surveys and experiments.See glossary of probability and _____ .

Exam Probability: **High**

45. *Answer choices:*
(see index for correct answer)

- a. Data Transmission
- b. Raw data
- c. Statistics

- d. Data acquisition

Guidance: level 1

:: Sound recording ::

_____ is a medium for magnetic recording, made of a thin, magnetizable coating on a long, narrow strip of plastic film. It was developed in Germany in 1928, based on magnetic wire recording. Devices that record and play back audio and video using _____ are tape recorders and video tape recorders respectively. A device that stores computer data on _____ is known as a tape drive.

Exam Probability: **High**

46. *Answer choices:*
(see index for correct answer)

- a. Tape recorder
- b. Magnetic tape
- c. Electrical network frequency analysis
- d. Sound recording and reproduction

Guidance: level 1

:: Enterprise architecture ::

Enterprise software, also known as _____ software , is computer software used to satisfy the needs of an organization rather than individual users. Such organizations include businesses, schools, interest-based user groups, clubs, charities, and governments. Enterprise software is an integral part of a information system.

Exam Probability: **High**

47. *Answer choices:*
(see index for correct answer)

- a. Enterprise life cycle
- b. ARID
- c. View model
- d. Enterprise application

Guidance: level 1

In computer main memory, auxiliary storage and computer buses, _____ is the existence of data that is additional to the actual data and permits correction of errors in stored or transmitted data. The additional data can simply be a complete copy of the actual data, or only select pieces of data that allow detection of errors and reconstruction of lost or damaged data up to a certain level.

Exam Probability: **High**

48. *Answer choices:*
(see index for correct answer)

- a. One Source Networks
- b. Metro Chicago Information Center
- c. Dummy data
- d. Data redundancy

Guidance: level 1

:: Information technology management ::

_____ is a good-practice framework created by international professional association ISACA for information technology management and IT governance. _____ provides an implementable "set of controls over information technology and organizes them around a logical framework of IT-related processes and enablers."

Exam Probability: **High**

49. *Answer choices:*
(see index for correct answer)

- a. Problem management
- b. Ubiquitous commerce
- c. Runbook
- d. Definitive Media Library

Guidance: level 1

:: ::

A _____ is an organized collection of data, generally stored and accessed electronically from a computer system. Where _____ s are more complex they are often developed using formal design and modeling techniques.

Exam Probability: **High**

50. *Answer choices:*

- a. levels of analysis
- b. deep-level diversity
- c. Database
- d. surface-level diversity

Guidance: level 1

:: ::

In linguistics, a _____ is the smallest element that can be uttered in isolation with objective or practical meaning.

Exam Probability: **High**

51. *Answer choices:*

- a. interpersonal communication
- b. Sarbanes-Oxley act of 2002
- c. personal values
- d. Word

Guidance: level 1

:: ::

A database is an organized collection of data, generally stored and accessed electronically from a computer system. Where databases are more complex they are often developed using formal design and modeling techniques.

Exam Probability: **Medium**

52. *Answer choices:*

- a. hierarchical perspective
- b. Database management system
- c. levels of analysis
- d. personal values

Guidance: level 1

:: Data transmission ::

In telecommunication a _____ is the means of connecting one location to another for the purpose of transmitting and receiving digital information. It can also refer to a set of electronics assemblies, consisting of a transmitter and a receiver and the interconnecting data telecommunication circuit. These are governed by a link protocol enabling digital data to be transferred from a data source to a data sink.

Exam Probability: **Medium**

53. *Answer choices:*
(see index for correct answer)

- a. Data link
- b. Bell 212A
- c. Transport Sample Protocol
- d. Transmission block

Guidance: level 1

:: ::

_____ , Inc. is an American online social media and social networking service company based in Menlo Park, California. It was founded by Mark Zuckerberg, along with fellow Harvard College students and roommates Eduardo Saverin, Andrew McCollum, Dustin Moskovitz and Chris Hughes. It is considered one of the Big Four technology companies along with Amazon, Apple, and Google.

Exam Probability: **Low**

54. *Answer choices:*
(see index for correct answer)

- a. corporate values
- b. personal values
- c. co-culture
- d. Facebook

:: Management ::

A _____ defines or constrains some aspect of business and always resolves to either true or false. _____ s are intended to assert business structure or to control or influence the behavior of the business. _____ s describe the operations, definitions and constraints that apply to an organization. _____ s can apply to people, processes, corporate behavior and computing systems in an organization, and are put in place to help the organization achieve its goals.

Exam Probability: **Medium**

55. *Answer choices:*
(see index for correct answer)

- a. Law practice management
- b. Goal
- c. Sales outsourcing
- d. Business rule

:: Monopoly (economics) ::

A _____ exists when a specific person or enterprise is the only supplier of a particular commodity. This contrasts with a monopsony which relates to a single entity`s control of a market to purchase a good or service, and with oligopoly which consists of a few sellers dominating a market. Monopolies are thus characterized by a lack of economic competition to produce the good or service, a lack of viable substitute goods, and the possibility of a high _____ price well above the seller`s marginal cost that leads to a high _____ profit. The verb monopolise or monopolize refers to the process by which a company gains the ability to raise prices or exclude competitors. In economics, a _____ is a single seller. In law, a _____ is a business entity that has significant market power, that is, the power to charge overly high prices. Although monopolies may be big businesses, size is not a characteristic of a _____ . A small business may still have the power to raise prices in a small industry .

56. *Answer choices:*

(see index for correct answer)

- a. Intellectual property
- b. Practice of law
- c. Special 301 Report
- d. Monopoly

Guidance: level 1

:: Computer security standards ::

The _____ for Information Technology Security Evaluation is an international standard for computer security certification. It is currently in version 3.1 revision 5.

Exam Probability: **High**

57. *Answer choices:*

(see index for correct answer)

- a. CVSS
- b. FIPS 199
- c. CTCPEC
- d. Common Criteria

Guidance: level 1

:: Information systems ::

_____ is the process of creating, sharing, using and managing the knowledge and information of an organisation. It refers to a multidisciplinary approach to achieving organisational objectives by making the best use of knowledge.

Exam Probability: **Medium**

58. *Answer choices:*

(see index for correct answer)

- a. Knowledge management
- b. Internavi
- c. Semantic desktop
- d. Digital marketing system

:: E-commerce ::

_____ is the activity of buying or selling of products on online services or over the Internet. Electronic commerce draws on technologies such as mobile commerce, electronic funds transfer, supply chain management, Internet marketing, online transaction processing, electronic data interchange , inventory management systems, and automated data collection systems.

Exam Probability: **Medium**

59. *Answer choices:*

(see index for correct answer)

- a. E-commerce
- b. CA/Browser Forum
- c. Electronic Money Association
- d. Discovery shopping

Marketing

Marketing is the study and management of exchange relationships. Marketing is the business process of creating relationships with and satisfying customers. With its focus on the customer, marketing is one of the premier components of business management.

Marketing is defined by the American Marketing Association as "the activity, set of institutions, and processes for creating, communicating, delivering, and exchanging offerings that have value for customers, clients, partners, and society at large."

:: ::

In financial markets, a share is a unit used as mutual funds, limited partnerships, and real estate investment trusts. The owner of _____ in the corporation/company is a shareholder of the corporation. A share is an indivisible unit of capital, expressing the ownership relationship between the company and the shareholder. The denominated value of a share is its face value, and the total of the face value of issued _____ represent the capital of a company, which may not reflect the market value of those _____ .

Exam Probability: **Low**

1. *Answer choices:*

(see index for correct answer)

- a. hierarchical
- b. co-culture
- c. Shares
- d. imperative

Guidance: level 1

:: Debt ::

_____ , in finance and economics, is payment from a borrower or deposit-taking financial institution to a lender or depositor of an amount above repayment of the principal sum , at a particular rate. It is distinct from a fee which the borrower may pay the lender or some third party. It is also distinct from dividend which is paid by a company to its shareholders from its profit or reserve, but not at a particular rate decided beforehand, rather on a pro rata basis as a share in the reward gained by risk taking entrepreneurs when the revenue earned exceeds the total costs.

Exam Probability: **High**

2. *Answer choices:*
(see index for correct answer)

- a. Extendible bond
- b. Consumer debt
- c. Interest
- d. Legal liability

Guidance: level 1

:: Data ::

Data has two ways of being created or generated. The first is what is called `captured data`, and is found through purposeful investigation or analysis. The second is called `exhaust data`, and is gathered usually by machines or terminals as a secondary function. For example, cash registers, smartphones, and speedometers serve a main function but may collect data as a secondary task. Exhaustive data is usually too large or of little use to process and becomes `transient` or thrown away.

Exam Probability: **Medium**

3. *Answer choices:*
(see index for correct answer)

- a. Data redundancy
- b. Primary data
- c. Humanities Indicators
- d. Metro Chicago Information Center

Guidance: level 1

:: Marketing ::

_____ , in marketing, manufacturing, call centres and management, is the use of flexible computer-aided manufacturing systems to produce custom output. Such systems combine the low unit costs of mass production processes with the flexibility of individual customization.

Exam Probability: **High**

4. *Answer choices:*

(see index for correct answer)

- a. HyTrust
- b. Mass customization
- c. Golden sample
- d. Market overhang

Guidance: level 1

:: Marketing techniques ::

_____ is the activity of dividing a broad consumer or business market, normally consisting of existing and potential customers, into sub-groups of consumers based on some type of shared characteristics. In dividing or segmenting markets, researchers typically look for common characteristics such as shared needs, common interests, similar lifestyles or even similar demographic profiles. The overall aim of segmentation is to identify high yield segments – that is, those segments that are likely to be the most profitable or that have growth potential – so that these can be selected for special attention .

Exam Probability: **Medium**

5. *Answer choices:*

(see index for correct answer)

- a. Market segmentation
- b. Marketing co-operation
- c. Blackout dates
- d. Virtual engagement

Guidance: level 1

_____ ship is the process of designing, launching and running a new business, which is often initially a small business. The people who create these businesses are called _____ s.

Exam Probability: **Low**

6. *Answer choices:*
(see index for correct answer)

- a. Geospatial information officer
- b. Business manager
- c. Store manager
- d. Entrepreneur

Guidance: level 1

:: Business terms ::

_____ occurs when a sales representative meets with a potential client for the purpose of transacting a sale. Many sales representatives rely on a sequential sales process that typically includes nine steps. Some sales representatives develop scripts for all or part of the sales process. The sales process can be used in face-to-face encounters and in telemarketing.

Exam Probability: **High**

7. *Answer choices:*
(see index for correct answer)

- a. customer base
- b. Personal selling
- c. back office
- d. granular

Guidance: level 1

:: Commerce ::

A _____ is a company or individual that purchases goods or services with the intention of selling them rather than consuming or using them. This is usually done for profit . One example can be found in the industry of telecommunications, where companies buy excess amounts of transmission capacity or call time from other carriers and resell it to smaller carriers.

Exam Probability: **High**

8. *Answer choices:*
(see index for correct answer)

- a. Reseller
- b. Issuing bank
- c. Return merchandise authorization
- d. Too cheap to meter

Guidance: level 1

:: Data interchange standards ::

_____ is the concept of businesses electronically communicating information that was traditionally communicated on paper, such as purchase orders and invoices. Technical standards for EDI exist to facilitate parties transacting such instruments without having to make special arrangements.

Exam Probability: **Low**

9. *Answer choices:*
(see index for correct answer)

- a. Data Interchange Standards Association
- b. Electronic data interchange
- c. Interaction protocol
- d. Common Alerting Protocol

Guidance: level 1

:: Types of marketing ::

_____ is "marketing on a worldwide scale reconciling or taking commercial advantage of global operational differences, similarities and opportunities in order to meet global objectives".

10. *Answer choices:*

- a. Social pull marketing
- b. Share of voice
- c. Consumer Generated Advertising
- d. Global marketing

Guidance: level 1

:: ::

In marketing jargon, product lining is offering several related products for sale individually. Unlike product bundling, where several products are combined into one group, which is then offered for sale as a units, product lining involves offering the products for sale separately. A line can comprise related products of various sizes, types, colors, qualities, or prices. Line depth refers to the number of subcategories a category has. Line consistency refers to how closely related the products that make up the line are. Line vulnerability refers to the percentage of sales or profits that are derived from only a few products in the line.

11. *Answer choices:*

- a. open system
- b. Product line
- c. levels of analysis
- d. Sarbanes-Oxley act of 2002

Guidance: level 1

:: Consumer theory ::

_____ is the quantity of a good that consumers are willing and able to purchase at various prices during a given period of time.

12. *Answer choices:*

- a. Income effect
- b. Engel curve
- c. Demand
- d. Marginal rate of substitution

Guidance: level 1

:: ::

According to the philosopher Piyush Mathur , "Tangibility is the property that a phenomenon exhibits if it has and/or transports mass and/or energy and/or momentum".

Exam Probability: **High**

13. *Answer choices:*
(see index for correct answer)

- a. surface-level diversity
- b. process perspective
- c. cultural
- d. Tangible

Guidance: level 1

:: Business law ::

A _____ is an arrangement where parties, known as partners, agree to cooperate to advance their mutual interests. The partners in a _____ may be individuals, businesses, interest-based organizations, schools, governments or combinations. Organizations may partner to increase the likelihood of each achieving their mission and to amplify their reach. A _____ may result in issuing and holding equity or may be only governed by a contract.

Exam Probability: **High**

14. *Answer choices:*
(see index for correct answer)

- a. Contract failure
- b. Unfair business practices
- c. Jurisdictional strike
- d. Administration

Guidance: level 1

A _____ is a research instrument consisting of a series of questions for the purpose of gathering information from respondents. The _____ was invented by the Statistical Society of London in 1838.

Exam Probability: **Medium**

15. *Answer choices:*
(see index for correct answer)

- a. open system
- b. empathy
- c. co-culture
- d. Questionnaire

Guidance: level 1

In communications and information processing, _____ is a system of rules to convert information—such as a letter, word, sound, image, or gesture—into another form or representation, sometimes shortened or secret, for communication through a communication channel or storage in a storage medium. An early example is the invention of language, which enabled a person, through speech, to communicate what they saw, heard, felt, or thought to others. But speech limits the range of communication to the distance a voice can carry, and limits the audience to those present when the speech is uttered. The invention of writing, which converted spoken language into visual symbols, extended the range of communication across space and time.

Exam Probability: **Medium**

16. *Answer choices:*
(see index for correct answer)

- a. Code
- b. co-culture
- c. imperative
- d. surface-level diversity

Guidance: level 1

_____ is change in the heritable characteristics of biological populations over successive generations. These characteristics are the expressions of genes that are passed on from parent to offspring during reproduction. Different characteristics tend to exist within any given population as a result of mutation, genetic recombination and other sources of genetic variation. _____ occurs when _____ ary processes such as natural selection and genetic drift act on this variation, resulting in certain characteristics becoming more common or rare within a population. It is this process of _____ that has given rise to biodiversity at every level of biological organisation, including the levels of species, individual organisms and molecules.

Exam Probability: **High**

17. *Answer choices:*
(see index for correct answer)

- a. open system
- b. hierarchical
- c. Evolution
- d. personal values

Guidance: level 1

:: Workplace ::

_____ is asystematic determination of a subject's merit, worth and significance, using criteria governed by a set of standards. It can assist an organization, program, design, project or any other intervention or initiative to assess any aim, realisable concept/proposal, or any alternative, to help in decision-making; or to ascertain the degree of achievement or value in regard to the aim and objectives and results of any such action that has been completed. The primary purpose of _____ , in addition to gaining insight into prior or existing initiatives, is to enable reflection and assist in the identification of future change.

Exam Probability: **Medium**

18. *Answer choices:*
(see index for correct answer)

- a. Workplace aggression
- b. Work motivation

- c. Workplace violence
- d. Feminisation of the workplace

Guidance: level 1

:: Marketing techniques ::

The _____ or unique selling point is a marketing concept first proposed as a theory to explain a pattern in successful advertising campaigns of the early 1940s. The USP states that such campaigns made unique propositions to customers that convinced them to switch brands. The term was developed by television advertising pioneer Rosser Reeves of Ted Bates & Company. Theodore Levitt, a professor at Harvard Business School, suggested that, "Differentiation is one of the most important strategic and tactical activities in which companies must constantly engage." The term has been used to describe one's "personal brand" in the marketplace. Today, the term is used in other fields or just casually to refer to any aspect of an object that differentiates it from similar objects.

Exam Probability: **High**

19. *Answer choices:*
(see index for correct answer)

- a. AIDA
- b. Unique selling proposition
- c. Premium
- d. Microsegment

Guidance: level 1

:: Advertising by type ::

_____ or advertising war is an advertisement in which a particular product, or service, specifically mentions a competitor by name for the express purpose of showing why the competitor is inferior to the product naming it. Also referred to as "knocking copy", it is loosely defined as advertising where "the advertised brand is explicitly compared with one or more competing brands and the comparison is obvious to the audience."

Exam Probability: **Medium**

20. *Answer choices:*

- a. Aerial advertising
- b. Comparative advertising
- c. Parody advertisement
- d. In-flight advertising

Guidance: level 1

:: Manufacturing ::

A _____ is a building for storing goods. _____ s are used by manufacturers, importers, exporters, wholesalers, transport businesses, customs, etc. They are usually large plain buildings in industrial parks on the outskirts of cities, towns or villages.

Exam Probability: **Medium**

21. *Answer choices:*

- a. Operations Execution System
- b. Initial Reject
- c. Warehouse
- d. Automated guided vehicle

Guidance: level 1

:: Marketing ::

_____ is a pricing strategy where the price of a product is initially set low to rapidly reach a wide fraction of the market and initiate word of mouth. The strategy works on the expectation that customers will switch to the new brand because of the lower price. _____ is most commonly associated with marketing objectives of enlarging market share and exploiting economies of scale or experience.

Exam Probability: **High**

22. *Answer choices:*

- a. Product bundling
- b. Penetration pricing
- c. customer-perceived value

- d. Adobe Experience Manager

Guidance: level 1

:: ::

_____ is the provision of service to customers before, during and after a purchase. The perception of success of such interactions is dependent on employees "who can adjust themselves to the personality of the guest". _____ concerns the priority an organization assigns to _____ relative to components such as product innovation and pricing. In this sense, an organization that values good _____ may spend more money in training employees than the average organization or may proactively interview customers for feedback.

Exam Probability: **High**

23. *Answer choices:*
(see index for correct answer)

- a. similarity-attraction theory
- b. empathy
- c. information systems assessment
- d. Customer service

Guidance: level 1

:: Marketing ::

A _____ is a group of customers within a business's serviceable available market at which a business aims its marketing efforts and resources. A _____ is a subset of the total market for a product or service. The _____ typically consists of consumers who exhibit similar characteristics and are considered most likely to buy a business's market offerings or are likely to be the most profitable segments for the business to service.

Exam Probability: **High**

24. *Answer choices:*
(see index for correct answer)

- a. Product planning
- b. Promotional mix
- c. All-commodity volume

- d. Mass marketing

Guidance: level 1

:: Business terms ::

A _____ is a short statement of why an organization exists, what its overall goal is, identifying the goal of its operations: what kind of product or service it provides, its primary customers or market, and its geographical region of operation. It may include a short statement of such fundamental matters as the organization's values or philosophies, a business's main competitive advantages, or a desired future state—the "vision".

Exam Probability: **Medium**

25. *Answer choices:*
(see index for correct answer)

- a. Personal selling
- b. centralization
- c. front office
- d. year-to-date

Guidance: level 1

:: Project management ::

A _____ is a source or supply from which a benefit is produced and it has some utility. _____ s can broadly be classified upon their availability—they are classified into renewable and non-renewable _____ s.Examples of non renewable _____ s are coal ,crude oil natural gas nuclear energy etc. Examples of renewable _____ s are air,water,wind,solar energy etc. They can also be classified as actual and potential on the basis of level of development and use, on the basis of origin they can be classified as biotic and abiotic, and on the basis of their distribution, as ubiquitous and localized . An item becomes a _____ with time and developing technology. Typically, _____ s are materials, energy, services, staff, knowledge, or other assets that are transformed to produce benefit and in the process may be consumed or made unavailable. Benefits of _____ utilization may include increased wealth, proper functioning of a system, or enhanced well-being. From a human perspective a natural _____ is anything obtained from the environment to satisfy human needs and wants. From a broader biological or ecological perspective a _____ satisfies the needs of a living organism .

Exam Probability: **High**

26. *Answer choices:*
(see index for correct answer)

- a. Test and evaluation master plan
- b. Project planning
- c. Cash flow diagram
- d. Resource

Guidance: level 1

:: Television commercials ::

_____ is a phenomenon whereby something new and somehow valuable is formed. The created item may be intangible or a physical object .

Exam Probability: **Low**

27. *Answer choices:*
(see index for correct answer)

- a. Old Lions
- b. Universal Business Adapter
- c. Creativity
- d. CM Yoko

:: Advertising ::

_____ is the behavioral and cognitive process of selectively concentrating on a discrete aspect of information, whether deemed subjective or objective, while ignoring other perceivable information. It is a state of arousal. It is the taking possession by the mind in clear and vivid form of one out of what seem several simultaneous objects or trains of thought. Focalization, the concentration of consciousness, is of its essence. _____ has also been described as the allocation of limited cognitive processing resources.

Exam Probability: **Medium**

28. *Answer choices:*
(see index for correct answer)

- a. Sponsorship broker
- b. Attention
- c. Bibliography of advertising
- d. Cost per acquisition

:: Marketing ::

_____ is a marketing practice of individuals or organizations . It allows them to sell products or services to other companies or organizations that resell them, use them in their products or services or use them to support their works.

Exam Probability: **Medium**

29. *Answer choices:*
(see index for correct answer)

- a. Mystery shopping
- b. Channel conflict
- c. The customer is always right
- d. Business marketing

In behavioral psychology, _____ is a consequence applied that will strengthen an organism's future behavior whenever that behavior is preceded by a specific antecedent stimulus. This strengthening effect may be measured as a higher frequency of behavior , longer duration , greater magnitude , or shorter latency . There are two types of _____ , known as positive _____ and negative _____ ; positive is where by a reward is offered on expression of the wanted behaviour and negative is taking away an undesirable element in the persons environment whenever the desired behaviour is achieved.

Exam Probability: **Medium**

30. *Answer choices:*
(see index for correct answer)

- a. Matching Law
- b. Reinforcement
- c. chaining
- d. Systematic desensitization

Guidance: level 1

_____ is a term frequently used in marketing. It is a measure of how products and services supplied by a company meet or surpass customer expectation. _____ is defined as "the number of customers, or percentage of total customers, whose reported experience with a firm, its products, or its services exceeds specified satisfaction goals."

Exam Probability: **Medium**

31. *Answer choices:*
(see index for correct answer)

- a. open system
- b. deep-level diversity
- c. surface-level diversity
- d. Customer satisfaction

Guidance: level 1

_____ is unwanted sound judged to be unpleasant, loud or disruptive to hearing. From a physics standpoint, _____ is indistinguishable from sound, as both are vibrations through a medium, such as air or water. The difference arises when the brain receives and perceives a sound.

32. *Answer choices:*

- a. Noise
- b. Martingale pricing
- c. Asymmetric price transmission
- d. Travel class

Guidance: level 1

:: ::

_____ or accountancy is the measurement, processing, and communication of financial information about economic entities such as businesses and corporations. The modern field was established by the Italian mathematician Luca Pacioli in 1494. _____ , which has been called the "language of business", measures the results of an organization's economic activities and conveys this information to a variety of users, including investors, creditors, management, and regulators. Practitioners of _____ are known as accountants. The terms " _____ " and "financial reporting" are often used as synonyms.

33. *Answer choices:*

- a. hierarchical perspective
- b. Accounting
- c. co-culture
- d. corporate values

Guidance: level 1

:: ::

A _____ or sample _____ is a single measure of some attribute of a sample . It is calculated by applying a function to the values of the items of the sample, which are known together as a set of data.

34. *Answer choices:*
(see index for correct answer)

- a. similarity-attraction theory
- b. co-culture
- c. process perspective
- d. Statistic

Guidance: level 1

:: Debt ::

_____ is the trust which allows one party to provide money or resources to another party wherein the second party does not reimburse the first party immediately , but promises either to repay or return those resources at a later date. In other words, _____ is a method of making reciprocity formal, legally enforceable, and extensible to a large group of unrelated people.

35. *Answer choices:*
(see index for correct answer)

- a. Compulsive buying disorder
- b. Credit
- c. Asset protection
- d. Zombie company

Guidance: level 1

:: Commercial item transport and distribution ::

In commerce, supply-chain management , the management of the flow of goods and services, involves the movement and storage of raw materials, of work-in-process inventory, and of finished goods from point of origin to point of consumption. Interconnected or interlinked networks, channels and node businesses combine in the provision of products and services required by end customers in a supply chain. Supply-chain management has been defined as the "design, planning, execution, control, and monitoring of supply-chain activities with the objective of creating net value, building a competitive infrastructure, leveraging worldwide logistics, synchronizing supply with demand and measuring performance globally."SCM practice draws heavily from the areas of industrial engineering, systems engineering, operations management, logistics, procurement, information technology, and marketing and strives for an integrated approach. Marketing channels play an important role in supply-chain management. Current research in supply-chain management is concerned with topics related to sustainability and risk management, among others. Some suggest that the "people dimension" of SCM, ethical issues, internal integration, transparency/visibility, and human capital/talent management are topics that have, so far, been underrepresented on the research agenda.

Exam Probability: **Medium**

36. *Answer choices:*
(see index for correct answer)

- a. Truck
- b. Supply chain management
- c. Humanitarian Logistics
- d. Wine shipping laws in the United States

Guidance: level 1

:: Business ethics ::

_____ is a microeconomic pricing strategy where identical or largely similar goods or services are transacted at different prices by the same provider in different markets. _____ is distinguished from product differentiation by the more substantial difference in production cost for the differently priced products involved in the latter strategy. Price differentiation essentially relies on the variation in the customers' willingness to pay and in the elasticity of their demand.

Exam Probability: **High**

37. *Answer choices:*
(see index for correct answer)

- a. Walmarting
- b. Center for Adult Development
- c. Bribery Act 2010
- d. Price discrimination

Guidance: level 1

:: Consumer theory ::

A _____ is a technical term in psychology, economics and philosophy usually used in relation to choosing between alternatives. For example, someone prefers A over B if they would rather choose A than B.

Exam Probability: **High**

38. *Answer choices:*
(see index for correct answer)

- a. Price elasticity of demand
- b. Business contract hire
- c. Preference
- d. Consumer choice

Guidance: level 1

:: ::

The _____ is an agreement signed by Canada, Mexico, and the United States, creating a trilateral trade bloc in North America. The agreement came into force on January 1, 1994, and superseded the 1988 Canada–United States Free Trade Agreement between the United States and Canada. The NAFTA trade bloc is one of the largest trade blocs in the world by gross domestic product.

Exam Probability: **Medium**

39. *Answer choices:*
(see index for correct answer)

- a. personal values
- b. Sarbanes-Oxley act of 2002
- c. North American Free Trade Agreement
- d. process perspective

Guidance: level 1

:: Project management ::

Contemporary business and science treat as a _____ any undertaking, carried out individually or collaboratively and possibly involving research or design, that is carefully planned to achieve a particular aim.

Exam Probability: **Low**

40. *Answer choices:*
(see index for correct answer)

- a. Sunk costs
- b. Project Management South Africa
- c. P3M3
- d. Theory X and Theory Y

Guidance: level 1

:: ::

_____ is the process whereby a business sets the price at which it will sell its products and services, and may be part of the business's marketing plan. In setting prices, the business will take into account the price at which it could acquire the goods, the manufacturing cost, the market place, competition, market condition, brand, and quality of product.

Exam Probability: **High**

41. *Answer choices:*
(see index for correct answer)

- a. hierarchical perspective
- b. levels of analysis
- c. cultural
- d. empathy

Guidance: level 1

:: Survey methodology ::

A _____ is the procedure of systematically acquiring and recording information about the members of a given population. The term is used mostly in connection with national population and housing _____ es; other common _____ es include agriculture, business, and traffic _____ es. The United Nations defines the essential features of population and housing _____ es as "individual enumeration, universality within a defined territory, simultaneity and defined periodicity", and recommends that population _____ es be taken at least every 10 years. United Nations recommendations also cover _____ topics to be collected, official definitions, classifications and other useful information to co-ordinate international practice.

Exam Probability: **Medium**

42. *Answer choices:*
(see index for correct answer)

- a. Group concept mapping
- b. Census
- c. Political forecasting
- d. Sampling

Guidance: level 1

In sales, commerce and economics, a _____ is the recipient of a good, service, product or an idea - obtained from a seller, vendor, or supplier via a financial transaction or exchange for money or some other valuable consideration.

Exam Probability: **Low**

43. *Answer choices:*
(see index for correct answer)

- a. Customer
- b. co-culture
- c. deep-level diversity
- d. empathy

Guidance: level 1

:: Data analysis ::

_____ is a process of inspecting, cleansing, transforming, and modeling data with the goal of discovering useful information, informing conclusions, and supporting decision-making. _____ has multiple facets and approaches, encompassing diverse techniques under a variety of names, and is used in different business, science, and social science domains. In today's business world, _____ plays a role in making decisions more scientific and helping businesses operate more effectively.

Exam Probability: **Low**

44. *Answer choices:*
(see index for correct answer)

- a. Univariate analysis
- b. Data analysis
- c. Training set
- d. Reification

Guidance: level 1

:: Management accounting ::

_____ s are costs that change as the quantity of the good or service that a business produces changes. _____ s are the sum of marginal costs over all units produced. They can also be considered normal costs. Fixed costs and _____ s make up the two components of total cost. Direct costs are costs that can easily be associated with a particular cost object. However, not all _____ s are direct costs. For example, variable manufacturing overhead costs are _____ s that are indirect costs, not direct costs. _____ s are sometimes called unit-level costs as they vary with the number of units produced.

Exam Probability: **Low**

45. *Answer choices:*
(see index for correct answer)

- a. Variable Costing
- b. Total benefits of ownership
- c. Bridge life-cycle cost analysis
- d. Inventory valuation

Guidance: level 1

:: ::

_____ is the study and management of exchange relationships. _____ is the business process of creating relationships with and satisfying customers. With its focus on the customer, _____ is one of the premier components of business management.

Exam Probability: **High**

46. *Answer choices:*
(see index for correct answer)

- a. Sarbanes-Oxley act of 2002
- b. cultural
- c. co-culture
- d. Character

Guidance: level 1

:: ::

_____ Motor Company is an American multinational automaker that has its main headquarter in Dearborn, Michigan, a suburb of Detroit. It was founded by Henry _____ and incorporated on June 16, 1903. The company sells automobiles and commercial vehicles under the _____ brand and most luxury cars under the Lincoln brand. _____ also owns Brazilian SUV manufacturer Troller, an 8% stake in Aston Martin of the United Kingdom and a 32% stake in Jiangling Motors. It also has joint-ventures in China , Taiwan , Thailand , Turkey , and Russia . The company is listed on the New York Stock Exchange and is controlled by the _____ family; they have minority ownership but the majority of the voting power.

Exam Probability: **Medium**

47. *Answer choices:*
(see index for correct answer)

- a. Ford
- b. Sarbanes-Oxley act of 2002
- c. cultural
- d. interpersonal communication

Guidance: level 1

:: Marketing ::

A _____ is the people, organizations, and activities necessary to transfer the ownership of goods from the point of production to the point of consumption. It is the way products get to the end-user, the consumer; and is also known as a distribution channel. A _____ is a useful tool for management, and is crucial to creating an effective and well-planned marketing strategy.

Exam Probability: **Low**

48. *Answer choices:*
(see index for correct answer)

- a. Marketing channel
- b. Discoverability
- c. Multicultural marketing
- d. Inbound marketing

Guidance: level 1

_____ is the process of gathering and measuring information on targeted variables in an established system, which then enables one to answer relevant questions and evaluate outcomes. _____ is a component of research in all fields of study including physical and social sciences, humanities, and business. While methods vary by discipline, the emphasis on ensuring accurate and honest collection remains the same. The goal for all _____ is to capture quality evidence that allows analysis to lead to the formulation of convincing and credible answers to the questions that have been posed.

Exam Probability: **High**

49. *Answer choices:*
(see index for correct answer)

- a. Sarbanes-Oxley act of 2002
- b. Data collection
- c. information systems assessment
- d. corporate values

Guidance: level 1

:: Legal terms ::

A _____ is a person who is called upon to issue a response to a communication made by another. The term is used in legal contexts, in survey methodology, and in psychological conditioning.

Exam Probability: **High**

50. *Answer choices:*
(see index for correct answer)

- a. Malice
- b. Issue
- c. Respondent
- d. Form of action

Guidance: level 1

:: Product management ::

A _____ is a professional role which is responsible for the development of products for an organization, known as the practice of product management. _____ s own the business strategy behind a product , specify its functional requirements and generally manage the launch of features. They coordinate work done by many other functions and are ultimately responsible for the business success of the product.

Exam Probability: **Low**

51. *Answer choices:*
(see index for correct answer)

- a. Product manager
- b. Swing tag
- c. Technology acceptance model
- d. Brand extension

Guidance: level 1

:: Marketing terminology ::

_____ is used in marketing to describe the inability to assess the value gained from engaging in an activity using any tangible evidence. It is often used to describe services where there is no tangible product that the customer can purchase, that can be seen or touched.

Exam Probability: **Low**

52. *Answer choices:*
(see index for correct answer)

- a. Corporate jargon
- b. Relational goods
- c. Low-end market
- d. Lifetime customer value

Guidance: level 1

:: Evaluation methods ::

In natural and social sciences, and sometimes in other fields, _____ is the systematic empirical investigation of observable phenomena via statistical, mathematical, or computational techniques. The objective of _____ is to develop and employ mathematical models, theories, and hypotheses pertaining to phenomena. The process of measurement is central to _____ because it provides the fundamental connection between empirical observation and mathematical expression of quantitative relationships.

Exam Probability: **Low**

53. *Answer choices:*
(see index for correct answer)

- a. Quantitative research
- b. Rubric
- c. Poll average
- d. Position weight matrix

Guidance: level 1

:: Commerce ::

_____ relates to "the exchange of goods and services, especially on a large scale". It includes legal, economic, political, social, cultural and technological systems that operate in a country or in international trade.

Exam Probability: **Medium**

54. *Answer choices:*
(see index for correct answer)

- a. V-commerce
- b. Acquiring bank
- c. Oxygen bar
- d. Commerce

Guidance: level 1

:: Cognitive dissonance ::

In the field of psychology, _____ is the mental discomfort experienced by a person who holds two or more contradictory beliefs, ideas, or values. This discomfort is triggered by a situation in which a person's belief clashes with new evidence perceived by the person. When confronted with facts that contradict beliefs, ideals, and values, people will try to find a way to resolve the contradiction to reduce their discomfort.

Exam Probability: **High**

55. *Answer choices:*
(see index for correct answer)

- a. Doublespeak
- b. Emotional conflict
- c. Self-refuting idea
- d. Hypocrisy

Guidance: level 1

:: ::

Management is the administration of an organization, whether it is a business, a not-for-profit organization, or government body. Management includes the activities of setting the strategy of an organization and coordinating the efforts of its employees to accomplish its objectives through the application of available resources, such as financial, natural, technological, and human resources. The term "management" may also refer to those people who manage an organization.

Exam Probability: **Medium**

56. *Answer choices:*
(see index for correct answer)

- a. information systems assessment
- b. corporate values
- c. similarity-attraction theory
- d. Manager

Guidance: level 1

:: Budgets ::

A _____ is a financial plan for a defined period, often one year. It may also include planned sales volumes and revenues, resource quantities, costs and expenses, assets, liabilities and cash flows. Companies, governments, families and other organizations use it to express strategic plans of activities or events in measurable terms.

Exam Probability: **High**

57. *Answer choices:*

- a. Budget
- b. Envelope system
- c. Railway Budget
- d. Personal budget

Guidance: level 1

:: Graphic design ::

An _____ is an artifact that depicts visual perception, such as a photograph or other two-dimensional picture, that resembles a subject—usually a physical object—and thus provides a depiction of it. In the context of signal processing, an _____ is a distributed amplitude of color.

Exam Probability: **Medium**

58. *Answer choices:*

- a. Image
- b. First Things First 2000 manifesto
- c. Type Directors Club
- d. Crowdspring

Guidance: level 1

:: Marketing ::

A business can use a variety of _____ when selling a product or service. The price can be set to maximize profitability for each unit sold or from the market overall. It can be used to defend an existing market from new entrants, to increase market share within a market or to enter a new market.

Exam Probability: **High**

59. *Answer choices:*

(see index for correct answer)

- a. Pick and pack
- b. Call to action
- c. Market intelligence
- d. Movie gimmick

Guidance: level 1

Manufacturing

Manufacturing is the production of merchandise for use or sale using labor and machines, tools, chemical and biological processing, or formulation. The term may refer to a range of human activity, from handicraft to high tech, but is most commonly applied to industrial design , in which raw materials are transformed into finished goods on a large scale. Such finished goods may be sold to other manufacturers for the production of other, more complex products, such as aircraft, household appliances, furniture, sports equipment or automobiles, or sold to wholesalers, who in turn sell them to retailers, who then sell them to end users and consumers.

:: Data management ::

_____ is the ability of a physical product to remain functional, without requiring excessive maintenance or repair, when faced with the challenges of normal operation over its design lifetime. There are several measures of _____ in use, including years of life, hours of use, and number of operational cycles. In economics, goods with a long usable life are referred to as durable goods.

Exam Probability: **High**

1. *Answer choices:*
(see index for correct answer)

- a. Schema crosswalk
- b. Durability
- c. Content Engineering
- d. World Wide Molecular Matrix

Guidance: level 1

:: Production and manufacturing ::

_____ is a set of techniques and tools for process improvement. Though as a shortened form it may be found written as 6S, it should not be confused with the methodology known as 6S .

2. *Answer choices:*
(see index for correct answer)

- a. production control
- b. Six Sigma
- c. production planning
- d. Division of labour

Guidance: level 1

:: Business planning ::

_____ is an organization's process of defining its strategy, or direction, and making decisions on allocating its resources to pursue this strategy. It may also extend to control mechanisms for guiding the implementation of the strategy. _____ became prominent in corporations during the 1960s and remains an important aspect of strategic management. It is executed by strategic planners or strategists, who involve many parties and research sources in their analysis of the organization and its relationship to the environment in which it competes.

3. *Answer choices:*
(see index for correct answer)

- a. Community Futures
- b. Exit planning
- c. Stakeholder management
- d. Strategic planning

Guidance: level 1

:: Industrial design ::

In physics and mathematics, the _____ of a mathematical space is informally defined as the minimum number of coordinates needed to specify any point within it. Thus a line has a _____ of one because only one coordinate is needed to specify a point on it for example, the point at 5 on a number line. A surface such as a plane or the surface of a cylinder or sphere has a _____ of two because two coordinates are needed to specify a point on it for example, both a latitude and longitude are required to locate a point on the surface of a sphere. The inside of a cube, a cylinder or a sphere is three- _____ al because three coordinates are needed to locate a point within these spaces.

Exam Probability: **Medium**

4. *Answer choices:*
(see index for correct answer)

- a. Industrial design rights in the European Union
- b. International Council of Societies of Industrial Design
- c. Form factor
- d. Dimension

Guidance: level 1

:: Packaging materials ::

_____ is a non-crystalline, amorphous solid that is often transparent and has widespread practical, technological, and decorative uses in, for example, window panes, tableware, and optoelectronics. The most familiar, and historically the oldest, types of manufactured _____ are "silicate _____ es" based on the chemical compound silica , the primary constituent of sand. The term _____ , in popular usage, is often used to refer only to this type of material, which is familiar from use as window _____ and in _____ bottles. Of the many silica-based _____ es that exist, ordinary glazing and container _____ is formed from a specific type called soda-lime _____ , composed of approximately 75% silicon dioxide , sodium oxide from sodium carbonate , calcium oxide , also called lime, and several minor additives.

Exam Probability: **Medium**

5. *Answer choices:*
(see index for correct answer)

- a. Tissue paper
- b. Corrugated fiberboard
- c. Polybutylene succinate
- d. Cellophane

Guidance: level 1

:: Semiconductor companies ::

_____ Corporation is a Japanese multinational conglomerate corporation headquartered in Konan, Minato, Tokyo. Its diversified business includes consumer and professional electronics, gaming, entertainment and financial services. The company owns the largest music entertainment business in the world, the largest video game console business and one of the largest video game publishing businesses, and is one of the leading manufacturers of electronic products for the consumer and professional markets, and a leading player in the film and television entertainment industry. _____ was ranked 97th on the 2018 Fortune Global 500 list.

Exam Probability: **Medium**

6. *Answer choices:*
(see index for correct answer)

- a. Fujitsu
- b. Semitool
- c. Nuvoton
- d. Hana Micron

Guidance: level 1

:: Distribution, retailing, and wholesaling ::

_____ measures the performance of a system. Certain goals are defined and the _____ gives the percentage to which those goals should be achieved. Fill rate is different from _____ .

Exam Probability: **High**

7. *Answer choices:*
(see index for correct answer)

- a. Wholesale list
- b. Service level
- c. Sales variance

- d. Chicago Review Press

Guidance: level 1

:: Information technology management ::

_____ is a collective term for all approaches to prepare , support and help individuals, teams, and organizations in making organizational change. The most common change drivers include: technological evolution, process reviews, crisis, and consumer habit changes; pressure from new business entrants, acquisitions, mergers, and organizational restructuring. It includes methods that redirect or redefine the use of resources, business process, budget allocations, or other modes of operation that significantly change a company or organization. Organizational _____ considers the full organization and what needs to change, while _____ may be used solely to refer to how people and teams are affected by such organizational transition. It deals with many different disciplines, from behavioral and social sciences to information technology and business solutions.

Exam Probability: **Low**

8. *Answer choices:*
(see index for correct answer)

- a. Open Cobalt
- b. Socitm
- c. Information protection policy
- d. Information Services Procurement Library

Guidance: level 1

:: ::

The _____ is a project plan of how the production budget will be spent over a given timescale, for every phase of a business project.

Exam Probability: **Low**

9. *Answer choices:*
(see index for correct answer)

- a. Production schedule
- b. hierarchical
- c. hierarchical perspective

- d. process perspective

Guidance: level 1

:: Metal forming ::

_____ is a type of motion that combines rotation and translation of that object with respect to a surface , such that, if ideal conditions exist, the two are in contact with each other without sliding.

Exam Probability: **Low**

10. *Answer choices:*
(see index for correct answer)

- a. Tube beading
- b. Forming limit diagram
- c. Rolling
- d. Roll slitting

Guidance: level 1

:: Information technology management ::

_____ within quality management systems and information technology systems is a process—either formal or informal—used to ensure that changes to a product or system are introduced in a controlled and coordinated manner. It reduces the possibility that unnecessary changes will be introduced to a system without forethought, introducing faults into the system or undoing changes made by other users of software. The goals of a _____ procedure usually include minimal disruption to services, reduction in back-out activities, and cost-effective utilization of resources involved in implementing change.

Exam Probability: **Medium**

11. *Answer choices:*
(see index for correct answer)

- a. Multichannel Group
- b. Enterprise information management
- c. Purchase order request
- d. Digital continuity

Guidance: level 1

:: Computer memory companies ::

_____ Corporation is a Japanese multinational conglomerate headquartered in Tokyo, Japan. Its diversified products and services include information technology and communications equipment and systems, electronic components and materials, power systems, industrial and social infrastructure systems, consumer electronics, household appliances, medical equipment, office equipment, as well as lighting and logistics.

Exam Probability: **Low**

12. *Answer choices:*
(see index for correct answer)

- a. Dataram
- b. Qimonda
- c. Toshiba
- d. GeIL

Guidance: level 1

:: Distribution, retailing, and wholesaling ::

The _____ is a distribution channel phenomenon in which forecasts yield supply chain inefficiencies. It refers to increasing swings in inventory in response to shifts in customer demand as one moves further up the supply chain. The concept first appeared in Jay Forrester's Industrial Dynamics and thus it is also known as the Forrester effect. The _____ was named for the way the amplitude of a whip increases down its length. The further from the originating signal, the greater the distortion of the wave pattern. In a similar manner, forecast accuracy decreases as one moves upstream along the supply chain. For example, many consumer goods have fairly consistent consumption at retail but this signal becomes more chaotic and unpredictable as the focus moves away from consumer purchasing behavior.

Exam Probability: **Low**

13. *Answer choices:*
(see index for correct answer)

- a. False designation of origin
- b. Bullwhip effect
- c. Independent Publishers Group
- d. Distribution center management system

:: Industrial organization ::

In economics, specifically general equilibrium theory, a perfect market is defined by several idealizing conditions, collectively called _____ . In theoretical models where conditions of _____ hold, it has been theoretically demonstrated that a market will reach an equilibrium in which the quantity supplied for every product or service, including labor, equals the quantity demanded at the current price. This equilibrium would be a Pareto optimum.

Exam Probability: **Medium**

14. *Answer choices:*
(see index for correct answer)

- a. Industrial inertia
- b. Path dependence
- c. Perfect competition
- d. American system of manufacturing

:: Insulators ::

A _____ is a piece of soft cloth large enough either to cover or to enfold a great portion of the user's body, usually when sleeping or otherwise at rest, thereby trapping radiant bodily heat that otherwise would be lost through convection, and so keeping the body warm.

Exam Probability: **High**

15. *Answer choices:*
(see index for correct answer)

- a. R-value
- b. Thermal pad
- c. Pentafluoropropane
- d. Vacuum insulated panel

:: Project management ::

_____ is a process of setting goals, planning and/or controlling the organizing and leading the execution of any type of activity, such as.

Exam Probability: **Medium**

16. *Answer choices:*
(see index for correct answer)

- a. The International Association of Project and Program Management
- b. Indian Institute of Project Management
- c. Management process
- d. Case competition

Guidance: level 1

:: Production and manufacturing ::

_____ is a concept in purchasing and project management for securing the quality and timely delivery of goods and components.

Exam Probability: **Low**

17. *Answer choices:*
(see index for correct answer)

- a. Craft production
- b. Profibus
- c. Expediting
- d. Back-story

Guidance: level 1

:: Promotion and marketing communications ::

The _____ of American Manufacturers, now ThomasNet, is an online platform for supplier discovery and product sourcing in the US and Canada. It was once known as the "big green books" and "Thomas Registry", and was a multi-volume directory of industrial product information covering 650,000 distributors, manufacturers and service companies within 67,000-plus industrial categories that is now published on ThomasNet.

Exam Probability: **High**

18. *Answer choices:*

- a. Thomas Register
- b. CollarCard
- c. Pressbook
- d. Word-of-mouth marketing

Guidance: level 1

:: Data management ::

_____ is an object-oriented program and library developed by CERN. It was originally designed for particle physics data analysis and contains several features specific to this field, but it is also used in other applications such as astronomy and data mining. The latest release is 6.16.00, as of 2018-11-14.

Exam Probability: **Medium**

19. *Answer choices:*

- a. Data storage device
- b. SciDB
- c. National Data Repository
- d. ROOT

Guidance: level 1

:: Information technology management ::

_____ is the discipline of engineering concerned with the principles and practice of product and service quality assurance and control. In the software development, it is the management, development, operation and maintenance of IT systems and enterprise architectures with a high quality standard.

Exam Probability: **Low**

20. *Answer choices:*

- a. Quality Engineering
- b. Lean IT
- c. Xinet
- d. SFIAPlus

:: Quality assurance ::

Organizations that issue credentials or certify third parties against official standards are themselves formally accredited by _____ bodies ; hence they are sometimes known as "accredited certification bodies". The _____ process ensures that their certification practices are acceptable, typically meaning that they are competent to test and certify third parties, behave ethically and employ suitable quality assurance.

Exam Probability: **High**

21. *Answer choices:*
(see index for correct answer)

- a. Silk Central
- b. Accreditation
- c. Trent Accreditation Scheme
- d. PCOLA-SOQ

:: Manufacturing ::

A _____ is an object used to extend the ability of an individual to modify features of the surrounding environment. Although many animals use simple _____ s, only human beings, whose use of stone _____ s dates back hundreds of millennia, use _____ s to make other _____ s. The set of _____ s needed to perform different tasks that are part of the same activity is called gear or equipment.

Exam Probability: **Medium**

22. *Answer choices:*
(see index for correct answer)

- a. Eneas
- b. Advanced planning and scheduling
- c. Interchangeable parts
- d. Tool

:: Unit operations ::

_____ is the process of separating the components or substances from a liquid mixture by using selective boiling and condensation. _____ may result in essentially complete separation , or it may be a partial separation that increases the concentration of selected components in the mixture. In either case, the process exploits differences in the volatility of the mixture's components. In industrial chemistry, _____ is a unit operation of practically universal importance, but it is a physical separation process, not a chemical reaction.

Exam Probability: **Low**

23. *Answer choices:*
(see index for correct answer)

- a. Distillation
- b. Homogenization
- c. Theoretical plate
- d. Solvent impregnated resin

Guidance: level 1

:: Product development ::

In business and engineering, _____ covers the complete process of bringing a new product to market. A central aspect of NPD is product design, along with various business considerations. _____ is described broadly as the transformation of a market opportunity into a product available for sale. The product can be tangible or intangible , though sometimes services and other processes are distinguished from "products." NPD requires an understanding of customer needs and wants, the competitive environment, and the nature of the market.Cost, time and quality are the main variables that drive customer needs. Aiming at these three variables, innovative companies develop continuous practices and strategies to better satisfy customer requirements and to increase their own market share by a regular development of new products. There are many uncertainties and challenges which companies must face throughout the process. The use of best practices and the elimination of barriers to communication are the main concerns for the management of the NPD .

Exam Probability: **Low**

24. *Answer choices:*
(see index for correct answer)

- a. New product development
- b. Modular function deployment
- c. Minimum viable product
- d. Collaborative product development

Guidance: level 1

:: Production and manufacturing ::

In industry, _____ is a system of maintaining and improving the integrity of production and quality systems through the machines, equipment, processes, and employees that add business value to an organization.

Exam Probability: **High**

25. *Answer choices:*
(see index for correct answer)

- a. Back-story
- b. Production
- c. Production part approval process
- d. Fixed position assembly

Guidance: level 1

:: Costs ::

The _____ is computed by dividing the total cost of goods available for sale by the total units available for sale. This gives a weighted-average unit cost that is applied to the units in the ending inventory.

Exam Probability: **High**

26. *Answer choices:*
(see index for correct answer)

- a. Quality costs
- b. Social cost
- c. Average cost
- d. Travel and subsistence

Guidance: level 1

_____ , also known as natural process limits, are horizontal lines drawn on a statistical process control chart, usually at a distance of ± 3 standard deviations of the plotted statistic from the statistic's mean.

Exam Probability: **Low**

27. *Answer choices:*
(see index for correct answer)

- a. Control limits
- b. Cross ownership
- c. Public sector consulting
- d. Success-oriented management

Guidance: level 1

:: Metal heat treatments ::

_____ is a group of industrial and metalworking processes used to alter the physical, and sometimes chemical, properties of a material. The most common application is metallurgical. Heat treatments are also used in the manufacture of many other materials, such as glass. Heat treatment involves the use of heating or chilling, normally to extreme temperatures, to achieve a desired result such as hardening or softening of a material. Heat treatment techniques include annealing, case hardening, precipitation strengthening, tempering, carburizing, normalizing and quenching. It is noteworthy that while the term heat treatment applies only to processes where the heating and cooling are done for the specific purpose of altering properties intentionally, heating and cooling often occur incidentally during other manufacturing processes such as hot forming or welding.

Exam Probability: **Medium**

28. *Answer choices:*
(see index for correct answer)

- a. Differential heat treatment
- b. Quenching
- c. Tempering
- d. Precipitation hardening

Guidance: level 1

:: Project management ::

_____ s can take many forms depending on the type of project being implemented and the nature of the organization. The _____ details the project deliverables and describes the major objectives. The objectives should include measurable success criteria for the project.

Exam Probability: **Medium**

29. *Answer choices:*
(see index for correct answer)

- a. Product-based planning
- b. Research program
- c. NEC Engineering and Construction Contract
- d. Scope statement

Guidance: level 1

:: Project management ::

A _____ is a type of bar chart that illustrates a project schedule, named after its inventor, Henry Gantt , who designed such a chart around the years 1910–1915. Modern _____ s also show the dependency relationships between activities and current schedule status.

Exam Probability: **Low**

30. *Answer choices:*
(see index for correct answer)

- a. Gantt chart
- b. Hammock activity
- c. ISO 31000
- d. Mandated lead arranger

Guidance: level 1

:: Mereology ::

_____ , in the abstract, is what belongs to or with something, whether as an attribute or as a component of said thing. In the context of this article, it is one or more components , whether physical or incorporeal, of a person's estate; or so belonging to, as in being owned by, a person or jointly a group of people or a legal entity like a corporation or even a society. Depending on the nature of the _____ , an owner of _____ has the right to consume, alter, share, redefine, rent, mortgage, pawn, sell, exchange, transfer, give away or destroy it, or to exclude others from doing these things, as well as to perhaps abandon it; whereas regardless of the nature of the _____ , the owner thereof has the right to properly use it , or at the very least exclusively keep it.

31. *Answer choices:*

- a. Mereological essentialism
- b. Mereotopology
- c. Property
- d. Mereology

Guidance: level 1

:: Gas technologies ::

A _____ is a device used to transfer heat between two or more fluids. _____ s are used in both cooling and heating processes. The fluids may be separated by a solid wall to prevent mixing or they may be in direct contact. They are widely used in space heating, refrigeration, air conditioning, power stations, chemical plants, petrochemical plants, petroleum refineries, natural-gas processing, and sewage treatment. The classic example of a _____ is found in an internal combustion engine in which a circulating fluid known as engine coolant flows through radiator coils and air flows past the coils, which cools the coolant and heats the incoming air. Another example is the heat sink, which is a passive _____ that transfers the heat generated by an electronic or a mechanical device to a fluid medium, often air or a liquid coolant.

32. *Answer choices:*

(see index for correct answer)

- a. Intercooler
- b. Gas cracker
- c. Condenser
- d. Heat exchanger

Guidance: level 1

:: Manufacturing ::

_____ or lean production, often simply "lean", is a systematic method for the minimization of waste within a manufacturing system without sacrificing productivity, which can cause problems. Lean also takes into account waste created through overburden and waste created through unevenness in work loads . Working from the perspective of the client who consumes a product or service, "value" is any action or process that a customer would be willing to pay for.

Exam Probability: **Medium**

33. *Answer choices:*

(see index for correct answer)

- a. Priming
- b. Notions
- c. ANSI/ISA-95
- d. Lean manufacturing

Guidance: level 1

:: Retailing ::

_____ is the process of selling consumer goods or services to customers through multiple channels of distribution to earn a profit. _____ ers satisfy demand identified through a supply chain. The term " _____ er" is typically applied where a service provider fills the small orders of a large number of individuals, who are end-users, rather than large orders of a small number of wholesale, corporate or government clientele. Shopping generally refers to the act of buying products. Sometimes this is done to obtain final goods, including necessities such as food and clothing; sometimes it takes place as a recreational activity. Recreational shopping often involves window shopping and browsing: it does not always result in a purchase.

Exam Probability: **Low**

34. *Answer choices:*
(see index for correct answer)

- a. Stock rotation
- b. Cash on Delivery
- c. Retail
- d. Window dresser

Guidance: level 1

:: Alchemical processes ::

In chemistry, a _____ is a special type of homogeneous mixture composed of two or more substances. In such a mixture, a solute is a substance dissolved in another substance, known as a solvent. The mixing process of a _____ happens at a scale where the effects of chemical polarity are involved, resulting in interactions that are specific to solvation. The _____ assumes the phase of the solvent when the solvent is the larger fraction of the mixture, as is commonly the case. The concentration of a solute in a _____ is the mass of that solute expressed as a percentage of the mass of the whole _____ . The term aqueous _____ is when one of the solvents is water.

Exam Probability: **High**

35. *Answer choices:*
(see index for correct answer)

- a. Projection
- b. Sublimation apparatus
- c. Putrefaction

- d. Corporification

Guidance: level 1

:: Debt ::

_____ is the trust which allows one party to provide money or resources to another party wherein the second party does not reimburse the first party immediately , but promises either to repay or return those resources at a later date. In other words, _____ is a method of making reciprocity formal, legally enforceable, and extensible to a large group of unrelated people.

Exam Probability: **Medium**

36. *Answer choices:*
(see index for correct answer)

- a. Extendible bond
- b. Credit
- c. Museum of Foreign Debt
- d. Odious debt

Guidance: level 1

:: Information systems ::

_____ is the process of creating, sharing, using and managing the knowledge and information of an organisation. It refers to a multidisciplinary approach to achieving organisational objectives by making the best use of knowledge.

Exam Probability: **Medium**

37. *Answer choices:*
(see index for correct answer)

- a. Notify NYC
- b. Physical Internet
- c. Identity correlation
- d. Knowledge management

Guidance: level 1

A _____ is a commercial document and first official offer issued by a
buyer to a seller indicating types, quantities, and agreed prices for products
or services. It is used to control the purchasing of products and services from
external suppliers. _____ s can be an essential part of enterprise
resource planning system orders.

Exam Probability: **High**

38. *Answer choices:*
(see index for correct answer)

- a. Air waybill
- b. Banknote
- c. Purchase order
- d. Bank statement

Guidance: level 1

A _____ is an accurate representation of the distribution of numerical
data. It is an estimate of the probability distribution of a continuous
variable and was first introduced by Karl Pearson. It differs from a bar
graph, in the sense that a bar graph relates two variables, but a _____
relates only one. To construct a _____ , the first step is to "bin" the
range of values—that is, divide the entire range of values into a series of
intervals—and then count how many values fall into each interval. The bins are
usually specified as consecutive, non-overlapping intervals of a variable. The
bins must be adjacent, and are often of equal size.

Exam Probability: **High**

39. *Answer choices:*
(see index for correct answer)

- a. Durbin test
- b. Histogram
- c. Kernel regression
- d. Concordant pair

Guidance: level 1

Catalysis is the process of increasing the rate of a chemical reaction by adding a substance known as a _____ , which is not consumed in the catalyzed reaction and can continue to act repeatedly. Because of this, only very small amounts of _____ are required to alter the reaction rate in principle.

Exam Probability: **Low**

40. *Answer choices:*
(see index for correct answer)

- a. corporate values
- b. hierarchical perspective
- c. interpersonal communication
- d. Sarbanes-Oxley act of 2002

Guidance: level 1

In sales, commerce and economics, a _____ is the recipient of a good, service, product or an idea - obtained from a seller, vendor, or supplier via a financial transaction or exchange for money or some other valuable consideration.

Exam Probability: **High**

41. *Answer choices:*
(see index for correct answer)

- a. Customer
- b. personal values
- c. imperative
- d. open system

Guidance: level 1

:: Management ::

_____ is a method of quality control which employs statistical methods to monitor and control a process. This helps to ensure that the process operates efficiently, producing more specification-conforming products with less waste . SPC can be applied to any process where the "conforming product" output can be measured. Key tools used in SPC include run charts, control charts, a focus on continuous improvement, and the design of experiments. An example of a process where SPC is applied is manufacturing lines.

Exam Probability: **Low**

42. *Answer choices:*
(see index for correct answer)

- a. Statistical process control
- b. Duality
- c. Business process mapping
- d. Target culture

Guidance: level 1

:: Production economics ::

_____ is the joint use of a resource or space. It is also the process of dividing and distributing. In its narrow sense, it refers to joint or alternating use of inherently finite goods, such as a common pasture or a shared residence. Still more loosely, " _____ " can actually mean giving something as an outright gift: for example, to "share" one's food really means to give some of it as a gift. _____ is a basic component of human interaction, and is responsible for strengthening social ties and ensuring a person's well-being.

Exam Probability: **High**

43. *Answer choices:*
(see index for correct answer)

- a. Factor price
- b. short run
- c. Peer production
- d. Sharing

Guidance: level 1

:: Management ::

A process is a unique combination of tools, materials, methods, and people engaged in producing a measurable output; for example a manufacturing line for machine parts. All processes have inherent statistical variability which can be evaluated by statistical methods.

Exam Probability: **Medium**

44. *Answer choices:*
(see index for correct answer)

- a. Event chain diagram
- b. Manager Tools Podcast
- c. Discovery-driven planning
- d. Process capability

Guidance: level 1

:: Costs ::

In microeconomic theory, the _____ , or alternative cost, of making a particular choice is the value of the most valuable choice out of those that were not taken. In other words, opportunity that will require sacrifices.

Exam Probability: **High**

45. *Answer choices:*
(see index for correct answer)

- a. Khozraschyot
- b. Cost of products sold
- c. Cost reduction
- d. Sliding scale fees

Guidance: level 1

:: Auditing ::

_____ is the process of systematic examination of a quality system carried out by an internal or external _____ or or an audit team. It is an important part of an organization's quality management system and is a key element in the ISO quality system standard, ISO 9001.

46. *Answer choices:*

- a. Forensic accounting
- b. Communication audit
- c. Audit management
- d. Quality audit

Guidance: level 1

:: Costs ::

In economics, _____ is the total economic cost of production and is made up of variable cost, which varies according to the quantity of a good produced and includes inputs such as labour and raw materials, plus fixed cost, which is independent of the quantity of a good produced and includes inputs that cannot be varied in the short term: fixed costs such as buildings and machinery, including sunk costs if any. Since cost is measured per unit of time, it is a flow variable.

47. *Answer choices:*

- a. Total cost
- b. Cost curve
- c. Sliding scale
- d. Explicit cost

Guidance: level 1

:: ::

An _____ is a company that produces parts and equipment that may be marketed by another manufacturer. For example, Foxconn, a Taiwanese electronics contract manufacturing company, which produces a variety of parts and equipment for companies such as Apple Inc., Dell, Google, Huawei, Nintendo, etc., is the largest OEM company in the world by both scale and revenue.

48. *Answer choices:*

(see index for correct answer)

- a. Character
- b. co-culture
- c. deep-level diversity
- d. Original equipment manufacturer

Guidance: level 1

:: Project management ::

In general usage, a _____ is a comprehensive evaluation of an individual's current pay and future financial state by using current known variables to predict future income, asset values and withdrawal plans. This often includes a budget which organizes an individual's finances and sometimes includes a series of steps or specific goals for spending and saving in the future. This plan allocates future income to various types of expenses, such as rent or utilities, and also reserves some income for short-term and long-term savings. A _____ is sometimes referred to as an investment plan, but in personal finance a _____ can focus on other specific areas such as risk management, estates, college, or retirement.

Exam Probability: **High**

49. *Answer choices:*
(see index for correct answer)

- a. Participatory impact pathways analysis
- b. Association for Project Management
- c. Case competition
- d. Trenegy Incorporated

Guidance: level 1

:: Management ::

_____ is the discipline of strategically planning for, and managing, all interactions with third party organizations that supply goods and/or services to an organization in order to maximize the value of those interactions. In practice, SRM entails creating closer, more collaborative relationships with key suppliers in order to uncover and realize new value and reduce risk of failure.

50. *Answer choices:*

(see index for correct answer)

- a. Personal offshoring
- b. Supplier relationship management
- c. Certified Project Management Professional
- d. Line of business

Guidance: level 1

:: Management accounting ::

_____ are costs that are not directly accountable to a cost object . _____ may be either fixed or variable. _____ include administration, personnel and security costs. These are those costs which are not directly related to production. Some _____ may be overhead. But some overhead costs can be directly attributed to a project and are direct costs.

Exam Probability: **Medium**

51. *Answer choices:*

(see index for correct answer)

- a. Job costing
- b. Indirect costs
- c. Pre-determined overhead rate
- d. Management accounting

Guidance: level 1

:: Industrial engineering ::

_____ , in its contemporary conceptualisation, is a comparison of perceived expectations of a service with perceived performance , giving rise to the equation SQ=P-E. This conceptualistion of _____ has its origins in the expectancy-disconfirmation paradigm.

Exam Probability: **Medium**

52. *Answer choices:*

(see index for correct answer)

- a. Pilot plant
- b. Activity relationship chart

- c. Flow process chart
- d. Industrial engineering and operations research

Guidance: level 1

:: Management ::

_____ is a formal technique useful where many possible courses of action are competing for attention. In essence, the problem-solver estimates the benefit delivered by each action, then selects a number of the most effective actions that deliver a total benefit reasonably close to the maximal possible one.

Exam Probability: **Low**

53. *Answer choices:*
(see index for correct answer)

- a. Bed management
- b. Dominant design
- c. Distributed management
- d. Event chain diagram

Guidance: level 1

:: Product management ::

_____ s, also known as Shewhart charts or process-behavior charts, are a statistical process control tool used to determine if a manufacturing or business process is in a state of control.

Exam Probability: **Medium**

54. *Answer choices:*
(see index for correct answer)

- a. Control chart
- b. Dwinell-Wright Company
- c. Crossing the Chasm
- d. Mid-life update

Guidance: level 1

:: Infographics ::

The _____ is a form used to collect data in real time at the location where the data is generated. The data it captures can be quantitative or qualitative. When the information is quantitative, the _____ is sometimes called a tally sheet.

Exam Probability: **Medium**

55. *Answer choices:*
(see index for correct answer)

- a. Chartjunk
- b. Admiralty chart
- c. SCaViS
- d. Texture advection

Guidance: level 1

:: Business process ::

_____ is the value to an enterprise which is derived from the techniques, procedures, and programs that implement and enhance the delivery of goods and services. _____ is one of the three components of structural capital, itself a component of intellectual capital. _____ can be seen as the value of processes to any entity, whether for profit or not-for profit, but is most commonly used in reference to for-profit entities.

Exam Probability: **High**

56. *Answer choices:*
(see index for correct answer)

- a. Extended Enterprise Modeling Language
- b. Process capital
- c. Software ecosystem
- d. Business process outsourcing

Guidance: level 1

:: Casting (manufacturing) ::

A _____ is a regularity in the world, man-made design, or abstract ideas. As such, the elements of a _____ repeat in a predictable manner. A geometric _____ is a kind of _____ formed of geometric shapes and typically repeated like a wallpaper design.

Exam Probability: **Low**

57. *Answer choices:*
(see index for correct answer)

- a. Continuous casting
- b. Die casting
- c. Ablation casting
- d. Bronze sculpture

Guidance: level 1

:: Project management ::

Rolling-wave planning is the process of project planning in waves as the project proceeds and later details become clearer; similar to the techniques used in agile software development approaches like Scrum..

Exam Probability: **High**

58. *Answer choices:*
(see index for correct answer)

- a. Collaborative project management
- b. Schedule
- c. Responsibility assignment matrix
- d. Sequence step algorithm

Guidance: level 1

:: Planning ::

_____ is a high level plan to achieve one or more goals under conditions of uncertainty. In the sense of the "art of the general," which included several subsets of skills including tactics, siegecraft, logistics etc., the term came into use in the 6th century C.E. in East Roman terminology, and was translated into Western vernacular languages only in the 18th century. From then until the 20th century, the word "_____" came to denote "a comprehensive way to try to pursue political ends, including the threat or actual use of force, in a dialectic of wills" in a military conflict, in which both adversaries interact.

Exam Probability: **High**

59. *Answer choices:*
(see index for correct answer)

- a. Event scheduling
- b. Strategy
- c. Parish plan
- d. Fragplan

Guidance: level 1

Commerce

Commerce relates to "the exchange of goods and services, especially on a large scale." It includes legal, economic, political, social, cultural and technological systems that operate in any country or internationally.

:: ::

An _____ is a systematic and independent examination of books, accounts, statutory records, documents and vouchers of an organization to ascertain how far the financial statements as well as non-financial disclosures present a true and fair view of the concern. It also attempts to ensure that the books of accounts are properly maintained by the concern as required by law. _____ ing has become such a ubiquitous phenomenon in the corporate and the public sector that academics started identifying an " _____ Society". The _____ or perceives and recognises the propositions before them for examination, obtains evidence, evaluates the same and formulates an opinion on the basis of his judgement which is communicated through their _____ ing report.

Exam Probability: **High**

1. *Answer choices:*
(see index for correct answer)

- a. deep-level diversity
- b. cultural
- c. Sarbanes-Oxley act of 2002
- d. Audit

Guidance: level 1

:: ::

Competition law is a law that promotes or seeks to maintain market competition by regulating anti-competitive conduct by companies. Competition law is implemented through public and private enforcement. Competition law is known as " _____ law" in the United States for historical reasons, and as "anti-monopoly law" in China and Russia. In previous years it has been known as trade practices law in the United Kingdom and Australia. In the European Union, it is referred to as both _____ and competition law.

Exam Probability: **Medium**

2. *Answer choices:*

(see index for correct answer)

- a. personal values
- b. Antitrust
- c. process perspective
- d. similarity-attraction theory

Guidance: level 1

:: Cash flow ::

_____ s are narrowly interconnected with the concepts of value, interest rate and liquidity.A _____ that shall happen on a future day tN can be transformed into a _____ of the same value in t0.

Exam Probability: **Medium**

3. *Answer choices:*

(see index for correct answer)

- a. Cash flow forecasting
- b. Cash flow statement
- c. Valuation using discounted cash flows
- d. First Chicago Method

Guidance: level 1

:: ::

A _____ is a structured form of play, usually undertaken for enjoyment and sometimes used as an educational tool. _____ s are distinct from work, which is usually carried out for remuneration, and from art, which is more often an expression of aesthetic or ideological elements. However, the distinction is not clear-cut, and many _____ s are also considered to be work or art .

Exam Probability: **Medium**

4. *Answer choices:*
(see index for correct answer)

- a. empathy
- b. hierarchical
- c. co-culture
- d. hierarchical perspective

Guidance: level 1

:: Commercial item transport and distribution ::

In a contract of carriage, the _____ is the entity who is financially responsible for the receipt of a shipment. Generally, but not always, the _____ is the same as the receiver.

Exam Probability: **High**

5. *Answer choices:*
(see index for correct answer)

- a. Cross-docking
- b. Consignee
- c. Fuel cell forklift
- d. Warehouse receipt

Guidance: level 1

:: Market research ::

_____ is an organized effort to gather information about target markets or customers. It is a very important component of business strategy. The term is commonly interchanged with marketing research; however, expert practitioners may wish to draw a distinction, in that marketing research is concerned specifically about marketing processes, while _____ is concerned specifically with markets.

Exam Probability: **Medium**

6. *Answer choices:*
(see index for correct answer)

- a. Sagacity segmentation
- b. Market research
- c. Industry analyst
- d. Media-Analyse

Guidance: level 1

:: Economics terminology ::

_____ is the total receipts a seller can obtain from selling goods or services to buyers. It can be written as P × Q, which is the price of the goods multiplied by the quantity of the sold goods.

Exam Probability: **Low**

7. *Answer choices:*
(see index for correct answer)

- a. Profit motive
- b. Bond issue
- c. Normal profit
- d. Total revenue

Guidance: level 1

:: Management occupations ::

_____ ship is the process of designing, launching and running a new business, which is often initially a small business. The people who create these businesses are called _____ s.

8. *Answer choices:*

(see index for correct answer)

- a. Corporate trainer
- b. Entrepreneur
- c. Chief business development officer
- d. City manager

Guidance: level 1

:: Trading posts of the Hanseatic League ::

_____ is a city and unitary authority area in North _____ shire, England, with a population of 208,200 as of 2017. Located at the confluence of the Rivers Ouse and Foss, it is the county town of the historic county of _____ shire and was the home of the House of _____ throughout its existence. The city is known for its famous historical landmarks such as _____ Minster and the city walls, as well as a variety of cultural and sporting activities, which makes it a popular tourist destination in England. The local authority is the City of _____ Council, a single tier governing body responsible for providing all local services and facilities throughout the city. The City of _____ local government district includes rural areas beyond the old city boundaries.

9. *Answer choices:*

(see index for correct answer)

- a. Antwerp
- b. York
- c. Novgorod Republic
- d. Polotsk

Guidance: level 1

:: Regulators ::

A _____ is a public authority or government agency responsible for exercising autonomous authority over some area of human activity in a regulatory or supervisory capacity. An independent _____ is a _____ that is independent from other branches or arms of the government.

Exam Probability: **Medium**

10. *Answer choices:*
(see index for correct answer)

- a. Alberta Energy Regulator
- b. Energy Resources Conservation Board
- c. Regulatory agency
- d. Croatian Regulatory Authority for Network Industries

Guidance: level 1

:: Land value taxation ::

_____ , sometimes referred to as dry _____ , is the solid surface of Earth that is not permanently covered by water. The vast majority of human activity throughout history has occurred in _____ areas that support agriculture, habitat, and various natural resources. Some life forms have developed from predecessor species that lived in bodies of water.

Exam Probability: **High**

11. *Answer choices:*
(see index for correct answer)

- a. Prosper Australia
- b. Land value tax
- c. Land
- d. Georgism

Guidance: level 1

:: ::

According to the philosopher Piyush Mathur , "Tangibility is the property that a phenomenon exhibits if it has and/or transports mass and/or energy and/or momentum".

12. *Answer choices:*
(see index for correct answer)

- a. cultural
- b. similarity-attraction theory
- c. information systems assessment
- d. co-culture

Guidance: level 1

:: Information technology management ::

B2B is often contrasted with business-to-consumer . In B2B commerce, it is often the case that the parties to the relationship have comparable negotiating power, and even when they do not, each party typically involves professional staff and legal counsel in the negotiation of terms, whereas B2C is shaped to a far greater degree by economic implications of information asymmetry. However, within a B2B context, large companies may have many commercial, resource and information advantages over smaller businesses. The United Kingdom government, for example, created the post of Small Business Commissioner under the Enterprise Act 2016 to "enable small businesses to resolve disputes" and "consider complaints by small business suppliers about payment issues with larger businesses that they supply."

13. *Answer choices:*
(see index for correct answer)

- a. Many-to-many
- b. EDIFACT
- c. Business-to-business
- d. National Biological Information Infrastructure

Guidance: level 1

:: E-commerce ::

_____ is a type of performance-based marketing in which a business rewards one or more affiliates for each visitor or customer brought by the affiliate's own marketing efforts.

14. *Answer choices:*

(see index for correct answer)

- a. Silent commerce
- b. TRANZ 330
- c. POLi Payments
- d. Affiliate marketing

Guidance: level 1

:: ::

An _____ is an area of the production, distribution, or trade, and consumption of goods and services by different agents. Understood in its broadest sense, `The _____ is defined as a social domain that emphasize the practices, discourses, and material expressions associated with the production, use, and management of resources`. Economic agents can be individuals, businesses, organizations, or governments. Economic transactions occur when two parties agree to the value or price of the transacted good or service, commonly expressed in a certain currency. However, monetary transactions only account for a small part of the economic domain.

15. *Answer choices:*

(see index for correct answer)

- a. information systems assessment
- b. Economy
- c. corporate values
- d. functional perspective

Guidance: level 1

:: ::

A _____ is monetary compensation paid by an employer to an employee in exchange for work done. Payment may be calculated as a fixed amount for each task completed , or at an hourly or daily rate , or based on an easily measured quantity of work done.

16. *Answer choices:*

- a. Sarbanes-Oxley act of 2002
- b. levels of analysis
- c. Wage
- d. surface-level diversity

Guidance: level 1

:: ::

_____ is the administration of an organization, whether it is a business, a not-for-profit organization, or government body. _____ includes the activities of setting the strategy of an organization and coordinating the efforts of its employees to accomplish its objectives through the application of available resources, such as financial, natural, technological, and human resources. The term "_____" may also refer to those people who manage an organization.

Exam Probability: **Medium**

17. *Answer choices:*

- a. similarity-attraction theory
- b. Management
- c. corporate values
- d. interpersonal communication

Guidance: level 1

:: E-commerce ::

A _____ is a hosted service offering that acts as an intermediary between business partners sharing standards based or proprietary data via shared business processes. The offered service is referred to as "_____ services".

Exam Probability: **High**

18. *Answer choices:*

- a. IBill

- b. Switchwise
- c. Value-added network
- d. Travel website

:: Credit cards ::

A _____ is a payment card issued to users to enable the cardholder to pay a merchant for goods and services based on the cardholder's promise to the card issuer to pay them for the amounts plus the other agreed charges. The card issuer creates a revolving account and grants a line of credit to the cardholder, from which the cardholder can borrow money for payment to a merchant or as a cash advance.

Exam Probability: **Low**

19. *Answer choices:*
(see index for correct answer)

- a. Credit card
- b. CardLab
- c. NexG PrePaid
- d. Japan Credit Bureau

:: Project management ::

Contemporary business and science treat as a _____ any undertaking, carried out individually or collaboratively and possibly involving research or design, that is carefully planned to achieve a particular aim.

Exam Probability: **Medium**

20. *Answer choices:*
(see index for correct answer)

- a. Project Management South Africa
- b. Project
- c. Identifying and Managing Project Risk
- d. Virtual design and construction

_____ is a means of protection from financial loss. It is a form of risk management, primarily used to hedge against the risk of a contingent or uncertain loss

Exam Probability: **High**

21. *Answer choices:*
(see index for correct answer)

- a. similarity-attraction theory
- b. hierarchical perspective
- c. co-culture
- d. Insurance

Guidance: level 1

:: Theories ::

A _____ union is a type of multinational political union where negotiated power is delegated to an authority by governments of member states.

Exam Probability: **High**

22. *Answer choices:*
(see index for correct answer)

- a. Supranational
- b. incrementalism

Guidance: level 1

:: Commodities ::

In economics, a _____ is an economic good or service that has full or substantial fungibility: that is, the market treats instances of the good as equivalent or nearly so with no regard to who produced them. Most commodities are raw materials, basic resources, agricultural, or mining products, such as iron ore, sugar, or grains like rice and wheat. Commodities can also be mass-produced unspecialized products such as chemicals and computer memory.

23. *Answer choices:*

(see index for correct answer)

- a. Commoditization
- b. Commodity pathway diversion
- c. IRely
- d. Commodity money

Guidance: level 1

:: ::

_____ , in general use, is a devotion and faithfulness to a nation, cause, philosophy, country, group, or person. Philosophers disagree on what can be an object of _____ , as some argue that _____ is strictly interpersonal and only another human being can be the object of _____ . The definition of _____ in law and political science is the fidelity of an individual to a nation, either one's nation of birth, or one's declared home nation by oath .

24. *Answer choices:*

(see index for correct answer)

- a. personal values
- b. hierarchical perspective
- c. empathy
- d. Loyalty

Guidance: level 1

:: Decision theory ::

Within economics the concept of _____ is used to model worth or value, but its usage has evolved significantly over time. The term was introduced initially as a measure of pleasure or satisfaction within the theory of utilitarianism by moral philosophers such as Jeremy Bentham and John Stuart Mill. But the term has been adapted and reapplied within neoclassical economics, which dominates modern economic theory, as a _____ function that represents a consumer's preference ordering over a choice set. As such, it is devoid of its original interpretation as a measurement of the pleasure or satisfaction obtained by the consumer from that choice.

Exam Probability: **Medium**

25. *Answer choices:*
(see index for correct answer)

- a. Utility
- b. Omission bias
- c. Clarity test
- d. Decision-making software

Guidance: level 1

:: Payment systems ::

_____ s are part of a payment system issued by financial institutions, such as a bank, to a customer that enables its owner to access the funds in the customer's designated bank accounts, or through a credit account and make payments by electronic funds transfer and access automated teller machines . Such cards are known by a variety of names including bank cards, ATM cards, MAC , client cards, key cards or cash cards.

Exam Probability: **High**

26. *Answer choices:*
(see index for correct answer)

- a. FreshBooks
- b. Visa Buxx
- c. Payment card
- d. VocaLink

Guidance: level 1

Business Model Canvas is a strategic management and lean startup template for developing new or documenting existing business models. It is a visual chart with elements describing a firm's or product's value proposition, infrastructure, customers, and finances. It assists firms in aligning their activities by illustrating potential trade-offs.

Exam Probability: **Low**

27. *Answer choices:*
(see index for correct answer)

- a. Cost structure
- b. deep-level diversity
- c. cultural
- d. Sarbanes-Oxley act of 2002

Guidance: level 1

:: Marketing ::

A _____ is an overall experience of a customer that distinguishes an organization or product from its rivals in the eyes of the customer. _____ s are used in business, marketing, and advertising. Name _____ s are sometimes distinguished from generic or store _____ s.

Exam Probability: **Medium**

28. *Answer choices:*
(see index for correct answer)

- a. Brand
- b. Gatefold
- c. Branding national myths and symbols
- d. Prommercial

Guidance: level 1

:: Auctioneering ::

A _____ is one of several similar kinds of auctions. Most commonly, it means an auction in which the auctioneer begins with a high asking price, and lowers it until some participant accepts the price, or it reaches a predetermined reserve price. This has also been called a clock auction or open-outcry descending-price auction. This type of auction is good for auctioning goods quickly, since a sale never requires more than one bid. Strategically, it's similar to a first-price sealed-bid auction.

Exam Probability: **High**

29. *Answer choices:*
(see index for correct answer)

- a. AntiqueWeek
- b. Wine auction
- c. Forward auction
- d. How Much Wood Would a Woodchuck Chuck

Guidance: level 1

:: Production economics ::

In microeconomics, _____ are the cost advantages that enterprises obtain due to their scale of operation , with cost per unit of output decreasing with increasing scale.

Exam Probability: **Medium**

30. *Answer choices:*
(see index for correct answer)

- a. Productivity Alpha
- b. Post-Fordism
- c. Marginal rate of technical substitution
- d. Economies of scale

Guidance: level 1

:: Manufacturing ::

A _____ is a building for storing goods. _____ s are used by manufacturers, importers, exporters, wholesalers, transport businesses, customs, etc. They are usually large plain buildings in industrial parks on the outskirts of cities, towns or villages.

Exam Probability: **High**

31. *Answer choices:*
(see index for correct answer)

- a. Ppc cycle
- b. Flexible manufacturing system
- c. Warehouse
- d. Glass production

Guidance: level 1

:: Industry ::

_____ describes various measures of the efficiency of production. Often , a _____ measure is expressed as the ratio of an aggregate output to a single input or an aggregate input used in a production process, i.e. output per unit of input. Most common example is the labour _____ measure, e.g., such as GDP per worker. There are many different definitions of _____ and the choice among them depends on the purpose of the _____ measurement and/or data availability. The key source of difference between various _____ measures is also usually related to how the outputs and the inputs are aggregated into scalars to obtain such a ratio-type measure of

_____ .

Exam Probability: **Low**

32. *Answer choices:*
(see index for correct answer)

- a. Unexpected events
- b. Industrial safety system
- c. Recommended exposure limit
- d. Productivity

Guidance: level 1

:: Marketing ::

_____ is the percentage of a market accounted for by a specific entity. In a survey of nearly 200 senior marketing managers, 67% responded that they found the revenue- "dollar _____" metric very useful, while 61% found "unit _____" very useful.

Exam Probability: **Low**

33. *Answer choices:*
(see index for correct answer)

- a. Corporate capabilities package
- b. Disruptive innovation
- c. Porter hypothesis
- d. Market share

Guidance: level 1

:: ::

_____ s is the linguistic and philosophical study of meaning, in language, programming languages, formal logics, and semiotics. It is concerned with the relationship between signifiers—like words, phrases, signs, and symbols—and what they stand for in reality, their denotation.

Exam Probability: **Medium**

34. *Answer choices:*
(see index for correct answer)

- a. Semantic
- b. empathy
- c. information systems assessment
- d. deep-level diversity

Guidance: level 1

:: Economic globalization ::

_____ is an agreement in which one company hires another company to be responsible for a planned or existing activity that is or could be done internally,and sometimes involves transferring employees and assets from one firm to another.

35. *Answer choices:*
(see index for correct answer)

- a. reshoring
- b. Outsourcing

Guidance: level 1

:: ::

In economics _____ is a theoretical concept where all markets are in equilibrium, and all prices and quantities have fully adjusted and are in equilibrium. The _____ contrasts with the short run where there are some constraints and markets are not fully in equilibrium.

Exam Probability: **Medium**

36. *Answer choices:*
(see index for correct answer)

- a. personal values
- b. corporate values
- c. deep-level diversity
- d. Long run

Guidance: level 1

:: Income ::

_____ is the application of disciplined analytics that predict consumer behaviour at the micro-market levels and optimize product availability and price to maximize revenue growth. The primary aim of _____ is selling the right product to the right customer at the right time for the right price and with the right pack. The essence of this discipline is in understanding customers' perception of product value and accurately aligning product prices, placement and availability with each customer segment.

Exam Probability: **High**

37. *Answer choices:*
(see index for correct answer)

- a. Net national income

- b. Real income
- c. Passive income
- d. Revenue management

Guidance: level 1

:: Consumer theory ::

A _____ is a technical term in psychology, economics and philosophy usually used in relation to choosing between alternatives. For example, someone prefers A over B if they would rather choose A than B.

Exam Probability: **Low**

38. *Answer choices:*
(see index for correct answer)

- a. End-of-life
- b. Preference
- c. Marginal rate of substitution
- d. Permanent income hypothesis

Guidance: level 1

:: Scientific method ::

In the social sciences and life sciences, a _____ is a research method involving an up-close, in-depth, and detailed examination of a subject of study , as well as its related contextual conditions.

Exam Probability: **High**

39. *Answer choices:*
(see index for correct answer)

- a. pilot project
- b. explanatory research
- c. Preference test
- d. Case study

Guidance: level 1

:: ::

_____ is the study and management of exchange relationships. _____ is the business process of creating relationships with and satisfying customers. With its focus on the customer, _____ is one of the premier components of business management.

Exam Probability: **Medium**

40. *Answer choices:*

(see index for correct answer)

- a. deep-level diversity
- b. hierarchical perspective
- c. cultural
- d. Marketing

Guidance: level 1

:: Supply chain management ::

A _____ is a type of auction in which the traditional roles of buyer and seller are reversed. Thus, there is one buyer and many potential sellers. In an ordinary auction , buyers compete to obtain goods or services by offering increasingly higher prices. In contrast, in a _____ , the sellers compete to obtain business from the buyer and prices will typically decrease as the sellers underbid each other.

Exam Probability: **High**

41. *Answer choices:*

(see index for correct answer)

- a. Reverse auction
- b. Calculating demand forecast accuracy
- c. Enterprise resource planning
- d. Supply chain management software

Guidance: level 1

:: ::

An _____ is the production of goods or related services within an economy. The major source of revenue of a group or company is the indicator of its relevant _____ . When a large group has multiple sources of revenue generation, it is considered to be working in different industries. Manufacturing _____ became a key sector of production and labour in European and North American countries during the Industrial Revolution, upsetting previous mercantile and feudal economies. This came through many successive rapid advances in technology, such as the production of steel and coal.

Exam Probability: **Medium**

42. *Answer choices:*
(see index for correct answer)

- a. similarity-attraction theory
- b. Industry
- c. hierarchical
- d. cultural

Guidance: level 1

:: Strategic alliances ::

A _____ is an agreement between two or more parties to pursue a set of agreed upon objectives needed while remaining independent organizations. A _____ will usually fall short of a legal partnership entity, agency, or corporate affiliate relationship. Typically, two companies form a _____ when each possesses one or more business assets or have expertise that will help the other by enhancing their businesses. _____ s can develop in outsourcing relationships where the parties desire to achieve long-term win-win benefits and innovation based on mutually desired outcomes.

Exam Probability: **Medium**

43. *Answer choices:*
(see index for correct answer)

- a. Strategic alliance
- b. Management contract
- c. International joint venture
- d. Bridge Alliance

Guidance: level 1

:: Auctioneering ::

A _____ is a type of sealed-bid auction. Bidders submit written bids without knowing the bid of the other people in the auction. The highest bidder wins but the price paid is the second-highest bid. This type of auction is strategically similar to an English auction and gives bidders an incentive to bid their true value. The auction was first described academically by Columbia University professor William Vickrey in 1961 though it had been used by stamp collectors since 1893. In 1797 Johann Wolfgang von Goethe sold a manuscript using a sealed-bid, second-price auction.

Exam Probability: **High**

44. *Answer choices:*
(see index for correct answer)

- a. Art auction
- b. Auction sniping
- c. Online travel auction
- d. Vickrey auction

Guidance: level 1

:: Management ::

In business, a _____ is the attribute that allows an organization to outperform its competitors. A _____ may include access to natural resources, such as high-grade ores or a low-cost power source, highly skilled labor, geographic location, high entry barriers, and access to new technology.

Exam Probability: **Medium**

45. *Answer choices:*
(see index for correct answer)

- a. Performance indicator
- b. Systems analysis
- c. Vendor relationship management
- d. Sales outsourcing

Guidance: level 1

:: Investment ::

In finance, the benefit from an _____ is called a return. The return may consist of a gain realised from the sale of property or an _____ , unrealised capital appreciation , or _____ income such as dividends, interest, rental income etc., or a combination of capital gain and income. The return may also include currency gains or losses due to changes in foreign currency exchange rates.

Exam Probability: **Medium**

46. *Answer choices:*
(see index for correct answer)

- a. Acertus Market Sentiment Indicator
- b. Buy and hold
- c. Investors United
- d. Certificate in Investment Performance Measurement

Guidance: level 1

:: Evaluation ::

_____ is a way of preventing mistakes and defects in manufactured products and avoiding problems when delivering products or services to customers; which ISO 9000 defines as "part of quality management focused on providing confidence that quality requirements will be fulfilled". This defect prevention in _____ differs subtly from defect detection and rejection in quality control and has been referred to as a shift left since it focuses on quality earlier in the process .

Exam Probability: **High**

47. *Answer choices:*
(see index for correct answer)

- a. Evaluation Assurance Level
- b. Commercial Product Assurance
- c. Defence Evaluation and Research Agency
- d. Quality assurance

Guidance: level 1

:: Business models ::

A _____ is "an autonomous association of persons united voluntarily to meet their common economic, social, and cultural needs and aspirations through a jointly-owned and democratically-controlled enterprise". _____ s may include.

Exam Probability: **Low**

48. *Answer choices:*

(see index for correct answer)

- a. Business Model Canvas
- b. Utility computing
- c. Cooperative
- d. Premium business model

Guidance: level 1

:: ::

The Walt _____ Company, commonly known as Walt _____ or simply _____ , is an American diversified multinational mass media and entertainment conglomerate headquartered at the Walt _____ Studios in Burbank, California.

Exam Probability: **Medium**

49. *Answer choices:*

(see index for correct answer)

- a. interpersonal communication
- b. levels of analysis
- c. open system
- d. Sarbanes-Oxley act of 2002

Guidance: level 1

:: Management accounting ::

_____ s are costs that change as the quantity of the good or service that a business produces changes. _____ s are the sum of marginal costs over all units produced. They can also be considered normal costs. Fixed costs and _____ s make up the two components of total cost. Direct costs are costs that can easily be associated with a particular cost object. However, not all _____ s are direct costs. For example, variable manufacturing overhead costs are _____ s that are indirect costs, not direct costs. _____ s are sometimes called unit-level costs as they vary with the number of units produced.

Exam Probability: **Low**

50. *Answer choices:*
(see index for correct answer)

- a. Cash and cash equivalents
- b. Variable cost
- c. Profit center
- d. Certified Management Accountants of Canada

Guidance: level 1

:: ::

A _____ is a professional who provides expert advice in a particular area such as security , management, education, accountancy, law, human resources, marketing , finance, engineering, science or any of many other specialized fields.

Exam Probability: **High**

51. *Answer choices:*
(see index for correct answer)

- a. deep-level diversity
- b. Consultant
- c. imperative
- d. information systems assessment

Guidance: level 1

:: Business law ::

A _____ is an arrangement where parties, known as partners, agree to cooperate to advance their mutual interests. The partners in a _____ may be individuals, businesses, interest-based organizations, schools, governments or combinations. Organizations may partner to increase the likelihood of each achieving their mission and to amplify their reach. A _____ may result in issuing and holding equity or may be only governed by a contract.

Exam Probability: **High**

52. *Answer choices:*
(see index for correct answer)

- a. Sole proprietorship
- b. Partnership
- c. Vehicle leasing
- d. Independent contractor

Guidance: level 1

:: Costs ::

In economics, _____ is the total economic cost of production and is made up of variable cost, which varies according to the quantity of a good produced and includes inputs such as labour and raw materials, plus fixed cost, which is independent of the quantity of a good produced and includes inputs that cannot be varied in the short term: fixed costs such as buildings and machinery, including sunk costs if any. Since cost is measured per unit of time, it is a flow variable.

Exam Probability: **High**

53. *Answer choices:*
(see index for correct answer)

- a. Opportunity cost
- b. Total cost
- c. Average cost
- d. Cost per paper

Guidance: level 1

:: Management ::

_____ is a process by which entities review the quality of all factors involved in production. ISO 9000 defines _____ as "A part of quality management focused on fulfilling quality requirements".

Exam Probability: **Low**

54. *Answer choices:*

- a. Goal
- b. Risk appetite
- c. Mobile sales enablement
- d. Tacit knowledge

Guidance: level 1

:: ::

_____ is a concept of English common law and is a necessity for simple contracts but not for special contracts . The concept has been adopted by other common law jurisdictions, including the US.

Exam Probability: **Medium**

55. *Answer choices:*

- a. imperative
- b. functional perspective
- c. co-culture
- d. Consideration

Guidance: level 1

:: ::

_____ is an American restaurant chain and international franchise which was founded in 1958 by Dan and Frank Carney. The company is known for its Italian-American cuisine menu, including pizza and pasta, as well as side dishes and desserts. _____ has 18,431 restaurants worldwide as of December 31, 2018, making it the world's largest pizza chain in terms of locations. It is a subsidiary of Yum! Brands, Inc., one of the world's largest restaurant companies.

56. *Answer choices:*
(see index for correct answer)

- a. Pizza Hut
- b. Sarbanes-Oxley act of 2002
- c. imperative
- d. surface-level diversity

Guidance: level 1

:: Basic financial concepts ::

_____ is a sustained increase in the general price level of goods and services in an economy over a period of time. When the general price level rises, each unit of currency buys fewer goods and services; consequently, _____ reflects a reduction in the purchasing power per unit of money a loss of real value in the medium of exchange and unit of account within the economy. The measure of _____ is the _____ rate, the annualized percentage change in a general price index, usually the consumer price index, over time. The opposite of _____ is deflation.

57. *Answer choices:*
(see index for correct answer)

- a. Leverage cycle
- b. Eurodollar
- c. Inflation
- d. Forward guidance

Guidance: level 1

:: Auctioneering ::

Unlike sealed-bid auctions , an _____ is "open" or fully transparent, as the identity of all bidders is disclosed to each other during the auction. More generally, an auction mechanism is considered "English" if it involves an iterative process of adjusting the price in a direction that is unfavorable to the bidders . In contrast, a Dutch auction would adjust the price in a direction that favored the bidders .

Exam Probability: **High**

58. *Answer choices:*
(see index for correct answer)

- a. Auction sniping
- b. English auction
- c. Virginity auction
- d. Online trading community

Guidance: level 1

:: Information technology ::

_____ is the use of computers to store, retrieve, transmit, and manipulate data, or information, often in the context of a business or other enterprise. IT is considered to be a subset of information and communications technology . An _____ system is generally an information system, a communications system or, more specifically speaking, a computer system – including all hardware, software and peripheral equipment – operated by a limited group of users.

Exam Probability: **Low**

59. *Answer choices:*
(see index for correct answer)

- a. E-Governance
- b. Geeks Without Bounds
- c. Information revolution
- d. Information technology

Guidance: level 1

Business ethics

Business ethics (also known as corporate ethics) is a form of applied ethics or professional ethics, that examines ethical principles and moral or ethical problems that can arise in a business environment. It applies to all aspects of business conduct and is relevant to the conduct of individuals and entire organizations. These ethics originate from individuals, organizational statements or from the legal system. These norms, values, ethical, and unethical practices are what is used to guide business. They help those businesses maintain a better connection with their stakeholders.

:: ::

The _____ is an institution of the European Union, responsible for proposing legislation, implementing decisions, upholding the EU treaties and managing the day-to-day business of the EU. Commissioners swear an oath at the European Court of Justice in Luxembourg City, pledging to respect the treaties and to be completely independent in carrying out their duties during their mandate. Unlike in the Council of the European Union, where members are directly and indirectly elected, and the European Parliament, where members are directly elected, the Commissioners are proposed by the Council of the European Union, on the basis of suggestions made by the national governments, and then appointed by the European Council after the approval of the European Parliament.

Exam Probability: **Low**

1. *Answer choices:*
(see index for correct answer)

- a. process perspective
- b. information systems assessment
- c. European Commission
- d. Sarbanes-Oxley act of 2002

Guidance: level 1

MCI, Inc. was an American telecommunication corporation, currently a subsidiary of Verizon Communications, with its main office in Ashburn, Virginia. The corporation was formed originally as a result of the merger of _____ and MCI Communications corporations, and used the name MCI _____ , succeeded by _____ , before changing its name to the present version on April 12, 2003, as part of the corporation's ending of its bankruptcy status. The company traded on NASDAQ as WCOM and MCIP . The corporation was purchased by Verizon Communications with the deal finalizing on January 6, 2006, and is now identified as that company's Verizon Enterprise Solutions division with the local residential divisions being integrated slowly into local Verizon subsidiaries.

Exam Probability: **Medium**

2. *Answer choices:*
(see index for correct answer)

- a. process perspective
- b. hierarchical perspective
- c. open system
- d. WorldCom

Guidance: level 1

The ABA _____ , created by the American Bar Association , are a set of rules that prescribe baseline standards of legal ethics and professional responsibility for lawyers in the United States. They were promulgated by the ABA House of Delegates upon the recommendation of the Kutak Commission in 1983. The rules are merely recommendations, or models, and are not themselves binding. However, having a common set of Model Rules facilitates a common discourse on legal ethics, and simplifies professional responsibility training as well as the day-to-day application of such rules. As of 2015, 49 states and four territories have adopted the rules in whole or in part, of which the most recent to do so was the Commonwealth of the Northern Mariana Islands in March 2015. California is the only state that has not adopted the ABA Model Rules, while Puerto Rico is the only U.S. jurisdiction outside of confederation has not adopted them but instead has its own Código de Ética Profesional.

Exam Probability: **Medium**

3. *Answer choices:*
(see index for correct answer)

- a. judgment notwithstanding the verdict
- b. Model Rules of Professional Conduct

Guidance: level 1

:: United States federal defense and national security legislation ::

The USA _____ is an Act of the U.S. Congress that was signed into law by President George W. Bush on October 26, 2001. The title of the Act is a contrived three letter initialism preceding a seven letter acronym , which in combination stand for Uniting and Strengthening America by Providing Appropriate Tools Required to Intercept and Obstruct Terrorism Act of 2001. The acronym was created by a 23 year old Congressional staffer, Chris Kyle.

Exam Probability: **Low**

4. *Answer choices:*
(see index for correct answer)

- a. USA PATRIOT Act
- b. Patriot Act

Guidance: level 1

_____ is an ethical framework and suggests that an entity, be it an organization or individual, has an obligation to act for the benefit of society at large. _____ is a duty every individual has to perform so as to maintain a balance between the economy and the ecosystems. A trade-off may exist between economic development, in the material sense, and the welfare of the society and environment, though this has been challenged by many reports over the past decade. _____ means sustaining the equilibrium between the two. It pertains not only to business organizations but also to everyone whose any action impacts the environment. This responsibility can be passive, by avoiding engaging in socially harmful acts, or active, by performing activities that directly advance social goals. _____ must be intergenerational since the actions of one generation have consequences on those following.

Exam Probability: **Low**

5. *Answer choices:*
(see index for correct answer)

- a. Minnie Cumnock Blodgett
- b. Home economics
- c. Family and consumer science
- d. Social responsibility

Guidance: level 1

The Ethics & Compliance Initiative was formed in 2015 and consists of three nonprofit organizations: the Ethics Research Center, the Ethics & Compliance Association, and the Ethics & Compliance Certification Institute. Based in Arlington, Virginia, United States, ECI is devoted to the advancement of high ethical standards and practices in public and private institutions, and provides research about ethical standards, workplace integrity, and compliance practices and processes.

Exam Probability: **High**

6. *Answer choices:*
(see index for correct answer)

- a. similarity-attraction theory

- b. Ethics Resource Center
- c. co-culture
- d. interpersonal communication

Guidance: level 1

:: Supply chain management terms ::

In business and finance, _____ is a system of organizations, people, activities, information, and resources involved inmoving a product or service from supplier to customer. _____ activities involve the transformation of natural resources, raw materials, and components into a finished product that is delivered to the end customer. In sophisticated _____ systems, used products may re-enter the _____ at any point where residual value is recyclable. _____ s link value chains.

Exam Probability: **High**

7. *Answer choices:*
(see index for correct answer)

- a. inventory management
- b. Stockout
- c. Work in process
- d. Widget

Guidance: level 1

:: ::

A _____ is a set of rules, often written, with regards to clothing. _____ s are created out of social perceptions and norms, and vary based on purpose, circumstances and occasions. Different societies and cultures are likely to have different _____ s.

Exam Probability: **Low**

8. *Answer choices:*
(see index for correct answer)

- a. levels of analysis
- b. imperative
- c. Dress code
- d. cultural

:: Anti-Revisionism ::

_____ , officially the German Democratic Republic , was a country that existed from 1949 to 1990, when the eastern portion of Germany was part of the Eastern Bloc during the Cold War. It described itself as a socialist "workers` and peasants` state", and the territory was administered and occupied by Soviet forces at the end of World War II — the Soviet Occupation Zone of the Potsdam Agreement, bounded on the east by the Oder–Neisse line. The Soviet zone surrounded West Berlin but did not include it; as a result, West Berlin remained outside the jurisdiction of the GDR.

Exam Probability: **Medium**

9. *Answer choices:*
(see index for correct answer)

- a. East Germany
- b. Anti-Revisionism
- c. Party of Labour of Albania
- d. Hoxhaism

:: Coal ::

_____ is a combustible black or brownish-black sedimentary rock, formed as rock strata called _____ seams. _____ is mostly carbon with variable amounts of other elements; chiefly hydrogen, sulfur, oxygen, and nitrogen. _____ is formed if dead plant matter decays into peat and over millions of years the heat and pressure of deep burial converts the peat into _____ . Vast deposits of _____ originates in former wetlands—called _____ forests—that covered much of the Earth`s tropical land areas during the late Carboniferous and Permian times.

Exam Probability: **Low**

10. *Answer choices:*
(see index for correct answer)

- a. Coal
- b. Coal shovel

- c. Azienda Nazionale Idrogenazione Combustibili
- d. Sub-bituminous coal

Guidance: level 1

:: Offshoring ::

A _____ is the temporary suspension or permanent termination of employment of an employee or, more commonly, a group of employees for business reasons, such as personnel management or downsizing an organization. Originally, _____ referred exclusively to a temporary interruption in work, or employment but this has evolved to a permanent elimination of a position in both British and US English, requiring the addition of "temporary" to specify the original meaning of the word. A _____ is not to be confused with wrongful termination. Laid off workers or displaced workers are workers who have lost or left their jobs because their employer has closed or moved, there was insufficient work for them to do, or their position or shift was abolished . Downsizing in a company is defined to involve the reduction of employees in a workforce. Downsizing in companies became a popular practice in the 1980s and early 1990s as it was seen as a way to deliver better shareholder value as it helps to reduce the costs of employers . Indeed, recent research on downsizing in the U.S., UK, and Japan suggests that downsizing is being regarded by management as one of the preferred routes to help declining organizations, cutting unnecessary costs, and improve organizational performance. Usually a _____ occurs as a cost cutting measure.

Exam Probability: **Medium**

11. *Answer choices:*
(see index for correct answer)

- a. Offshoring Research Network
- b. Antex
- c. Layoff
- d. Advanced Contact Solutions

Guidance: level 1

:: Management ::

_____ is the identification, evaluation, and prioritization of risks followed by coordinated and economical application of resources to minimize, monitor, and control the probability or impact of unfortunate events or to maximize the realization of opportunities.

Exam Probability: **High**

12. *Answer choices:*
(see index for correct answer)

- a. Swarm Development Group
- b. Director
- c. Risk management
- d. Strategic management

Guidance: level 1

:: Employment compensation ::

A _____ is the minimum income necessary for a worker to meet their basic needs. Needs are defined to include food, housing, and other essential needs such as clothing. The goal of a _____ is to allow a worker to afford a basic but decent standard of living. Due to the flexible nature of the term "needs", there is not one universally accepted measure of what a _____ is and as such it varies by location and household type.

Exam Probability: **Medium**

13. *Answer choices:*
(see index for correct answer)

- a. Gender pay gap
- b. Living wage
- c. Sick leave
- d. Take-home vehicle

Guidance: level 1

:: Business ethics ::

_____ is an area of applied ethics which deals with the moral principles behind the operation and regulation of marketing. Some areas of _____ overlap with media ethics.

Exam Probability: **Low**

14. *Answer choices:*
(see index for correct answer)

- a. Business Ethics Quarterly
- b. Evolution of corporate social responsibility in India
- c. Sustainability Accounting Standards Board
- d. Ethical corporate social responsibility

Guidance: level 1

:: Business ethics ::

_____ is a persistent pattern of mistreatment from others in the workplace that causes either physical or emotional harm. It can include such tactics as verbal, nonverbal, psychological, physical abuse and humiliation. This type of workplace aggression is particularly difficult because, unlike the typical school bully, workplace bullies often operate within the established rules and policies of their organization and their society. In the majority of cases, bullying in the workplace is reported as having been by someone who has authority over their victim. However, bullies can also be peers, and occasionally subordinates. Research has also investigated the impact of the larger organizational context on bullying as well as the group-level processes that impact on the incidence and maintenance of bullying behaviour. Bullying can be covert or overt. It may be missed by superiors; it may be known by many throughout the organization. Negative effects are not limited to the targeted individuals, and may lead to a decline in employee morale and a change in organizational culture. It can also take place as overbearing supervision, constant criticism, and blocking promotions.

Exam Probability: **Low**

15. *Answer choices:*
(see index for correct answer)

- a. Society for Business Ethics
- b. Workplace bullying
- c. Price discrimination

- d. Accounting ethics

Guidance: level 1

:: ::

In ecology, a _____ is the type of natural environment in which a particular species of organism lives. It is characterized by both physical and biological features. A species' _____ is those places where it can find food, shelter, protection and mates for reproduction.

Exam Probability: **Low**

16. *Answer choices:*
(see index for correct answer)

- a. process perspective
- b. hierarchical
- c. empathy
- d. cultural

Guidance: level 1

:: Private equity ::

In finance, a high-yield bond is a bond that is rated below investment grade. These bonds have a higher risk of default or other adverse credit events, but typically pay higher yields than better quality bonds in order to make them attractive to investors.

Exam Probability: **Low**

17. *Answer choices:*
(see index for correct answer)

- a. IDFC Project Equity
- b. Pledge fund
- c. Junk bond
- d. Business Development Company

Guidance: level 1

:: Commercial crimes ::

_____ is an agreement between participants on the same side in a market to buy or sell a product, service, or commodity only at a fixed price, or maintain the market conditions such that the price is maintained at a given level by controlling supply and demand.

Exam Probability: **High**

18. *Answer choices:*
(see index for correct answer)

- a. Copyfraud
- b. pilferage
- c. Price fixing
- d. Wage theft

Guidance: level 1

:: White-collar criminals ::

_____ refers to financially motivated, nonviolent crime committed by businesses and government professionals. It was first defined by the sociologist Edwin Sutherland in 1939 as "a crime committed by a person of respectability and high social status in the course of their occupation". Typical _____ s could include wage theft, fraud, bribery, Ponzi schemes, insider trading, labor racketeering, embezzlement, cybercrime, copyright infringement, money laundering, identity theft, and forgery. Lawyers can specialize in _____ .

Exam Probability: **Low**

19. *Answer choices:*
(see index for correct answer)

- a. White-collar crime
- b. Tongsun Park

Guidance: level 1

:: United States federal trade legislation ::

The _____ of 1914 established the Federal Trade Commission. The Act, signed into law by Woodrow Wilson in 1914, outlaws unfair methods of competition and outlaws unfair acts or practices that affect commerce.

Exam Probability: **High**

20. *Answer choices:*
(see index for correct answer)

- a. Federal Trade Commission Act
- b. Act to Protect the Commerce of the United States and Punish the Crime of Piracy
- c. Trade Expansion Act
- d. Cargo Preference Act

Guidance: level 1

:: ::

_____ is "property consisting of land and the buildings on it, along with its natural resources such as crops, minerals or water; immovable property of this nature; an interest vested in this an item of real property, buildings or housing in general. Also: the business of _____ ; the profession of buying, selling, or renting land, buildings, or housing." It is a legal term used in jurisdictions whose legal system is derived from English common law, such as India, England, Wales, Northern Ireland, United States, Canada, Pakistan, Australia, and New Zealand.

Exam Probability: **High**

21. *Answer choices:*
(see index for correct answer)

- a. personal values
- b. Real estate
- c. corporate values
- d. hierarchical

Guidance: level 1

:: Patent law ::

A _____ is generally any statement intended to specify or delimit the scope of rights and obligations that may be exercised and enforced by parties in a legally recognized relationship. In contrast to other terms for legally operative language, the term _____ usually implies situations that involve some level of uncertainty, waiver, or risk.

Exam Probability: **Medium**

22. *Answer choices:*
(see index for correct answer)

- a. Patent family
- b. Disclaimer
- c. Research exemption
- d. Divisional patent application

Guidance: level 1

:: ::

The _____ Group is a global financial investment management and insurance company headquartered in Des Moines, Iowa.

Exam Probability: **Low**

23. *Answer choices:*
(see index for correct answer)

- a. hierarchical perspective
- b. process perspective
- c. similarity-attraction theory
- d. Principal Financial

Guidance: level 1

:: United States federal labor legislation ::

The _____ of 1988 is a United States federal law that generally prevents employers from using polygraph tests, either for pre-employment screening or during the course of employment, with certain exemptions.

Exam Probability: **Medium**

24. *Answer choices:*

(see index for correct answer)

- a. Employee Polygraph Protection Act
- b. Adamson Act
- c. National Whistleblowers Center
- d. Uniformed Services Employment and Reemployment Rights Act

Guidance: level 1

:: Corporate scandals ::

_____ was a bank based in the Caribbean, which operated from 1986 to 2009 when it went into receivership. It was an affiliate of the Stanford Financial Group and failed when the its parent was seized by United States authorities in early 2009 as part of the investigation into Allen Stanford.

Exam Probability: **Low**

25. *Answer choices:*

(see index for correct answer)

- a. Stanford Financial Group
- b. Polly Peck
- c. ExtenZe
- d. Stanford International Bank

Guidance: level 1

:: Globalization-related theories ::

_____ is an economic system based on the private ownership of the means of production and their operation for profit. Characteristics central to _____ include private property, capital accumulation, wage labor, voluntary exchange, a price system, and competitive markets. In a capitalist market economy, decision-making and investment are determined by every owner of wealth, property or production ability in financial and capital markets, whereas prices and the distribution of goods and services are mainly determined by competition in goods and services markets.

Exam Probability: **Low**

26. *Answer choices:*

(see index for correct answer)

- a. Economic Development
- b. postmodernism
- c. Capitalism

Guidance: level 1

:: Product certification ::

_____ is food produced by methods that comply with the standards of organic farming. Standards vary worldwide, but organic farming features practices that cycle resources, promote ecological balance, and conserve biodiversity. Organizations regulating organic products may restrict the use of certain pesticides and fertilizers in the farming methods used to produce such products. _____ s typically are not processed using irradiation, industrial solvents, or synthetic food additives.

Exam Probability: **Low**

27. *Answer choices:*
(see index for correct answer)

- a. Organic Food Development Center
- b. Organic certification
- c. Organic food
- d. TCO Certification

Guidance: level 1

:: ::

The _____ of 1977 is a United States federal law known primarily for two of its main provisions: one that addresses accounting transparency requirements under the Securities Exchange Act of 1934 and another concerning bribery of foreign officials. The Act was amended in 1988 and in 1998, and has been subject to continued congressional concerns, namely whether its enforcement discourages U.S. companies from investing abroad.

Exam Probability: **Low**

28. *Answer choices:*
(see index for correct answer)

- a. Sarbanes-Oxley act of 2002
- b. hierarchical

- c. co-culture
- d. Foreign Corrupt Practices Act

Guidance: level 1

:: Timber industry ::

The _____ is an international non-profit, multi-stakeholder organization established in 1993 to promote responsible management of the world's forests. The FSC does this by setting standards on forest products, along with certifying and labeling them as eco-friendly.

Exam Probability: **Low**

29. *Answer choices:*
(see index for correct answer)

- a. Brettstapel
- b. Greenheart Group
- c. Naval stores
- d. Resistograph

Guidance: level 1

:: Financial regulatory authorities of the United States ::

The _____ is an agency of the United States government responsible for consumer protection in the financial sector. CFPB's jurisdiction includes banks, credit unions, securities firms, payday lenders, mortgage-servicing operations, foreclosure relief services, debt collectors and other financial companies operating in the United States.

Exam Probability: **Low**

30. *Answer choices:*
(see index for correct answer)

- a. Office of Thrift Supervision
- b. Federal Reserve Board
- c. Municipal Securities Rulemaking Board
- d. Federal Deposit Insurance Corporation

Guidance: level 1

:: Management ::

The term _____ refers to measures designed to increase the degree of autonomy and self-determination in people and in communities in order to enable them to represent their interests in a responsible and self-determined way, acting on their own authority. It is the process of becoming stronger and more confident, especially in controlling one's life and claiming one's rights. _____ as action refers both to the process of self- _____ and to professional support of people, which enables them to overcome their sense of powerlessness and lack of influence, and to recognize and use their resources. To do work with power.

Exam Probability: **Medium**

31. *Answer choices:*
(see index for correct answer)

- a. Project team builder
- b. Mushroom management
- c. Empowerment
- d. Situational crisis communication theory

Guidance: level 1

:: United Kingdom labour law ::

The _____ was a series of programs, public work projects, financial reforms, and regulations enacted by President Franklin D. Roosevelt in the United States between 1933 and 1936. It responded to needs for relief, reform, and recovery from the Great Depression. Major federal programs included the Civilian Conservation Corps , the Civil Works Administration , the Farm Security Administration , the National Industrial Recovery Act of 1933 and the Social Security Administration . They provided support for farmers, the unemployed, youth and the elderly. The _____ included new constraints and safeguards on the banking industry and efforts to re-inflate the economy after prices had fallen sharply. _____ programs included both laws passed by Congress as well as presidential executive orders during the first term of the presidency of Franklin D. Roosevelt.

Exam Probability: **Medium**

32. *Answer choices:*
(see index for correct answer)

- a. Working Time Regulations 1998
- b. New Deal
- c. Police Act 1919
- d. Legal abstentionism

Guidance: level 1

:: ::

A _____ is an organization, usually a group of people or a company, authorized to act as a single entity and recognized as such in law. Early incorporated entities were established by charter. Most jurisdictions now allow the creation of new _____ s through registration.

Exam Probability: **Low**

33. *Answer choices:*
(see index for correct answer)

- a. cultural
- b. open system
- c. Corporation
- d. information systems assessment

Guidance: level 1

:: Public relations terminology ::

_____ , also called "green sheen", is a form of spin in which green PR or green marketing is deceptively used to promote the perception that an organization's products, aims or policies are environmentally friendly. Evidence that an organization is _____ often comes from pointing out the spending differences: when significantly more money or time has been spent advertising being "green", than is actually spent on environmentally sound practices. _____ efforts can range from changing the name or label of a product to evoke the natural environment on a product that contains harmful chemicals to multimillion-dollar marketing campaigns portraying highly polluting energy companies as eco-friendly.Publicized accusations of _____ have contributed to the term's increasing use.

Exam Probability: **High**

34. *Answer choices:*

(see index for correct answer)

- a. Photo op
- b. Crisis communication
- c. Greenwashing
- d. Green PR

Guidance: level 1

:: Renewable energy ::

A _____ is a fuel that is produced through contemporary biological processes, such as agriculture and anaerobic digestion, rather than a fuel produced by geological processes such as those involved in the formation of fossil fuels, such as coal and petroleum, from prehistoric biological matter. If the source biomatter can regrow quickly, the resulting fuel is said to be a form of renewable energy.

Exam Probability: **High**

35. *Answer choices:*

(see index for correct answer)

- a. Biofuel
- b. Renewable energy debate
- c. Biomass Energy Centre
- d. Tidal power

Guidance: level 1

:: Natural gas ::

_____ is a naturally occurring hydrocarbon gas mixture consisting primarily of methane, but commonly including varying amounts of other higher alkanes, and sometimes a small percentage of carbon dioxide, nitrogen, hydrogen sulfide, or helium. It is formed when layers of decomposing plant and animal matter are exposed to intense heat and pressure under the surface of the Earth over millions of years. The energy that the plants originally obtained from the sun is stored in the form of chemical bonds in the gas.

Exam Probability: **Medium**

36. *Answer choices:*
(see index for correct answer)

- a. Eurogas
- b. Moisture analysis
- c. Natural gas
- d. Liquefied natural gas

Guidance: level 1

:: ::

The Catholic Church, also known as the Roman Catholic Church, is the largest Christian church, with approximately 1.3 billion baptised Catholics worldwide as of 2017. As the world's oldest continuously functioning international institution, it has played a prominent role in the history and development of Western civilisation. The church is headed by the Bishop of Rome, known as the pope. Its central administration, the Holy See, is in the Vatican City, an enclave within the city of Rome in Italy.

Exam Probability: **High**

37. *Answer choices:*
(see index for correct answer)

- a. personal values
- b. process perspective
- c. Catholicism
- d. Sarbanes-Oxley act of 2002

Guidance: level 1

:: Corporations law ::

A normal _____ consists of various departments that contribute to the company's overall mission and goals. Common departments include Marketing, [Finance, [[Operations managementOperations, Human Resource, and IT. These five divisions represent the major departments within a publicly traded company, though there are often smaller departments within autonomous firms. There is typically a CEO, and Board of Directors composed of the directors of each department. There are also company presidents, vice presidents, and CFOs. There is a great diversity in corporate forms as enterprises may range from single company to multi-corporate conglomerate. The four main _____ s are Functional, Divisional, Geographic, and the Matrix. Realistically, most corporations tend to have a "hybrid" structure, which is a combination of different models with one dominant strategy.

Exam Probability: **Medium**

38. *Answer choices:*
(see index for correct answer)

- a. Articles of association
- b. Corporate law
- c. Corporate structure
- d. Benihana of Tokyo, Inc. v. Benihana, Inc.

Guidance: level 1

:: ::

_____ is the introduction of contaminants into the natural environment that cause adverse change. _____ can take the form of chemical substances or energy, such as noise, heat or light. Pollutants, the components of _____ , can be either foreign substances/energies or naturally occurring contaminants. _____ is often classed as point source or nonpoint source _____ .In 2015, _____ killed 9 million people in the world.

Exam Probability: **High**

39. *Answer choices:*
(see index for correct answer)

- a. imperative
- b. similarity-attraction theory
- c. Pollution
- d. corporate values

:: Advertising techniques ::

The _____ is a story from the Trojan War about the subterfuge that the Greeks used to enter the independent city of Troy and win the war. In the canonical version, after a fruitless 10-year siege, the Greeks constructed a huge wooden horse, and hid a select force of men inside including Odysseus. The Greeks pretended to sail away, and the Trojans pulled the horse into their city as a victory trophy. That night the Greek force crept out of the horse and opened the gates for the rest of the Greek army, which had sailed back under cover of night. The Greeks entered and destroyed the city of Troy, ending the war.

Exam Probability: **High**

40. *Answer choices:*
(see index for correct answer)

- a. Two Cunts in a Kitchen
- b. Soft sell
- c. Trojan horse
- d. FAST marketing

:: Marketing ::

_____ is the marketing of products that are presumed to be environmentally safe. It incorporates a broad range of activities, including product modification, changes to the production process, sustainable packaging, as well as modifying advertising. Yet defining _____ is not a simple task where several meanings intersect and contradict each other; an example of this will be the existence of varying social, environmental and retail definitions attached to this term. Other similar terms used are environmental marketing and ecological marketing.

Exam Probability: **Low**

41. *Answer choices:*
(see index for correct answer)

- a. Green marketing

- b. Pre-order
- c. Consumer complaint
- d. Nutraceutical

:: Television terminology ::

A _____ organization , also known as a non-business entity, not-for-profit organization, or _____ institution, is dedicated to furthering a particular social cause or advocating for a shared point of view. In economic terms, it is an organization that uses its surplus of the revenues to further achieve its ultimate objective, rather than distributing its income to the organization's shareholders, leaders, or members. _____ s are tax exempt or charitable, meaning they do not pay income tax on the money that they receive for their organization. They can operate in religious, scientific, research, or educational settings.

Exam Probability: **Low**

42. *Answer choices:*
(see index for correct answer)

- a. Nonprofit
- b. not-for-profit
- c. multiplexing
- d. distance learning

:: Labor rights ::

The _____ is the concept that people have a human _____ , or engage in productive employment, and may not be prevented from doing so. The _____ is enshrined in the Universal Declaration of Human Rights and recognized in international human rights law through its inclusion in the International Covenant on Economic, Social and Cultural Rights, where the _____ emphasizes economic, social and cultural development.

Exam Probability: **High**

43. *Answer choices:*
(see index for correct answer)

- a. Right to work
- b. China Labour Bulletin
- c. The Hyatt 100
- d. Kate Mullany House

Guidance: level 1

:: Business ::

_____ , or built-in obsolescence, in industrial design and economics is a policy of planning or designing a product with an artificially limited useful life, so that it becomes obsolete after a certain period of time. The rationale behind this strategy is to generate long-term sales volume by reducing the time between repeat purchases .

Exam Probability: **Low**

44. *Answer choices:*
(see index for correct answer)

- a. Kingdomality
- b. Planned obsolescence
- c. Procurement PunchOut
- d. Hellenic Australian Business Council

Guidance: level 1

:: ::

_____ or accountancy is the measurement, processing, and communication of financial information about economic entities such as businesses and corporations. The modern field was established by the Italian mathematician Luca Pacioli in 1494. _____ , which has been called the "language of business", measures the results of an organization's economic activities and conveys this information to a variety of users, including investors, creditors, management, and regulators. Practitioners of _____ are known as accountants. The terms " _____ " and "financial reporting" are often used as synonyms.

Exam Probability: **Low**

45. *Answer choices:*
(see index for correct answer)

- a. levels of analysis
- b. Accounting
- c. corporate values
- d. personal values

Guidance: level 1

:: Electronic feedback ::

_____ occurs when outputs of a system are routed back as inputs as part of a chain of cause-and-effect that forms a circuit or loop. The system can then be said to feed back into itself. The notion of cause-and-effect has to be handled carefully when applied to _____ systems.

Exam Probability: **Low**

46. *Answer choices:*
(see index for correct answer)

- a. feedback loop
- b. Positive feedback

Guidance: level 1

:: Power (social and political) ::

_____ is a form of reverence gained by a leader who has strong interpersonal relationship skills. _____ , as an aspect of personal power, becomes particularly important as organizational leadership becomes increasingly about collaboration and influence, rather than command and control.

Exam Probability: **High**

47. *Answer choices:*
(see index for correct answer)

- a. Referent power
- b. need for power
- c. Expert power

Guidance: level 1

:: ::

_____ ism is a form of government characterized by strong central power and limited political freedoms. Individual freedoms are subordinate to the state and there is no constitutional accountability and rule of law under an _____ regime. _____ regimes can be autocratic with power concentrated in one person or it can be more spread out between multiple officials and government institutions. Juan Linz's influential 1964 description of _____ ism characterized _____ political systems by four qualities.

Exam Probability: **Medium**

48. *Answer choices:*
(see index for correct answer)

- a. surface-level diversity
- b. personal values
- c. open system
- d. empathy

Guidance: level 1

:: Social philosophy ::

The _____ describes the unintended social benefits of an individual's self-interested actions. Adam Smith first introduced the concept in The Theory of Moral Sentiments, written in 1759, invoking it in reference to income distribution. In this work, however, the idea of the market is not discussed, and the word "capitalism" is never used.

Exam Probability: **High**

49. *Answer choices:*
(see index for correct answer)

- a. vacancy chain
- b. Societal attitudes towards abortion
- c. Veil of Ignorance
- d. Freedom to contract

Guidance: level 1

:: ::

An _____ is the release of a liquid petroleum hydrocarbon into the environment, especially the marine ecosystem, due to human activity, and is a form of pollution. The term is usually given to marine _____ s, where oil is released into the ocean or coastal waters, but spills may also occur on land. _____ s may be due to releases of crude oil from tankers, offshore platforms, drilling rigs and wells, as well as spills of refined petroleum products and their by-products, heavier fuels used by large ships such as bunker fuel, or the spill of any oily refuse or waste oil.

Exam Probability: **Low**

50. *Answer choices:*
(see index for correct answer)

- a. co-culture
- b. cultural
- c. Oil spill
- d. imperative

Guidance: level 1

:: ::

Competition law is a law that promotes or seeks to maintain market competition by regulating anti-competitive conduct by companies. Competition law is implemented through public and private enforcement. Competition law is known as " _____ law" in the United States for historical reasons, and as "anti-monopoly law" in China and Russia. In previous years it has been known as trade practices law in the United Kingdom and Australia. In the European Union, it is referred to as both _____ and competition law.

Exam Probability: **High**

51. *Answer choices:*
(see index for correct answer)

- a. Antitrust
- b. levels of analysis
- c. surface-level diversity
- d. process perspective

Guidance: level 1

:: ::

Cannabis, also known as _____ among other names, is a psychoactive drug from the Cannabis plant used for medical or recreational purposes. The main psychoactive part of cannabis is tetrahydrocannabinol , one of 483 known compounds in the plant, including at least 65 other cannabinoids. Cannabis can be used by smoking, vaporizing, within food, or as an extract.

Exam Probability: **High**

52. *Answer choices:*
(see index for correct answer)

- a. information systems assessment
- b. hierarchical
- c. open system
- d. Marijuana

Guidance: level 1

:: Socialism ::

_____ is a label used to define the first currents of modern socialist thought as exemplified by the work of Henri de Saint-Simon, Charles Fourier, Étienne Cabet and Robert Owen.

Exam Probability: **High**

53. *Answer choices:*
(see index for correct answer)

- a. Goulash Communism
- b. Utopian socialism
- c. Socialist state
- d. Socialism of the 21st century

Guidance: level 1

:: Leadership ::

_____ is a theory of leadership where a leader works with teams to identify needed change, creating a vision to guide the change through inspiration, and executing the change in tandem with committed members of a group; it is an integral part of the Full Range Leadership Model. _____ serves to enhance the motivation, morale, and job performance of followers through a variety of mechanisms; these include connecting the follower's sense of identity and self to a project and to the collective identity of the organization; being a role model for followers in order to inspire them and to raise their interest in the project; challenging followers to take greater ownership for their work, and understanding the strengths and weaknesses of followers, allowing the leader to align followers with tasks that enhance their performance.

Exam Probability: **Medium**

54. *Answer choices:*
(see index for correct answer)

- a. The Saint, the Surfer, and the CEO
- b. Transformational leadership
- c. Ethical leadership
- d. Leadership analysis

Guidance: level 1

:: Cultural appropriation ::

_____ is a social and economic order that encourages the acquisition of goods and services in ever-increasing amounts. With the industrial revolution, but particularly in the 20th century, mass production led to an economic crisis: there was overproduction—the supply of goods would grow beyond consumer demand, and so manufacturers turned to planned obsolescence and advertising to manipulate consumer spending. In 1899, a book on _____ published by Thorstein Veblen, called The Theory of the Leisure Class, examined the widespread values and economic institutions emerging along with the widespread "leisure time" in the beginning of the 20th century. In it Veblen "views the activities and spending habits of this leisure class in terms of conspicuous and vicarious consumption and waste. Both are related to the display of status and not to functionality or usefulness."

Exam Probability: **High**

55. *Answer choices:*
(see index for correct answer)

- a. Metrosexual
- b. Representation of African Americans in media
- c. Blackface
- d. Jynx

Guidance: level 1

:: Social responsibility ::

The United Nations Global Compact is a non-binding United Nations pact to encourage businesses worldwide to adopt sustainable and socially responsible policies, and to report on their implementation. The _____ is a principle-based framework for businesses, stating ten principles in the areas of human rights, labor, the environment and anti-corruption. Under the Global Compact, companies are brought together with UN agencies, labor groups and civil society. Cities can join the Global Compact through the Cities Programme.

Exam Probability: **Low**

56. *Answer choices:*
(see index for correct answer)

- a. Mallen Baker
- b. Socially responsible marketing
- c. Social impact
- d. United Nations Academic Impact

Guidance: level 1

:: Production and manufacturing ::

_____ is a set of techniques and tools for process improvement. Though as a shortened form it may be found written as 6S, it should not be confused with the methodology known as 6S .

Exam Probability: **Medium**

57. *Answer choices:*
(see index for correct answer)

- a. Six Sigma
- b. Agricultural cooperative

- c. Traditional engineering
- d. MAPICS

Guidance: level 1

:: Data management ::

_____ is a form of intellectual property that grants the creator of an original creative work an exclusive legal right to determine whether and under what conditions this original work may be copied and used by others, usually for a limited term of years. The exclusive rights are not absolute but limited by limitations and exceptions to _____ law, including fair use. A major limitation on _____ on ideas is that _____ protects only the original expression of ideas, and not the underlying ideas themselves.

Exam Probability: **Low**

58. *Answer choices:*
(see index for correct answer)

- a. Copyright
- b. Master data management
- c. Cloud Data Management Interface
- d. Content format

Guidance: level 1

:: Business ethics ::

_____ is a type of international private business self-regulation. While once it was possible to describe CSR as an internal organisational policy or a corporate ethic strategy, that time has passed as various international laws have been developed and various organisations have used their authority to push it beyond individual or even industry-wide initiatives. While it has been considered a form of corporate self-regulation for some time, over the last decade or so it has moved considerably from voluntary decisions at the level of individual organisations, to mandatory schemes at regional, national and even transnational levels.

Exam Probability: **High**

59. *Answer choices:*
(see index for correct answer)

- a. Sweatshop
- b. Pension spiking
- c. Cost the limit of price
- d. Corporate social responsibility

Guidance: level 1

Accounting

Accounting or accountancy is the measurement, processing, and communication of financial information about economic entities such as businesses and corporations. The modern field was established by the Italian mathematician Luca Pacioli in 1494. Accounting, which has been called the "language of business", measures the results of an organization's economic activities and conveys this information to a variety of users, including investors, creditors, management, and regulators.

:: Budgets ::

A _____ is a financial plan for a defined period, often one year. It may also include planned sales volumes and revenues, resource quantities, costs and expenses, assets, liabilities and cash flows. Companies, governments, families and other organizations use it to express strategic plans of activities or events in measurable terms.

Exam Probability: **High**

1. *Answer choices:*

(see index for correct answer)

- a. Budget
- b. Budget set
- c. Performance-based budgeting
- d. Marginal budgeting for bottlenecks

Guidance: level 1

:: Management accounting ::

A _____ is an organizational unit headed by a manager, who is responsible for its activities and results. In responsibility accounting, revenues and cost information are collected and reported on by _____ s.

2. *Answer choices:*
(see index for correct answer)

- a. Constraints accounting
- b. Responsibility center
- c. Double counting
- d. Total benefits of ownership

Guidance: level 1

:: Business economics ::

_____ is one of the constituents of a leasing calculus or operation. It describes the future value of a good in terms of absolute value in monetary terms and it is sometimes abbreviated into a percentage of the initial price when the item was new.

3. *Answer choices:*
(see index for correct answer)

- a. Residual value
- b. Business ecosystem
- c. Model audit
- d. Incremental operating margin

Guidance: level 1

:: Debt ::

A _____ is a party that has a claim on the services of a second party. It is a person or institution to whom money is owed. The first party, in general, has provided some property or service to the second party under the assumption that the second party will return an equivalent property and service. The second party is frequently called a debtor or borrower. The first party is called the _____ , which is the lender of property, service, or money.

Exam Probability: **High**

4. *Answer choices:*

(see index for correct answer)

- a. Compulsive buying disorder
- b. Peak debt
- c. Financial assistance
- d. Borrowing base

Guidance: level 1

:: Expense ::

An _____ , operating expenditure, operational expense, operational expenditure or opex is an ongoing cost for running a product, business, or system. Its counterpart, a capital expenditure , is the cost of developing or providing non-consumable parts for the product or system. For example, the purchase of a photocopier involves capex, and the annual paper, toner, power and maintenance costs represents opex. For larger systems like businesses, opex may also include the cost of workers and facility expenses such as rent and utilities.

Exam Probability: **Low**

5. *Answer choices:*

(see index for correct answer)

- a. Accretion expense
- b. Expense account
- c. Operating expense
- d. expenditure

Guidance: level 1

:: Financial ratios ::

The _____ is a financial ratio indicating the relative proportion of shareholders' equity and debt used to finance a company's assets. Closely related to leveraging, the ratio is also known as risk, gearing or leverage. The two components are often taken from the firm's balance sheet or statement of financial position , but the ratio may also be calculated using market values for both, if the company's debt and equity are publicly traded, or using a combination of book value for debt and market value for equity financially.

Exam Probability: **High**

6. *Answer choices:*
(see index for correct answer)

- a. Return on assets
- b. Put/call ratio
- c. PB ratio
- d. Debt-to-equity ratio

Guidance: level 1

:: Accounting terminology ::

_____ is an accounting system for recording resources whose use has been limited by the donor, grant authority, governing agency, or other individuals or organisations or by law. It emphasizes accountability rather than profitability, and is used by Nonprofit organizations and by governments. In this method, a fund consists of a self-balancing set of accounts and each are reported as either unrestricted, temporarily restricted or permanently restricted based on the provider-imposed restrictions.

Exam Probability: **Low**

7. *Answer choices:*
(see index for correct answer)

- a. Fund accounting
- b. Accrued liabilities
- c. double-entry bookkeeping
- d. managerial accounting

Guidance: level 1

:: Accounting in the United States ::

_____ refers to a Memorandum of Understanding signed in September 2002 between the Financial Accounting Standards Board , the US standard setter, and the International Accounting Standards Board . The agreement is so called as it was reached in Norwalk.

Exam Probability: **Medium**

8. *Answer choices:*
(see index for correct answer)

- a. Revolving fund
- b. Uniform Certified Public Accountant Examination
- c. Association of Government Accountants
- d. Norwalk Agreement

Guidance: level 1

:: Corporations law ::

_____ , also referred to as the certificate of incorporation or the corporate charter, are a document or charter that establishes the existence of a corporation in the United States and Canada. They generally are filed with the Secretary of State or other company registrar.

Exam Probability: **Low**

9. *Answer choices:*
(see index for correct answer)

- a. Corporate law
- b. Company seal
- c. For-profit corporation
- d. Internal affairs doctrine

Guidance: level 1

:: Management accounting ::

_____ is a method of identifying and evaluating activities that a business performs, using activity-based costing to carry out a value chain analysis or a re-engineering initiative to improve strategic and operational decisions in an organization.

10. *Answer choices:*
(see index for correct answer)

- a. Activity-based management
- b. Variable cost
- c. Factory overhead
- d. Inventory valuation

Guidance: level 1

:: Real estate ::

An _____ is to, interest in, or legal liability on real property that does not prohibit passing title to the property but that may diminish its value. _____ s can be classified in several ways. They may be financial or non-financial . Alternatively, they may be divided into those that affect title or those that affect the use or physical condition of the encumbered property . _____ s include security interests, liens, servitudes , leases, restrictions, encroachments, and air and subsurface rights. Also, those considered as potentially making the title defeasible are _____ s, for example, charging orders, building orders and structure alteration. _____ : charge upon or claim against land arising out of private grant or a contract.

Exam Probability: **Low**

11. *Answer choices:*
(see index for correct answer)

- a. Severance
- b. Overseas property
- c. Encumbrance
- d. Equity stripping

Guidance: level 1

:: Management accounting ::

_____ s are costs that change as the quantity of the good or service that a business produces changes. _____ s are the sum of marginal costs over all units produced. They can also be considered normal costs. Fixed costs and _____ s make up the two components of total cost. Direct costs are costs that can easily be associated with a particular cost object. However, not all _____ s are direct costs. For example, variable manufacturing overhead costs are _____ s that are indirect costs, not direct costs. _____ s are sometimes called unit-level costs as they vary with the number of units produced.

Exam Probability: **Medium**

12. *Answer choices:*
(see index for correct answer)

- a. Cost driver
- b. Chartered Cost Accountant
- c. Resource consumption accounting
- d. Invested capital

Guidance: level 1

:: Taxation ::

A _____ is a person or organization subject to pay a tax. _____ s have an Identification Number, a reference number issued by a government to its citizens.

Exam Probability: **High**

13. *Answer choices:*
(see index for correct answer)

- a. Directorate-General for Taxation and Customs Union
- b. Taxpayer
- c. Sales tax token
- d. User charge

Guidance: level 1

:: Capital gains taxes ::

A _____ refers to profit that results from a sale of a capital asset, such as stock, bond or real estate, where the sale price exceeds the purchase price. The gain is the difference between a higher selling price and a lower purchase price. Conversely, a capital loss arises if the proceeds from the sale of a capital asset are less than the purchase price.

Exam Probability: **High**

14. *Answer choices:*
(see index for correct answer)

- a. Capital cost tax factor
- b. Capital gain
- c. Capital Cost Allowance

Guidance: level 1

:: Financial ratios ::

_____ or asset turns is a financial ratio that measures the efficiency of a company's use of its assets in generating sales revenue or sales income to the company.

Exam Probability: **Low**

15. *Answer choices:*
(see index for correct answer)

- a. Asset turnover
- b. AlphaIC
- c. Debt service coverage ratio
- d. Payout ratio

Guidance: level 1

:: International accounting organizations ::

The _____ is the global organization for the accountancy profession. Founded in 1977, IFAC has more than 175 members and associates in more than 130 countries and jurisdictions, representing nearly 3 million accountants employed in public practice, industry and commerce, government, and academe. The organization supports the development, adoption and implementation of international standards for accounting education, ethics, and the public sector as well as audit and assurance. It supports four independent standard-setting boards, which establish international standards on ethics, auditing and assurance, accounting education, and public sector accounting. It also issues guidance to encourage high quality performance by professional accountants in business and small and medium accounting practices.

Exam Probability: **Low**

16. *Answer choices:*
(see index for correct answer)

- a. International Federation of Accountants
- b. World Congress of Accountants
- c. International Accounting Education Standards Board
- d. International Federation of Francophone Accountants

Guidance: level 1

:: ::

_____ is a process whereby a person assumes the parenting of another, usually a child, from that person's biological or legal parent or parents. Legal _____ s permanently transfers all rights and responsibilities, along with filiation, from the biological parent or parents.

Exam Probability: **Low**

17. *Answer choices:*
(see index for correct answer)

- a. information systems assessment
- b. Character
- c. Adoption
- d. open system

Guidance: level 1

:: Management accounting ::

A _____ is a part of a business which is expected to make an identifiable contribution to the organization's profits.

Exam Probability: **High**

18. *Answer choices:*
(see index for correct answer)

- a. Bridge life-cycle cost analysis
- b. Relevant cost
- c. Profit center
- d. Grenzplankostenrechnung

Guidance: level 1

:: Banking terms ::

An _____ occurs when money is withdrawn from a bank account and the available balance goes below zero. In this situation the account is said to be "overdrawn". If there is a prior agreement with the account provider for an _____ , and the amount overdrawn is within the authorized _____ limit, then interest is normally charged at the agreed rate. If the negative balance exceeds the agreed terms, then additional fees may be charged and higher interest rates may apply.

Exam Probability: **Medium**

19. *Answer choices:*
(see index for correct answer)

- a. Infopro Sdn Bhd
- b. Hard count
- c. Wholesale funding
- d. Overdraft

Guidance: level 1

:: Pricing ::

_____ is the difference between a lower selling price and a higher purchase price, resulting in a financial loss for the seller.

Exam Probability: **High**

20. *Answer choices:*

(see index for correct answer)

- a. Best Rate Guaranteed
- b. Transfer mispricing
- c. Menu cost
- d. Capital loss

Guidance: level 1

:: ::

_____ is the act of compensating someone for an out-of-pocket expense by giving them an amount of money equal to what was spent.

Exam Probability: **Medium**

21. *Answer choices:*

(see index for correct answer)

- a. personal values
- b. Character
- c. process perspective
- d. Reimbursement

Guidance: level 1

:: Insolvency ::

_____ is the process in accounting by which a company is brought to an end in the United Kingdom, Republic of Ireland and United States. The assets and property of the company are redistributed. _____ is also sometimes referred to as winding-up or dissolution, although dissolution technically refers to the last stage of _____ . The process of _____ also arises when customs, an authority or agency in a country responsible for collecting and safeguarding customs duties, determines the final computation or ascertainment of the duties or drawback accruing on an entry.

22. *Answer choices:*

(see index for correct answer)

- a. Liquidator
- b. Liquidation
- c. United Kingdom insolvency law
- d. Preferential creditor

Guidance: level 1

:: Accounting terminology ::

Accounts are typically defined by an identifier and a caption or header and are coded by account type. In computerized accounting systems with computable quantity accounting, the accounts can have a quantity measure definition.

Exam Probability: **High**

23. *Answer choices:*

(see index for correct answer)

- a. Capital expenditure
- b. Chart of accounts
- c. Accounts receivable
- d. Accrual

Guidance: level 1

:: Basic financial concepts ::

In finance, maturity or _____ refers to the final payment date of a loan or other financial instrument, at which point the principal is due to be paid.

Exam Probability: **Low**

24. *Answer choices:*

(see index for correct answer)

- a. Lodgement
- b. Future-oriented
- c. Financial transaction
- d. Leverage cycle

Guidance: level 1

A nonprofit organization , also known as a non-business entity, _____ organization, or nonprofit institution, is dedicated to furthering a particular social cause or advocating for a shared point of view. In economic terms, it is an organization that uses its surplus of the revenues to further achieve its ultimate objective, rather than distributing its income to the organization's shareholders, leaders, or members. Nonprofits are tax exempt or charitable, meaning they do not pay income tax on the money that they receive for their organization. They can operate in religious, scientific, research, or educational settings.

Exam Probability: **High**

25. *Answer choices:*
(see index for correct answer)

- a. Satellite television
- b. multiplexing
- c. Not-for-profit
- d. distance learning

Guidance: level 1

_____ are liabilities that reflect expenses that have not yet been paid or logged under accounts payable during an accounting period; in other words, a company's obligation to pay for goods and services that have been provided for which invoices have not yet been received. Examples would include accrued wages payable, accrued sales tax payable, and accrued rent payable.

Exam Probability: **Low**

26. *Answer choices:*
(see index for correct answer)

- a. Checkoff
- b. double-entry bookkeeping
- c. Accrued liabilities
- d. Accounting equation

Guidance: level 1

_____ is a style of business management that focuses on identifying and handling cases that deviate from the norm, recommended as best practice by the project management method PRINCE2.

Exam Probability: **Medium**

27. *Answer choices:*
(see index for correct answer)

- a. Management by exception
- b. Concept of operations
- c. Focused improvement
- d. Scrum

Guidance: level 1

:: Business ::

The seller, or the provider of the goods or services, completes a sale in response to an acquisition, appropriation, requisition or a direct interaction with the buyer at the point of sale. There is a passing of title of the item, and the settlement of a price, in which agreement is reached on a price for which transfer of ownership of the item will occur. The seller, not the purchaser typically executes the sale and it may be completed prior to the obligation of payment. In the case of indirect interaction, a person who sells goods or service on behalf of the owner is known as a _____ man or _____ woman or _____ person, but this often refers to someone selling goods in a store/shop, in which case other terms are also common, including _____ clerk, shop assistant, and retail clerk.

Exam Probability: **Medium**

28. *Answer choices:*
(see index for correct answer)

- a. Professional services
- b. Fast-moving consumer goods
- c. Sales
- d. Religion and business

Guidance: level 1

:: Financial ratios ::

Earnings per share is the monetary value of earnings per outstanding share of common stock for a company.

Exam Probability: **High**

29. *Answer choices:*
(see index for correct answer)

- a. Debt ratio
- b. Sortino ratio
- c. Return on capital employed
- d. Average accounting return

Guidance: level 1

:: Debt ::

A _____ is a monetary amount owed to a creditor that is unlikely to be paid and, or which the creditor is not willing to take action to collect for various reasons, often due to the debtor not having the money to pay, for example due to a company going into liquidation or insolvency. There are various technical definitions of what constitutes a _____ , depending on accounting conventions, regulatory treatment and the institution provisioning. In the USA, bank loans with more than ninety days` arrears become "problem loans". Accounting sources advise that the full amount of a _____ be written off to the profit and loss account or a provision for _____ s as soon as it is foreseen.

Exam Probability: **High**

30. *Answer choices:*
(see index for correct answer)

- a. Debt compliance
- b. Creditor
- c. Phantom debt
- d. Exchangeable bond

Guidance: level 1

:: Accounting source documents ::

_____ is a letter sent by a customer to a supplier to inform the supplier that their invoice has been paid. If the customer is paying by cheque, the _____ often accompanies the cheque. The advice may consist of a literal letter or of a voucher attached to the side or top of the cheque.

Exam Probability: **High**

31. *Answer choices:*
(see index for correct answer)

- a. Bank statement
- b. Banknote
- c. Parcel audit
- d. Purchase order

Guidance: level 1

:: Land value taxation ::

_____ , sometimes referred to as dry _____ , is the solid surface of Earth that is not permanently covered by water. The vast majority of human activity throughout history has occurred in _____ areas that support agriculture, habitat, and various natural resources. Some life forms have developed from predecessor species that lived in bodies of water.

Exam Probability: **Low**

32. *Answer choices:*
(see index for correct answer)

- a. Georgism
- b. Henry George
- c. Land value tax
- d. Harry Gunnison Brown

Guidance: level 1

:: Accounting source documents ::

A _____ or account statement is a summary of financial transactions which have occurred over a given period on a bank account held by a person or business with a financial institution.

33. *Answer choices:*

(see index for correct answer)

- a. Superbill
- b. Purchase order
- c. Banknote
- d. Bank statement

Guidance: level 1

:: Banking ::

A _____ is a financial institution that accepts deposits from the public and creates credit. Lending activities can be performed either directly or indirectly through capital markets. Due to their importance in the financial stability of a country, _____ s are highly regulated in most countries. Most nations have institutionalized a system known as fractional reserve _____ ing under which _____ s hold liquid assets equal to only a portion of their current liabilities. In addition to other regulations intended to ensure liquidity, _____ s are generally subject to minimum capital requirements based on an international set of capital standards, known as the Basel Accords.

Exam Probability: **High**

34. *Answer choices:*

(see index for correct answer)

- a. Bank
- b. Coin wrapper
- c. zero balance account
- d. Standing order

Guidance: level 1

:: Business models ::

A _____ is a company that owns enough voting stock in another firm to control management and operation by influencing or electing its board of directors. The company is deemed a subsidiary of the _____ .

Exam Probability: **High**

35. *Answer choices:*
(see index for correct answer)

- a. Trade printing
- b. Small business
- c. IASME
- d. Parent company

Guidance: level 1

:: Accounting ::

_____ examines how accounting is used by individuals, organizations and government as well as the consequences that these practices have. Starting from the assumption that accounting both measures and makes visible certain economic events, _____ has studied the roles of accounting in organizations and society and the consequences that these practices have for individuals, organizations, governments and capital markets. It encompasses a broad range of topics including financial _____ , management _____ , auditing research, capital market research, accountability research, social responsibility research and taxation research.

Exam Probability: **Low**

36. *Answer choices:*
(see index for correct answer)

- a. Cash sweep
- b. Accounting research
- c. Russian GAAP
- d. Special journals

Guidance: level 1

:: ::

An _____ is a contingent motivator. Traditional _____ s are extrinsic motivators which reward actions to yield a desired outcome. The effectiveness of traditional _____ s has changed as the needs of Western society have evolved. While the traditional _____ model is effective when there is a defined procedure and goal for a task, Western society started to require a higher volume of critical thinkers, so the traditional model became less effective. Institutions are now following a trend in implementing strategies that rely on intrinsic motivations rather than the extrinsic motivations that the traditional _____ s foster.

Exam Probability: **Medium**

37. *Answer choices:*
(see index for correct answer)

- a. process perspective
- b. open system
- c. deep-level diversity
- d. Incentive

Guidance: level 1

:: Information systems ::

_____ are formal, sociotechnical, organizational systems designed to collect, process, store, and distribute information. In a sociotechnical perspective, _____ are composed by four components: task, people, structure , and technology.

Exam Probability: **High**

38. *Answer choices:*
(see index for correct answer)

- a. Knowledge management
- b. Formative context
- c. Ignorance management
- d. Information systems

Guidance: level 1

:: Tax law ::

_____ or revenue law is an area of legal study which deals with the constitutional, common-law, statutory, tax treaty, and regulatory rules that constitute the law applicable to taxation.

Exam Probability: **High**

39. *Answer choices:*
(see index for correct answer)

- a. Tax Court of Canada
- b. Tax Law Rewrite Project
- c. Taxable wages
- d. Territorial nexus

Guidance: level 1

:: Inventory ::

It requires a detailed physical count, so that the company knows exactly how many of each goods brought on specific dates remained at year end inventory. When this information is found, the amount of goods are multiplied by their purchase cost at their purchase date, to get a number for the ending inventory cost.

Exam Probability: **Medium**

40. *Answer choices:*
(see index for correct answer)

- a. Inventory optimization
- b. Safety stock
- c. Specific identification
- d. just-in-time manufacturing

Guidance: level 1

:: Notes (finance) ::

A _____ , sometimes referred to as a note payable, is a legal instrument , in which one party promises in writing to pay a determinate sum of money to the other , either at a fixed or determinable future time or on demand of the payee, under specific terms.

41. *Answer choices:*
(see index for correct answer)

- a. Promissory note
- b. Capital note
- c. Equity-linked note
- d. Federal Reserve Note

Guidance: level 1

:: Business models ::

A _____, _____ company or daughter company is a company that is owned or controlled by another company, which is called the parent company, parent, or holding company. The _____ can be a company, corporation, or limited liability company. In some cases it is a government or state-owned enterprise. In some cases, particularly in the music and book publishing industries, subsidiaries are referred to as imprints.

Exam Probability: **Medium**

42. *Answer choices:*
(see index for correct answer)

- a. Subsidiary
- b. Co-operative economics
- c. Business-agile enterprise
- d. Utility computing

Guidance: level 1

:: Employment classifications ::

Generally, tax authorities will view a person as self-employed if the person chooses to be recognized as such, or is generating income such that the person is required to file a tax return under legislation in the relevant jurisdiction. In the real world, the critical issue for the taxing authorities is not that the person is trading but is whether the person is profitable and hence potentially taxable. In other words, the activity of trading is likely to be ignored if no profit is present, so occasional and hobby- or enthusiast-based economic activity is generally ignored by authorities.

43. *Answer choices:*
(see index for correct answer)

- a. Young professional
- b. Freelancer
- c. Self-employment
- d. Full-time

Guidance: level 1

:: SEC filings ::

_____ is a prescribed regulation under the US Securities Act of 1933 that lays out reporting requirements for various SEC filings used by public companies. Companies are also often called issuers , filers or registrants .

Exam Probability: **Low**

44. *Answer choices:*
(see index for correct answer)

- a. Form 8-K
- b. Regulation S-K
- c. Form 3
- d. Form 10-Q

Guidance: level 1

:: ::

A tax is a compulsory financial charge or some other type of levy imposed upon a taxpayer by a governmental organization in order to fund various public expenditures. A failure to pay, along with evasion of or resistance to _____ , is punishable by law. Taxes consist of direct or indirect taxes and may be paid in money or as its labour equivalent.

Exam Probability: **Low**

45. *Answer choices:*
(see index for correct answer)

- a. corporate values
- b. Taxation
- c. empathy

- d. Character

Guidance: level 1

:: Economic globalization ::

_____ is an agreement in which one company hires another company to be responsible for a planned or existing activity that is or could be done internally,and sometimes involves transferring employees and assets from one firm to another.

Exam Probability: **Low**

46. *Answer choices:*
(see index for correct answer)

- a. global financial
- b. reshoring

Guidance: level 1

:: Generally Accepted Accounting Principles ::

In accounting, an economic item`s _____ is the original nominal monetary value of that item. _____ accounting involves reporting assets and liabilities at their _____ s, which are not updated for changes in the items' values. Consequently, the amounts reported for these balance sheet items often differ from their current economic or market values.

Exam Probability: **Low**

47. *Answer choices:*
(see index for correct answer)

- a. Deferred income
- b. Pro forma
- c. Historical cost
- d. Petty cash

Guidance: level 1

:: Legal terms ::

A _____ is a gathering of people who have been invited by a host for the purposes of socializing, conversation, recreation, or as part of a festival or other commemoration of a special occasion. A _____ will typically feature food and beverages, and often music and dancing or other forms of entertainment. In many Western countries, parties for teens and adults are associated with drinking alcohol such as beer, wine, or distilled spirits.

Exam Probability: **Low**

48. *Answer choices:*
(see index for correct answer)

- a. Quasi-legislative capacity
- b. Antedated
- c. Party
- d. Pursuer

Guidance: level 1

:: Management accounting ::

_____ , or dollar contribution per unit, is the selling price per unit minus the variable cost per unit. "Contribution" represents the portion of sales revenue that is not consumed by variable costs and so contributes to the coverage of fixed costs. This concept is one of the key building blocks of break-even analysis.

Exam Probability: **High**

49. *Answer choices:*
(see index for correct answer)

- a. Hedge accounting
- b. Environmental full-cost accounting
- c. Standard cost
- d. Revenue center

Guidance: level 1

:: Management accounting ::

_____ is the profit the firm makes from serving a customer or customer group over a specified period of time, specifically the difference between the revenues earned from and the costs associated with the customer relationship in a specified period. According to Philip Kotler,"a profitable customer is a person, household or a company that overtime, yields a revenue stream that exceeds by an acceptable amount the company's cost stream of attracting, selling and servicing the customer."

Exam Probability: **Medium**

50. *Answer choices:*
(see index for correct answer)

- a. Customer profitability
- b. Bridge life-cycle cost analysis
- c. Total benefits of ownership
- d. Management control system

Guidance: level 1

:: Generally Accepted Accounting Principles ::

An _____ or profit and loss account is one of the financial statements of a company and shows the company's revenues and expenses during a particular period.

Exam Probability: **Low**

51. *Answer choices:*
(see index for correct answer)

- a. Net profit
- b. Generally accepted accounting principles
- c. deferred revenue
- d. Trial balance

Guidance: level 1

:: Inventory ::

_____ is the amount of inventory a company has in stock at the end of its fiscal year. It is closely related with _____ cost, which is the amount of money spent to get these goods in stock. It should be calculated at the lower of cost or market.

Exam Probability: **Low**

52. *Answer choices:*

(see index for correct answer)

- a. Ending inventory
- b. GMROII
- c. Stock-taking
- d. Specific identification

Guidance: level 1

:: Management accounting ::

_____ are costs that are not directly accountable to a cost object . _____ may be either fixed or variable. _____ include administration, personnel and security costs. These are those costs which are not directly related to production. Some _____ may be overhead. But some overhead costs can be directly attributed to a project and are direct costs.

Exam Probability: **High**

53. *Answer choices:*

(see index for correct answer)

- a. Indirect costs
- b. Job costing
- c. Target costing
- d. Profit center

Guidance: level 1

:: ::

_____ is the income that is gained by governments through taxation. Taxation is the primary source of income for a state. Revenue may be extracted from sources such as individuals, public enterprises, trade, royalties on natural resources and/or foreign aid. An inefficient collection of taxes is greater in countries characterized by poverty, a large agricultural sector and large amounts of foreign aid.

Exam Probability: **Low**

54. *Answer choices:*
(see index for correct answer)

- a. Sarbanes-Oxley act of 2002
- b. co-culture
- c. levels of analysis
- d. imperative

Guidance: level 1

:: Negotiable instrument law ::

_____ of a financial instrument, such as a cheque, is only a signature, not indicating the payee. The effect of this is that it is payable only to the bearer – legally, it transforms an order instrument into a bearer instrument. It is one of the types of endorsement of a negotiable instrument.

Exam Probability: **Low**

55. *Answer choices:*
(see index for correct answer)

- a. Expedited Funds Availability Act
- b. Negotiable Instruments Act, 1881
- c. Swift v. Tyson
- d. Burton v. United States

Guidance: level 1

:: Management accounting ::

_____ is the process of reviewing and analyzing a company's financial statements to make better economic decisions to earn income in future. These statements include the income statement, balance sheet, statement of cash flows, notes to accounts and a statement of changes in equity . _____ is a method or process involving specific techniques for evaluating risks, performance, financial health, and future prospects of an organization.

Exam Probability: **Low**

56. *Answer choices:*
(see index for correct answer)

- a. Hedge accounting
- b. Institute of Management Accountants
- c. Management accounting
- d. Pre-determined overhead rate

Guidance: level 1

:: ::

A _____ is an organization, usually a group of people or a company, authorized to act as a single entity and recognized as such in law. Early incorporated entities were established by charter . Most jurisdictions now allow the creation of new _____ s through registration.

Exam Probability: **High**

57. *Answer choices:*
(see index for correct answer)

- a. imperative
- b. hierarchical
- c. Corporation
- d. surface-level diversity

Guidance: level 1

:: Financial statements ::

In financial accounting, a _____ or statement of financial position or statement of financial condition is a summary of the financial balances of an individual or organization, whether it be a sole proprietorship, a business partnership, a corporation, private limited company or other organization such as Government or not-for-profit entity. Assets, liabilities and ownership equity are listed as of a specific date, such as the end of its financial year. A _____ is often described as a "snapshot of a company's financial condition". Of the four basic financial statements, the _____ is the only statement which applies to a single point in time of a business' calendar year.

Exam Probability: **Low**

58. *Answer choices:*
(see index for correct answer)

- a. Balance sheet
- b. Consolidated financial statement
- c. Statements on auditing standards
- d. Clean surplus accounting

Guidance: level 1

:: Value theory ::

Within philosophy, it can be known as ethics or axiology. Early philosophical investigations sought to understand good and evil and the concept of "the good". Today, much of _____ aspires to the scientifically empirical, recording what people do value and attempting to understand why they value it in the context of psychology, sociology, and economics.

Exam Probability: **Low**

59. *Answer choices:*
(see index for correct answer)

- a. Value theory
- b. economic value
- c. Intrinsic theory of value
- d. Law of value

Guidance: level 1

INDEX: Correct Answers

Foundations of Business

1. b: Loan

2. c: Good

3. : Patent

4. a: Procurement

5. b: Analysis

6. a: Logistics

7. : Present value

8. c: Payment

9. a: Political risk

10. : Federal Trade Commission

11. a: Employment

12. : Stock

13. c: Project

14. a: Outsourcing

15. d: E-commerce

16. c: Opportunity cost

17. c: Error

18. : Raw material

19. : Preferred stock

20. : Document

21. c: Evaluation

22. b: Focus group

23. c: Interest rate

24. d: Social security

25. c: Accounts receivable

26. a: Supply chain

27. : Free trade

28. a: Stock market

29. c: Purchasing

30. c: Image

31. c: Mission statement

32. : Competition

33. : Foreign direct investment

34. : Income statement

35. d: Bribery

36. c: Entrepreneur

37. : Competitor

38. c: Meeting

39. a: Feedback

40. a: Ownership

41. : Problem

42. : Stock exchange

43. d: Corporate governance

44. c: Sales

45. d: Decision-making

46. : Budget

47. b: Affirmative action

48. c: Competitive advantage

49. a: Direct investment

50. : Consumer Protection

51. d: Planning

52. b: Board of directors

53. a: Business model

54. b: System

55. d: SWOT analysis

56. b: Organizational structure

57. d: Corporation

58. : Capital market

59. b: Explanation

Management

1. d: Corporate governance

2. d: Logistics

3. b: Emotional intelligence

4. b: Bureaucracy

5. d: Goal

6. b: Management by objectives

7. a: Resource management

8. a: Product design

9. c: Budget

10. a: Shareholder

11. c: Research and development

12. a: Virtual team

13. b: Sharing

14. a: Sexual harassment

15. a: Firm

16. c: Overtime

17. : Collective bargaining

18. d: Sales

19. c: Efficiency

20. a: Size

21. c: Utility

22. a: Arbitration

23. c: Bias

24. a: Lead

25. a: Glass ceiling

26. : Social capital

27. : Decentralization

28. : Information

29. d: Joint venture

30. d: Senior management

31. b: Job description

32. b: Control chart

33. c: Mass customization

34. b: Intellectual property

35. c: Six Sigma

36. c: Problem solving

37. d: Career

38. a: Proactive

39. a: Market research

40. : Job design

41. : Expatriate

42. d: Case study

43. c: Partnership

44. b: Analysis

45. a: Risk management

46. : Quality circle

47. : Collaboration

48. a: Labor force

49. a: Interdependence

50. a: Balanced scorecard

51. c: Leadership development

52. c: Competitive advantage

53. c: Initiative

54. d: Human resources

55. b: Entrepreneurship

56. a: Franchising

57. d: Economies of scale

58. b: Procurement

59. : Officer

Business law

1. b: Merger

2. b: Standing

3. : Adoption

4. b: Breach of contract

5. a: Bad faith

6. a: Warehouse receipt

7. a: Bailee

8. b: Punitive damages

9. : Securities and Exchange Commission

10. b: Risk

11. b: Sherman Act

12. d: Creditor

13. : Securities Act

14. a: Revenue

15. d: Purchasing

16. a: Amendment

17. a: First Amendment

18. a: Relevant market

19. b: Utilitarianism

20. c: Assignee

21. b: Contract law

22. b: Sexual harassment

23. d: Environmental Protection

24. c: Jurisdiction

25. : Shareholder

26. d: Reasonable person

27. c: Cooperative

28. c: Asset

29. c: Dividend

30. d: Prima facie

31. d: Complaint

32. c: Credit

33. b: Puffery

34. b: Statutory Law

35. d: Resource

36. d: Disparagement

37. b: Constitutional law

38. c: Apparent authority

39. c: Operating agreement

40. d: Social responsibility

41. : Option contract

42. : Criminal law

43. a: Insider trading

44. : Partnership

45. c: Federal question

46. : Res ipsa

47. d: Argument

48. a: Unconscionability

49. c: Indictment

50. d: Accounting

51. c: Litigation

52. b: Requirements contract

53. b: Mediation

54. d: Delegation

55. d: Investment

56. c: Embezzlement

57. : Auction

58. c: Injunction

59. d: Voidable contract

Finance

1. b: Partnership

2. c: Fixed cost

3. : Revenue recognition

4. d: Par value

5. : Consideration

6. c: Capital lease

7. a: Market risk

8. c: Capital budgeting

9. d: Patent

10. d: Tax rate

11. b: Break-even

12. : Pension

13. a: Tax expense

14. : Cash equivalent

15. a: Shareholder

16. a: Fair value

17. a: Risk assessment

18. c: Internal rate of return

19. a: Normal balance

20. b: Investment

21. a: Debit card

22. c: Cost of capital

23. b: Cost object

24. a: Preference

25. b: Write-off

26. a: Cash flow

27. d: Double taxation

28. d: Bond market

29. d: WorldCom

30. c: Financial management

31. c: Net asset

32. a: Future value

33. : Marketing

34. : Yield curve

35. a: Income tax

36. c: Market price

37. c: Rate risk

38. b: Interest rate risk

39. d: Specific identification

40. c: Total cost

41. : Opportunity cost

42. : Present value

43. d: Asset management

44. : Capital expenditure

45. d: Indirect costs

46. d: Ledger

47. b: Net worth

48. : Interest expense

49. b: Inventory

50. a: Long-term liabilities

51. c: Derivative

52. b: Liquidity

53. a: Advertising

54. a: Variable cost

55. c: Financial analysis

56. c: Schedule

57. a: Periodic inventory

58. c: Put option

59. a: Rate of return

Human resource management

1. a: Disability insurance

2. : Data collection

3. d: Eustress

4. a: Asset

5. : Aggression

6. a: Human capital

7. : Union shop

8. b: Card check

9. d: Layoff

10. c: Social loafing

11. d: Information overload

12. : Grievance

13. c: Executive officer

14. b: Employee Polygraph Protection Act

15. d: Action learning

16. b: Part-time

17. c: Wage

18. c: Profession

19. c: Enforcement

20. c: Cross-functional team

21. d: Tacit knowledge

22. b: Workplace bullying

23. d: Management

24. c: Virtual team

25. b: Training and development

26. : Recession

27. a: Workforce

28. b: Workplace violence

29. d: Empowerment

30. b: Work ethic

31. b: Succession planning

32. c: Golden parachute

33. b: Severance package

34. b: Questionnaire

35. b: Minimum wage

36. d: Rating scale

37. : Meeting

38. b: Performance improvement

39. d: Job satisfaction

40. c: Scientific management

41. b: Right-to-work law

42. a: Retirement

43. b: Independent contractor

44. b: Decentralization

45. b: Love contract

46. d: Best practice

47. a: Departmentalization

48. d: Predictive validity

49. c: Piece rate

50. : Interview

51. : Cost

52. b: Pay grade

53. b: Professional association

54. : Nearshoring

55. b: Career development

56. d: Nepotism

57. a: Interactional justice

58. b: Construct validity

59. b: Organizational learning

Information systems

1. b: Service level

2. : Cybersquatting

3. : Data integrity

4. b: Information security

5. c: Service level agreement

6. : Web analytics

7. d: Security management

8. a: Mozy

9. a: Web server

10. : Business analytics

11. d: Automation

12. b: Payment system

13. d: Consumer-to-business

14. c: Virtual reality

15. a: Data integration

16. b: Galileo

17. b: Extranet

18. c: Information literacy

19. : Vulnerability

20. c: Security controls

21. b: Avatar

22. c: Master data

23. c: Supply chain management

24. c: Phishing

25. b: Vertical integration

26. c: Semantic Web

27. d: Service-oriented architecture

28. b: Random access

29. : Balanced scorecard

30. : Management information system

31. d: Bit rate

32. b: Unstructured data

33. a: Government-to-government

34. a: Telnet

35. : Decision-making

36. a: Wiki

37. c: Content management

38. : Click-through rate

39. c: Reputation management

40. : Interoperability

41. b: Extensible Markup Language

42. b: Availability

43. : Master data management

44. d: Dashboard

45. c: Statistics

46. b: Magnetic tape

47. d: Enterprise application

48. d: Data redundancy

49. : COBIT

50. c: Database

51. d: Word

52. b: Database management system

53. a: Data link

54. d: Facebook

55. d: Business rule

56. d: Monopoly

57. d: Common Criteria

58. a: Knowledge management

59. a: E-commerce

Marketing

1. c: Shares

2. c: Interest

3. b: Primary data

4. b: Mass customization

5. a: Market segmentation

6. d: Entrepreneur

7. b: Personal selling

8. a: Reseller

9. b: Electronic data interchange

10. d: Global marketing

11. b: Product line

12. c: Demand

13. d: Tangible

14. : Partnership

15. d: Questionnaire

16. a: Code

17. c: Evolution

18. : Evaluation

19. b: Unique selling proposition

20. b: Comparative advertising

21. c: Warehouse

22. b: Penetration pricing

23. d: Customer service

24. : Target market

25. : Mission statement

26. d: Resource

27. c: Creativity

28. b: Attention

29. d: Business marketing

30. b: Reinforcement

31. d: Customer satisfaction

32. a: Noise

33. b: Accounting

34. d: Statistic

35. b: Credit

36. b: Supply chain management

37. d: Price discrimination

38. c: Preference

39. c: North American Free Trade Agreement

40. : Project

41. : Pricing

42. b: Census

43. a: Customer

44. b: Data analysis

45. : Variable cost

46. : Marketing

47. a: Ford

48. a: Marketing channel

49. b: Data collection

50. c: Respondent

51. a: Product manager

52. : Intangibility

53. a: Quantitative research

54. d: Commerce

55. : Cognitive dissonance

56. d: Manager

57. a: Budget

58. a: Image

59. : Pricing strategies

Manufacturing

1. b: Durability

2. b: Six Sigma

3. d: Strategic planning

4. d: Dimension

5. : Glass

6. : Sony

7. b: Service level

8. : Change management

9. a: Production schedule

10. c: Rolling

11. : Change control

12. c: Toshiba

13. b: Bullwhip effect

14. c: Perfect competition

15. : Blanket

16. c: Management process

17. c: Expediting

18. a: Thomas Register

19. d: ROOT

20. a: Quality Engineering

21. b: Accreditation

22. d: Tool

23. a: Distillation

24. a: New product development

25. : Total productive maintenance

26. c: Average cost

27. a: Control limits

28. : Heat treating

29. d: Scope statement

30. a: Gantt chart

31. c: Property

32. d: Heat exchanger

33. d: Lean manufacturing

34. c: Retail

35. : Solution

36. b: Credit

37. d: Knowledge management

38. c: Purchase order

39. b: Histogram

40. : Catalyst

41. a: Customer

42. a: Statistical process control

43. d: Sharing

44. d: Process capability

45. : Opportunity cost

46. d: Quality audit

47. a: Total cost

48. d: Original equipment manufacturer

49. : Financial plan

50. b: Supplier relationship management

51. b: Indirect costs

52. : Service quality

53. : Pareto analysis

54. a: Control chart

55. : Check sheet

56. b: Process capital

57. : Pattern

58. : Rolling Wave planning

59. b: Strategy

Commerce

1. d: Audit

2. b: Antitrust

3. : Cash flow

4. : Game

5. b: Consignee

6. b: Market research

7. d: Total revenue

8. b: Entrepreneur

9. b: York

10. c: Regulatory agency

11. c: Land

12. : Tangible

13. c: Business-to-business

14. d: Affiliate marketing

15. b: Economy

16. c: Wage

17. b: Management

18. c: Value-added network

19. a: Credit card

20. b: Project

21. d: Insurance

22. a: Supranational

23. : Commodity

24. d: Loyalty

25. a: Utility

26. c: Payment card

27. a: Cost structure

28. a: Brand

29. : Dutch auction

30. d: Economies of scale

31. c: Warehouse

32. d: Productivity

33. d: Market share

34. a: Semantic

35. b: Outsourcing

36. d: Long run

37. d: Revenue management

38. b: Preference

39. d: Case study

40. d: Marketing

41. a: Reverse auction

42. b: Industry

43. a: Strategic alliance

44. d: Vickrey auction

45. : Competitive advantage

46. : Investment

47. d: Quality assurance

48. c: Cooperative

49. : Disney

50. b: Variable cost

51. b: Consultant

52. b: Partnership

53. b: Total cost

54. : Quality control

55. d: Consideration

56. a: Pizza Hut

57. c: Inflation

58. b: English auction

59. d: Information technology

Business ethics

1. c: European Commission

2. d: WorldCom

3. b: Model Rules of Professional Conduct

4. b: Patriot Act

5. d: Social responsibility

6. b: Ethics Resource Center

7. : Supply Chain

8. c: Dress code

9. a: East Germany

10. a: Coal

11. c: Layoff

12. c: Risk management

13. b: Living wage

14. : Marketing ethics

15. b: Workplace bullying

16. : Habitat

17. c: Junk bond

18. c: Price fixing

19. a: White-collar crime

20. a: Federal Trade Commission Act

21. b: Real estate

22. b: Disclaimer

23. d: Principal Financial

24. a: Employee Polygraph Protection Act

25. d: Stanford International Bank

26. c: Capitalism

27. c: Organic food

28. d: Foreign Corrupt Practices Act

29. : Forest Stewardship Council

30. : Consumer Financial Protection Bureau

31. c: Empowerment

32. b: New Deal

33. c: Corporation

34. c: Greenwashing

35. a: Biofuel

36. c: Natural gas

37. c: Catholicism

38. c: Corporate structure

39. c: Pollution

40. c: Trojan horse

41. a: Green marketing

42. a: Nonprofit

43. a: Right to work

44. b: Planned obsolescence

45. b: Accounting

46. c: Feedback

47. a: Referent power

48. : Authoritarian

49. : Invisible hand

50. c: Oil spill

51. a: Antitrust

52. d: Marijuana

53. b: Utopian socialism

54. b: Transformational leadership

55. : Consumerism

56. : UN Global Compact

57. a: Six Sigma

58. a: Copyright

59. d: Corporate social responsibility

Accounting

1. a: Budget

2. b: Responsibility center

3. a: Residual value

4. : Creditor

5. c: Operating expense

6. d: Debt-to-equity ratio

7. a: Fund accounting

8. d: Norwalk Agreement

9. : Articles of incorporation

10. a: Activity-based management

11. c: Encumbrance

12. : Variable cost

13. b: Taxpayer

14. b: Capital gain

15. a: Asset turnover

16. a: International Federation of Accountants

17. c: Adoption

18. c: Profit center

19. d: Overdraft

20. d: Capital loss

21. d: Reimbursement

22. b: Liquidation

23. b: Chart of accounts

24. : Maturity date

25. c: Not-for-profit

26. c: Accrued liabilities

27. a: Management by exception

28. c: Sales

29. : Diluted earnings per share

30. : Bad debt

31. : Remittance advice

32. : Land

33. d: Bank statement

34. a: Bank

35. d: Parent company

36. b: Accounting research

37. d: Incentive

38. d: Information systems

39. : Tax law

40. c: Specific identification

41. a: Promissory note

42. a: Subsidiary

43. c: Self-employment

44. b: Regulation S-K

45. b: Taxation

46. c: Outsourcing

47. c: Historical cost

48. c: Party

49. : Contribution margin

50. a: Customer profitability

51. : Income statement

52. a: Ending inventory

53. a: Indirect costs

54. : Tax revenue

55. ... endorsement

56. : Financial statement analysis

57. c: Corporation

58. a: Balance sheet

59. a: Value theory

55. : Blank endorsement

56. : Financial statement analysis

57. c: Corporation

58. a: Balance sheet

59. a: Value theory

CPSIA information can be obtained
at www.ICGtesting.com
Printed in the USA
LVHW051624301019
635718LV00005B/745/P